Following Characters into Meaning

VOLUME 1

ENVISIONMENT, PREDICTION, AND INFERENCE

LUCY CALKINS ◆ KATHLEEN TOLAN

firsthand

HEINEMANN

DEDICATED TO TEACHERS

Dedicated to Melanie Brown, with thanks for unending support and generosity.

DEDICATED TO TEACHERS

*first*hand
An imprint of Heinemann
361 Hanover Street, Portsmouth, NH 03801
www.heinemann.com

Offices and agents throughout the world

"Dedicated to Teachers" is a trademark of Greenwood Publishing Group, Inc.

The authors and publisher wish to thank those who have generously given permission to reprint borrowed material:

Excerpts from THE TIGER RISING. Copyright ©2001 by Kate DiCamillo. Reproduced by permission of the publisher, Candlewick Press, Somerville, MA.

Photographers: Peter Cunningham and Melanie Brown
Cover and Interior Design: Jenny Jensen Greenleaf
Composition: Publishers' Design and Production Services, Inc.

Library of Congress Cataloging-in-Publication Data
CIP data on file with the Library of Congress

ISBN 10: 0-325-03043-X
ISBN 13: 978-0-325-03043-2

Printed in the United States of America on acid-free paper
14   13   12   11   10   ML   1   2   3   4   5

Following Characters into Meaning

VOLUME 1

ENVISIONMENT, PREDICTION, AND INFERENCE

Units of Study for Teaching Reading, Grades 3–5

In the acknowledgments to *Building a Reading Life*, I described the context out of which these books have emerged and thanked our larger community including the sixty-plus staff developers at the Teachers College Reading and Writing Project (TCRWP), the several hundred principals, and the thousands of teachers with whom we work closely. That text (and all the other acknowledgments) pertains also to the entire series. Although I mentioned the TCRWP staff as a whole, a few have been especially instrumental in developing ideas that are important in this book. Kathleen and I are grateful to Cory Gillette, who has co-led much of our work with formative assessments of reading as well as the effort to think about the bands of text difficulty. We're grateful also to our senior reading specialist, Joe Yukish, who provided shoulders on which our organization could stand. Joe was a leader in Reading Recovery before coming to the TCRWP, and we owe a debt to that entire organization. Shana Frazin championed children's literature and has been an especially generous leader at the Project.

As I mentioned earlier, a few teachers piloted the final iteration of these units. How grateful we are to Erin Hanley Cain, a fifth-grade teacher at PS 28, a Title I school in Upper Manhattan. Erin teaches a class of thirty fifth-graders, almost all of whom are English language learners. You'll watch her children on the DVD—listen to their partnership work with *Old Yeller*, watch their small group conversation about Colonial America, witness Kathleen's small group strategy lesson in which she teaches Erin's children to envision. Erin provides the scaffolds necessary to move kids from work that is simple to work that is complex, and teaches with urgency and incredible levels of accountability. We're honored to stand on her shoulders.

Erin is supported by Elsa Nuñez, a mentor principal. On a shoestring budget, Elsa has turned around her school for 1,000 high-need ELLs, creating the structures necessary to mentor all her teachers and to support all her kids. Teaching reading doesn't happen in isolated classrooms. It is a whole-school endeavor, and Elsa has created a place where everyone—including Kathleen and I—can work and learn.

Although the series is written as if the units of study have been taught to a single classroom of children, the most recent iteration of them has actually been taught to children from six grade 3-5 classrooms in five very different schools. The children featured in the book are a composite group, drawn from all these classrooms. Some of the fifth graders who especially come to the foreground in this unit are Kathy Doyle's youngsters. People who have read my books over the years will recognize Kathy's distinctive teaching because I've used her room as a learning laboratory for more than twenty years now. Kathy's students' consistently produce work that is breathtaking. Because of her vast knowledge of books, her unbounded love of literacy, and her continued dedication to her own professional learning, Kathy is able to turn each child in her care toward reading, and to keep each devouring books with passion.

Katie Even's third-grade inclusion classroom has also been a laboratory for these units. You can watch Katie teach a nonfiction minilesson on the DVD, and even just that glimpse of her will help you understand what a joy it's been to study one evening a week in a think tank that includes Katie, to research in her classroom, and to learn alongside her class. Whenever we gather together to think about teaching, Katie can re-create the drama of particular moments—usually in self-deprecating ways—that leave us laughing until our sides hurt. When the laughter subsides, the conversation always gets down to the hard work of thinking about how our teaching can be more kid-centered and responsive, so that we reach even hard-to-reach readers.

A terrific supporting cast has surrounded these books, and let me bring them onstage for a moment. You will get to know Hareem Khan when you read her spunky, wise teaching in *Constructing Curriculum: Alternate Units of Study*. You may not, however, recognize her contributions to this and other books, so let me describe her role. One of the challenges in writing this series was that for every session, I needed to write a prelude that created the ethical, philosophical, theoretical, and human context for that day's teaching. I am convinced that when we impose our teaching on a class-full of kids, it is incumbent on us to be deeply invested in what we are teaching. But it is not easy to ground teaching in that sort of depth every day for well over a hundred days. When my well ran dry, I sometimes said to Hareem, "Can you do some free-writing to help me get started on a prelude to this session?" and three days later, some paragraphs would come across my screen that said what I wanted to say in ways that gave me unbelievable starter dough for completing that prelude. Hareem was a Fulbright student of mine for a tiny window of time and is now home on the border of Pakistan and Afghanistan. That she can write, think, and teach as she does, situated where she is, is one of the great miracles in my life.

I also want to thank the people who have made these books beautiful. First, I am grateful to the entire community at Heinemann for joining me in upholding the highest of standards for aesthetic beauty. In these days when everyone is carrying two jobs on their shoulders, when pressures to produce are greater than ever, it's incredibly rare and special for a publishing company to stand by an author in her insistence that every aspect of the product must be perfect, even when perfection can only be achieved through that old fashioned process of trial and error. The tiniest details—the bookmarks, for example—were revised half a dozen times. The design of the books is the handicraft of artist and designer Jenny Greenleaf, who is simply extraordinary. Those who know my other books will recognize the trademark photographs. Peter Cunningham is one of the world's great photographers, returned home from photo trips across the world to stand tip-toe on tables and lie belly-down in meeting areas to capture the heart and soul of the children with whom these units of study were piloted. Thanks to all.

Contents

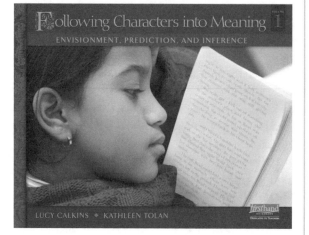

FOLLOWING CHARACTERS INTO MEANING

VOLUME 2: Building Theories, Gathering Evidence

PART TWO   BUILDING THEORIES ABOUT CHARACTERS

Contents

Introduction

The Unit in a Nutshell

t is essential that stories ignite a vital sort of imagination, one that allows readers to live inside the world of the story, to identify with the characters, seeing and sensing situations from inside the characters' minds. This, the first portion of the unit, highlights personal response, envisionment, and empathy to strengthen that connection between readers and characters. In this volume, you'll also learn how to use informal assessment to help you clarify several reading skill progressions—learning what predicting can look like in early stages and then in advanced stages, for example—so that you can lay out learning pathways for readers, helping them to develop more powerful reading skills.

The first portion of this unit, contained in Volume I, helps children approach their study of character *aesthetically* (walking in the shoes of characters, seeing through the characters' eyes, empathizing, and predicting), while the second volume shifts focus so that now we help readers approach texts *efferently* (pulling back to develop a bird's-eye view of a text, gleaning facts and insights about characters that they then carry away from the text, synthesizing this information into evidence-based theories and talking about these theories with others). Our goal by the end of the unit is for readers to be able to shift between these stances—with aesthetic reading enriching the efferent reading and vice versa—blending together the advantages of being lost in the text with the advantages of being analytical about it.

SOME HIGHLIGHTED SKILLS

Volume 1: empathizing, envisioning, predicting, building engagement
Volume 2: inferring, developing theories about characters, synthesizing

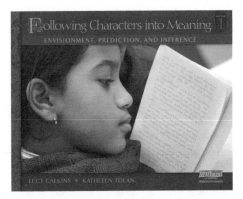

OVERVIEW OF THE UNIT

It is impossible to read a novel well and not think and care about the characters, making a unit of study on character feel somewhat inevitable. The unit is also easier to provision than some, because children can grow ideas about characters when reading any fiction book at all, so you do not need a specialized library.

At the start of any unit, it is important to clarify the reading goals for the unit. Children will hear that this is a unit on "characters," and that topic will be so concrete and clear to them that they'll be ready to get started, no question. You, on the other hand, will probably want to give the focus of the unit a bit of thought because although characters are crucial in any story, there is no reading skill called "characters." The *children* will think this is simply a unit on characters, but *you* will know that this is a unit on a set of skills that you'll bring forth as children read fiction, thinking and caring about characters. And those skills can be chosen by you, the teacher.

The Goals and Plan for Volume 1: Teach in Ways that Support Lost-in-the-Book Reading

Supporting Students' Reading Volume

Although your teaching may emphasize envisionment and prediction during the first portion of the unit and close reading, inference, and growing theories during the second portion of the unit, throughout the whole unit children will be engaged in similar work: reading, reading, and reading more fiction books. If they read books that are levels K, L, or M, they'll read at least five of these a week. If they are reading books that are levels U, V, or above, they'll read more like one a week. If they are reading something in between, their reading volume will also be something in between. Either way, they'll be reading a lot—and this matters more than anything else I will say in this write-up!

Continuing Partner Work

Meanwhile, it also matters that your children meet with a partner for five minutes or so at the end of every day's reading workshop. Depending on the availability of books in your classroom library, partners can be reading the same books or books from the same series or just different books they swap. If partners have a character in common, the conversation can focus on the shared characters. If you don't have enough series books in your classroom for partners to read within the same series, you'll need to do more work teaching each partner to listen carefully to follow the development of characters across their partners' texts.

Supporting the Lost-in-a-Book Feeling with an Absorbing Read-Aloud

During the first portion of the unit, then, you'll teach toward that lost-in-a-book feeling that comes when one identifies with the protagonist in a good story. The easiest way to guide children into this lost-in-a-book feeling of being caught up in the story is to read aloud an absorbing chapter book, helping children imagine the world of the story and identify with the main character. During the preceding unit, you will have demonstrated and supported that lost-in-the-book work by encouraging empathy with characters during the read-aloud, and now you'll continue and extend this work, again reading aloud an enthralling text. Again you'll pause in the midst of read-aloud to say, "I can see, it, can't you?" and then paint a picture that is drawn from earlier information in the text, from identifications with characters, and from your own life experiences, too. Another time you might look up from the text and say, "I'm trying to imagine in my mind what

this looks like. I've never been to this school, but I'm kind of picturing it is like our school—red brick, three stories tall—I'll read on and see." As you read on in the story about the school, it's likely that new information in the text will lead you to revise your initial mental pictures. "Oh, now I realize it's a *white clapboard* schoolhouse! And I'm getting the idea it's much smaller than our school, because…." You'll definitely want to point out explicitly the ways in which close reading informs your mental pictures, helping you continually revise those pictures in light of new information.

The point, of course, is not only to help readers picture the text, almost as if it was the film of a movie being run through the projector of the reader's own mind, but also to help readers read with a sense of identification. As you read aloud, then, you'll sometimes say, "How do you think he's feeling right now? Turn and talk." Or "I'm worried about him. Aren't you? Turn and tell your partner about your worries." Or you may say, "Show me on your faces what Rob is feeling *now*," or, a bit later, "Use your body to show me what's happening to Rob n*ow*. Things are changing, aren't they! "

Supporting the Lost-in-a-Book Feeling in Independent Reading: Mental Pictures and Dramatization

Of course, the goal is not only for children to envision and lose themselves in the books that *you* read aloud. The goal is also for children to do this *for themselves* when they read. You'll want to teach children to envision through every means possible. During independent reading and the follow-up partnership times, you'll probably encourage children to talk about their mental pictures. What do the places in the book look like? What has the reader seen before that can help him or her picture the character, the character's home, or the locale in which the book is situated? You might encourage a reader to quickly sketch a character or a setting as he or she reads, and then in his or her partnership conversation, to talk through the reasons for this particular image. "What's going on around the character?" you could prompt. "Who else is there? What's the scene like?" You'll tell readers if they're not sure what a scene entails, this is how reading goes. The reader's job is to draw on all we have read and then guess—imagining as best we are able.

When children meet in partnerships, you'll suggest that sometimes readers return to passages that matter in a text, rereading those and almost acting them out as we do this. You might say to two children who are reading *Because of Winn Dixie*, "Sometimes it helps to actually try to act out a little bit of what we are reading. Why don't you try it? Why doesn't one of you pretend you are Opal. Tell your father why you need this dog. And the other one of you—your dad. You are looking at that stray dog. What are you thinking? Say your thoughts aloud." Of course, you have an array of ways to nudge children to immerse themselves in whatever they are reading. With that same partnership, you could alternatively have said, "Your right finger puppet is Opal. Opal, tell your father (he's your left finger-puppet) why you need to adopt this dog! And father (you could hold up your left hand to indicate that finger-puppet), get ready to talk back to your daughter." Alternatively, you could suggest a child try little bits of fast-writing. "Sometimes it helps to use writing to get us pretending we are the characters in a story we are reading. Try it, for just a second. Pretend you are Opal. You are standing outside that trailer, getting ready to talk to your father. Winn Dixie is right beside you. What are you thinking right now? Jot your thoughts."

> *It is essential in reading imaginative literature, as fiction is called, that stories ignite a vital sort of imagination, one that allows readers to piece together and live inside the world of the story.*

Using Informal Assessments to Inform Our Teaching of Prediction

This summary of the unit has emphasized the skill of envisionment, but you'll want to teach prediction with equal gusto. You'll learn how to use informal assessment to help you clarify in your own mind what it is that skilled predictors do so that you can lay out a learning pathway for readers, helping them to progress from where they are as predictors to where they can go next. This work will be informed by your knowledge of the level of text difficulty at which a reader reads. Children who are reading texts at level K/L/M can predict by relying on knowledge of simple, straightforward story structure. A character has a problem and tries, tries, tries to resolve that problem. Readers who are working with texts at level U/V/W will need to do quite different work as they predict, thinking, "How might all the subplots come together into something cohesive at the end? Which characters that seemed minor or subplots that seemed tangential at first might return to bring this story toward its conclusion?"

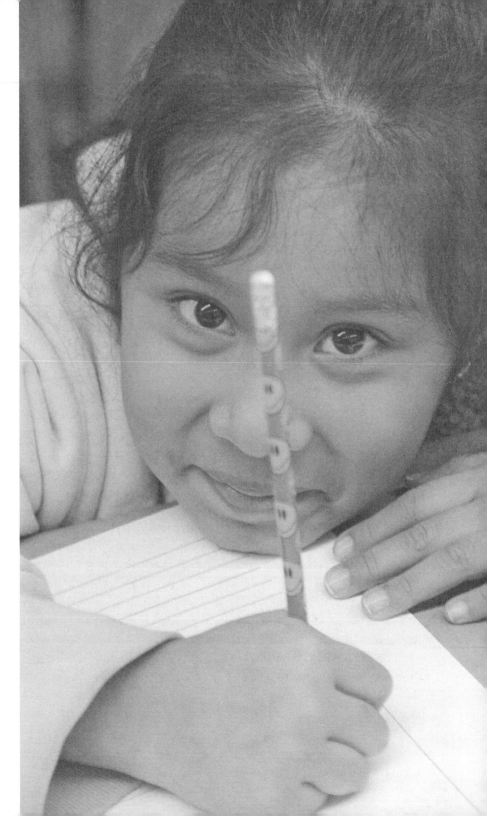

The Goals and Plan for Volume 2: Growing Theories About Characters

During the second bend in the road of this unit, you'll shift your emphasis and this time teach readers to read closely, inferring to grow theories about the character, and then reading with those theories in hand, altering them according to incoming information.

Learning About Characters by Noticing Details; Using Details to Infer

We often launch this work by teaching children that in life as well as in books, we watch how people act, noticing especially how they respond to events. From this we formulate tentative theories about them. You might say something like, "I noticed the way you all pulled together the other day when Jeremy was hurt. I saw Randalio making a band-aid out of a paper towel, and from his actions I got the idea that he is quick-thinking and resourceful. And I watched the way Leo kept out of everyone's way and then found quiet ways to help, and I thought, 'That's just the way Leo acts during morning jobs, too.' I saw a pattern! So I thought, 'This gives me the idea that Leo is observant, and that his quietness helps him be especially thoughtful.'" Then you could debrief by saying something like, "Do you see how I made theories about Leo and Randalio based on their actions? Readers do that too." You can tell children that just as we grow theories about people around us, we can also grow theories about characters in books.

For me it is important to emphasize that readers pay attention not only to *what* a character does but also to *how* the character does these things. Does the text give any clues about the character's gestures? About the way a character walks or sits or closes the door? If the text says that a character slumps in the chair, then the reader needs to ask, "Why does she sit like that? Is she tired? Bored? What's going on?" Readers also pay attention to the way characters talk: the words they choose, their tone of voice, the emotional cues the author adds with dialogue. All of these give hints about what kind of people live in the world of a story. Sometimes the author offers windows into a character's mind: passages of thinking or an explanation of a character's motives.

The techniques sound easy to teach, but children often struggle trying to do this work. As I watch their struggles, I invent teaching in response to what they show me. For example, many children need to be taught that readers glean information about a character not only from passages pertaining directly to that char-

acter but also from many other passages—those telling about the character's home, for example, or the character's family. "Let's read this story together and think, 'Which part tells me something about Robert,'" I might say, and then proceed to show that passages describing Robert's home provide windows into his character.

Reaching for Rich, Precise, Truthful Words

Children also need to be taught that the story will *tell* specifics, and that readers can *infer* generalizations. If the story says that Robert started his essay five times, each time crumpling his discarded lead into a wad, then the author is expecting that the reader will supply the generalizations that name the sort of person this character seems to be. The reader won't find those words in the text but must instead bring those words to the text. Many children will reach first for generic terms: A character is nice, mean, or good. I find it helps to create a literary word chart so that children realize that a nice character might be generous or encouraging or loyal or patient. A mean character might be intolerant or snide or jealous or even malicious. I sometimes suggest kids rate the synonyms for nice along a gradient of niceness for children to begin to grasp the nuances of each word. A child who has marked passages in a story that reveal the character's traits can profit from being invited to reach for the precisely true word that captures the character's personality.

Seeking Characters' Complexity and Evolution

Of course, once a child has read attending to specifics in the story and using those specifics to help spark insights about the character, that child will need to be taught that characters are complicated; they are not just one way. Then too, characters change. Either way, a reader will need to read on in the text, thinking, "Do these new sections of the text confirm or challenge my ideas about the character?" When I approach a unit intending to teach readers to grow ideas about characters, I know that as part of this I will teach children to think between several related sections of a text—say, a passage at the start, one at the middle, and one at the end—to talk and think very specifically about a character's evolution across the story line. Children tend to rely on sweeping generalizations when talking about the ways a character changes or the lessons a character learns, and our goal is to teach children to grow grounded, accountable, and especially, precise ideas.

As part of this, it is important to teach readers to use their knowledge of how stories tend to go to remind them of what's worth noticing in a story and to inform their thinking about character change. In literature, stories are often built around a central structure in which a main character faces challenges, some explicit and some more nebulous. The character draws on what's inside himself or herself to meet these challenges and often changes in the process, developing new inner resources. Often not only the main character changes in this process, but other characters change as well. This way, readers come to realize that events in stories are consequential; the choices made by one character affect others, and single events often have a significant impact on other events.

Overcoming the Particular Challenges in Each Band of Text Difficulty

In helping young readers to grow ideas about characters, I am informed by my understanding of bands of text difficulty. I know, for example, that readers who are working with K/L/M texts will probably find that those texts feature one or two main characters, each of whom is characterized by a couple of dominant character traits, and those will usually be very much related to the story line. Cherry Sue is overly friendly and generous, and the story line is that Poppleton eventually decides he's had enough of her generosity and he wants a bit of space from her. It will not require a lot of inference for readers of these texts to deduce what their characters are like as people. Their characters won't tend to change, either, although their feelings will. Meanwhile, once readers are reading texts in the N/Q band of text difficulty, characters will become more ambivalent. They'll feel one thing and something contrary to that as well. Readers will often find that the text comes right out and tells them about this emotional complexity. At this band of text difficulty, it is common for a character to change at the end of the story.

Using Post-Its and Conversation Prompts to Build Theories and Inform Conversations About Characters

When I teach children to think about the protagonist's traits, motivations, problems (or struggles), lessons, and/or changes, I tend to suggest children keep Post-its (and perhaps "theory charts") as they read, and I suggest they meet for five minutes with a partner at the end of every reading workshop to "talk off their Post-its."

If children are accustomed to working with "boxes and bullets" (see the essay unit in *Units of Study for Teaching Writing*), I help them jot main ideas in a boxes-and-bullets form as they prepare for partner conversations. Either way, once they meet with a partner, I teach readers that one child can get the conversation started by sharing something provocative and central to the text, and then the partner can listen and extend the remark, perhaps using conversation prompts such as these:

"What in the text makes you say that?"
"I thought that too, because…"
"Another example of that is…"
"I thought something different because…"
"I agree because…"
"Wait. I'm confused. Are you saying…"
"Have you found the same thing with the character in your story?"
"Can you say more about that?"
"Can you show me the part in the story where you got that idea?"

I encourage partners to "talk long" about an idea because actually what they are doing as they extend their conversations is learning to think in some depth.

Growing Complex Theories: Revising Our Thinking as We Go

As this unit progresses, there'll come a time when I teach children to look over their Post-its to develop bigger theories about their characters. One way children or partners might do this is to take their Post-its out of their books and sort them into piles that seem to go together. They might sort them into piles that are about one particular character or another. Children can delve into a stack of Post-its (a cluster of related ideas) looking for contrasts and patterns. They can try to develop a new idea out of those Post-its. (We tend to call these bigger ideas theories.) Once children have developed a couple of theories, they can revisit earlier parts of the text in light of their theories. They can also read forward, gathering more evidence to support their theories, making individual theory charts.

Whenever we teach children anything, it is important to have in mind ways to ratchet up the level of what they do. We need to know what it means to do this work fairly well, better, and really well so that we can move youngsters along a trajectory of development. Children, too, need to be part of the conversation about what it means to grow theories about characters really well. I sometimes ask them to do something simple such as starring the Post-its or entries that they thought did an especially good job of carrying ideas, and then I ask them to articulate what it was about this particular Post-it or entry that made it work, and then use it as a mentor Post-it, a mentor entry. Then the children can continue to read, this time with the goal of producing equally thoughtful responses to reading.

Once children have developed a theory or multiple theories, teach them to read on, expecting that their theories will become more complex (which generally means longer, with qualifiers added) or that they will change. It's crucial to teach children to revise their initial ideas in light of new information. A child might start off with a theory that "Gilly is mean," and then learn first to open up the word *mean* by using more specific ways to talk and think about Gilly. Then the reader might read on, focusing on more parts of the book and thinking about how those parts fit or don't fit with the theory. Such a child could end up thinking not, "Gilly is mean," but "Gilly hurts others so they don't get close to her and don't matter to her, and so that they, like her mother, don't hurt her."

Sustaining Previous Work as You Continue to Teach

Of course, as we rally children to do *new* work within this unit, it is also important to remind them to continue doing all they have already been taught. That is, our teaching must be cumulative. Early in this new unit, I'll shine a spotlight on something I especially emphasized during last month's unit, and I'll act absolutely baffled if any child in the room is not carrying all that I taught last month. For example, I will certainly have emphasized keeping daily logs during Unit 1. I can't forget those logs now! And of course, I will want to make sure that this unit does not overwhelm children's reading, so I will continue to emphasize that children need to actually read, eyes on print, for at least forty minutes each day in school and for close to that same amount of time at home.

Walking in a Character's Shoes

IN THIS SESSION,
you will teach students
that readers come to understand our characters by
making movies in our minds
and envisioning their
experiences.

PART ONE

Making Movies in Our Minds As We Read

hen J.K. Rowling, author of the "Harry Potter" series, spoke at Harvard's commencement recently, she devoted most of her attention to the crucial importance of the human imagination. She emphasized not the imagination that allows one to create sorcerers, wizards, and other inventions of the human mind but rather the imagination that allows us to walk in the shoes of another person, to empathize with people whose experiences we have never shared. She told the graduates and their families that one of the most formative experiences of her life was the year she spent as a researcher for Amnesty International. She said, "There in my little office I read hastily scribbled letters smuggled out of totalitarian regimes by men and women who were risking imprison-

GETTING READY

- Reflect upon and be prepared to share with the children a personal story about a time in your life when words on a page brought a distant person to life.

- Begin a selected read-aloud that will thread through this unit. We recommend *The Tiger Rising*, by Kate DiCamillo. If you go with this book, read Chapter 1 to your children prior to this session.

- Study the read-aloud book you selected—we'll assume it is *The Tiger Rising*. Identify a section of your read-aloud book that invites readers to envision, one that is written in a way that nudges readers to draw on their own prior knowledge of places similar to those in the book. If you are using *The Tiger Rising*, expect to reread a passage from Chapter 1 aloud to the children.

- You'll be referring to the chart from Unit 1, "'Ways You and Another Reader Can Talk About Your Books'"" during the session, so you'll want to move it closer to the meeting area. Be prepared with markers so you can add to this chart.

- In Unit 1, you stressed that children should bring their "My Reading Life" folders to the meeting area. If they now have reading notebooks, expect that they'll also bring these. Supply students with extra-large Post-its.

- Toward the end of the minilesson, you'll set children up to do work differently, depending on whether they are Partner 1 or Partner 2. Be sure each partner knows if he or she is Partner 1 or Partner 2.

- Readers' independent reading work can flow seamlessly into this new unit.

- In Session II's minilesson, you will read aloud the beginning of Chapter 2 in *The Tiger Rising*.

ment to inform the outside world of what was happening to them." Rowling told those who'd gathered, "I read the testimonies of torture victims, eye witness accounts of trials and executions, kidnapping and rape." She went on to say that she came, through that work, to realize that "Unlike any other creature on this planet, human beings can learn and understand without having experienced. We can *think* ourselves into other people's minds, *imagine* ourselves into other people's places." Rowling began having nightmares after reading these letters, and to this day she carries with her the memory of an African torture victim—a young man no older than she was at the time—who became mentally ill

> We read, and one word takes the hand of the next, drawing us toward another place, another time.

after all he'd endured. Rowling met him eventually and said that he trembled uncontrollably. "I was given the job of escorting him to the underground station, and this man whose life had been shattered by cruelty took my hand with exquisite courtesy, and wished me future happiness." Rowling simply shared this detail—she didn't elaborate on it—but for me it was unspeakably moving to imagine a man who had lived through such terror and agony having the grace to bless the young J.K. Rowling as she continued on her journey.

Rowling went on to say that she watched the letters from those victims affect other readers, too, people who like her had never been tortured or imprisoned for their beliefs. She watched those people read, she watched them imagine, and above all she watched them respond, and she saw the power of collective response. "The power of human empathy, leading to collective action, saves lives. . . ."

I begin this book with J.K. Rowling's important words, because she is right to shine a spotlight on the crucial role of the imagination in reading. We read, and one word takes the hand of the next, drawing us toward another place, another time. We read, and suddenly we are with C.S. Lewis's Lucy, Peter, Susan, and Edmund entering a wardrobe, pushing past coats, and then we, with Lucy, feel cold in our faces. Something icy brushes against us: a snow-covered branch. We look down and see we are standing in snow. Ahead, a light gleams golden, and from far off, we hear the sound of the sleigh bells, and then the evil Snow Queen approaches and lures Edmund away, and soon Lucy, Peter, and Susan and the rest of us take off to save a kingdom and to learn that mere children can make the world a better place. That's reading.

Too often, our methods of teaching don't spotlight the role of imagination. We hurry kids to name a character's trait and supply evidence for that trait, to predict the end of the story or to extract a thesis that could fit inside a fortune cookie, yet rarely rally them to read with imagination.

This minilesson marks the start of a unit, and more specifically, the start of a bend in the road, a part of that unit that is designed to lead children toward that lost-in-a-story, nose-in-the-book reading that is hard to teach but impossible to ignore. The reading that you will be teaching is not unlike drama. When we read, we almost assume a part in the story, and when we share books with others, one way to do so is to reread and reenact sections of a book. One child takes the role of one character, her partner is a second character, and together the readers bring the text to life. This sort of reading requires imagination, empathy, and envisionment—and it leads inevitably to predictions. Later, in the next part, or bend in the road, of this unit of study, you'll help readers realize that they can shift from being lost in the story to thinking critically and analytically about the text, from passion hot to critic cold. But for now, it's all about passion hot.

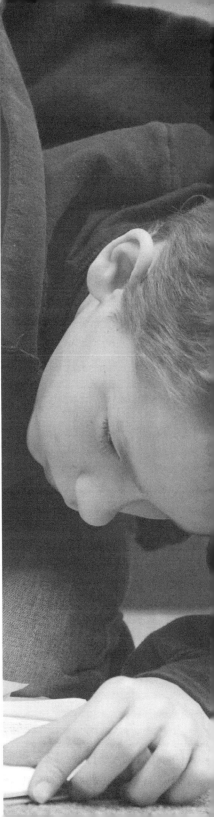

MINILESSON

Making Movies in Our Minds As We Read

CONNECTION

Tell children about a time when words on a page brought a distant person to life for you.

"Reading is a miracle, if you think of it. My father recently decided to pull out the trunks of family papers that had been passed from one person to another in our family until they finally ended up in the closets of his house. From those trunks, my father pulled logs, written hundreds of years ago, all by people I have never met."

"I hold a log, like a message in a bottle, sent not across the seas, but across time. I read those words now, 250 years after some of them were written, and poof! It is like magic. Suddenly I am on Webster Street in old Boston, not far from where the character Johnny Tremain worked as a blacksmith's assistant. Charlotte—my great, great, great, great grandmother—is making toast in a big brick fireplace, using an iron rack to hold the slices of bread. I read her description: 'Tubs were brought in here, before the kitchen fireplace and we had our Saturday night scrubs, preparatory for the Sabbath,' and *I can picture it*."

Leaning close to the children, I said, "Do you remember the fairy-tale story of Aladdin, who found a magic lamp? He lit that oil lamp and poof! People from far away and long ago appeared before him, real as life. For me, reading is like Aladdin's magic lamp."

You'll find your own stories to illustrate the way that reading evokes imagination. Perhaps in your stash of cherished items at home, you have a letter, sent from overseas, perhaps on that light blue airmail paper that was so common when I was a child. Bring that letter in and tell your children how the scrawled words on those thin pages bring a person to life for you. Or you can retell Rowling's story, as told in the prelude.

If you can't think of written texts that have brought a person to life, listen to the news and you'll hear stories of what writing has done for others. During his presidential campaign, Barack Obama told stories of how he got to know his absent father by reading the letters he had written to American universities, pleading for the chance to study there. Barack tells of what it meant to him to see his father's dreams, there on those pages. On the news, I also heard the story of how, just before he died, Tim Russert found that his son, Luke, had gotten himself a tattoo. Before Tim could get angry at the news of what his son had done, he learned that the tattoo Luke had made were the initials TJR, inscribed onto his rib cage. Those are the initials of Tim's father, Big Russ, and of Tim Russert himself. Luke explained to his dad, "I want you guys with me always." I can only imagine what it must be like for Luke now, to rub his arm against those initials and to conjure up his father, real as life. Reading does that. It brings distant people to life. Tell children stories such as these.

Name your teaching point. Specifically, tell children that when we read, we make a movie in the mind and we become one of the characters.

"Today and for upcoming days, I want to teach you that if we read well, we *become* the character in a book. We read the words and then poof! We are one of the characters in the mental movie we're making. Poof! I'm Willy, bundled up on that sled, snow flying into my eyes, my heart racing, urging Searchlight on.

TEACHING

Reread an intense but brief section of your read-aloud book, and as you read, pause often to visualize, describing what you see and enacting it.

"Right now I'm going to go back and reread a bit of *The Tiger Rising,* and we're going to almost *become* Rob. We will see what he sees, as if we were right there with him at the Kentucky Star Motel. To do this, we'll have *to fill in stuff* that's missing. We'll draw on details from the earlier parts of the book and from our own experiences of motels, rainy days, funerals, and tigers.

"Let's read and create a movie in the mind, almost becoming Rob.

That morning, after he discovered the tiger, Rob went and stood under the Kentucky Star Motel sign and waited for the school bus just like it was any other day. The Kentucky Star sign was composed of a yellow neon star that rose and fell over a piece of blue neon in the shape of the state of Kentucky. . . .

"I can see Rob standing under a huge neon Kentucky Star sign (I gestured above my head) in front of the motel. He's looking for the school bus." (I tilted my head and looked to the left as if to see if the school bus was coming.)

It's important that our teaching leaves footprints, that yesterday's teaching points and yesterday's texts leave a mark that lasts. Time and again during this unit and across the year, you'll refer back to the books and insights from Unit I.

Notice that usually the amount of text read in a minilesson is very small. You can make your point without covering a lot of ground. Also notice that often in a minilesson, we take the class back to a familiar bit of the read-aloud text.

It is worth noting a couple things about the text. First, within just the first two pages of this book, time has jumped forward and backward half a dozen times. You might note this on a Post-it because if you are conferring with a child who is reading a text that is similarly difficult (levels S-U), you might find that time jumps around in that text as well. You could use these pages to demonstrate that readers need to monitor for time changes, and to "move the clock forward and back."

You will be alternating between reading aloud and thinking aloud. It may be confusing for children to differentiate between the two processes. Help children differentiate by finding a way to act-out that you are reading and a contrasting way to act out that you are thinking aloud. Usually teachers find that when reading, it helps to hold the book up in front of you, with posture that conveys that this is story time. When you shift to thinking aloud, many teachers find it helps to lower the book and slide back in the chair, to sit upright, and to lift your eyes up toward the ceiling in a way that conveys you are searching your thoughts. After a bit, you'll shift back to reading. You'll lean toward the children, raise the book, and they'll understand what is going on.

Rob liked the sign; he harbored a dim but abiding notion that it would bring him good luck.

Looking up toward the ceiling, I said, "I see Rob, looking up at the sign, smiling. He likes it.

> Finding the tiger had been luck, he knew that. He had been out in the woods behind the Kentucky Star Motel, way out in the woods, not really looking for anything, just wandering. . . .

"Oh, right. Rob is remembering what had happened earlier that morning.

> . . . hoping that maybe he would get lost or get eaten by a bear and not have to go to school ever again. That's when he saw the old Beauchamp gas station building, all boarded up and tumbling down; next to it, there was a cage, and inside the cage, unbelievably, there was a tiger—a real-life, very large tiger pacing back and forth. He was orange and gold and so bright, it was like staring at the sun itself, angry and trapped in a cage.

I went back and reread a bit.

> He [Rob] had been out in the woods . . . not really looking for anything, just wandering, hoping that maybe he would get lost or get eaten by a bear and not have to go to school ever again."

"I picture Rob walking around in the woods, wandering, pushing a branch out of the way, maybe kicking at a stone." (I acted aimless, halfheartedly pushing a branch out of the way and scuffing at a stone.)

> That's when he saw the old Beauchamp gas station building, all boarded up and tumbling down; next to it, there was a cage, and inside the cage, unbelievably, there was a tiger—a real-life, very large tiger pacing back and forth. He was orange and gold and so bright, it was like staring at the sun itself, angry and trapped in a cage.

Your voice as you read "Finding the tiger had been . . ." might convey a little bit of disorientation, because time has just moved backwards in the text and most readers will take a second to realize what's going on. You can show kids that you monitor for sense enough to experience dislocation for a second, and to ask, "What?" Then as you read on, you'll quickly figure out what's going on, leading you to perhaps mutter to yourself, "Oh, right, he is remembering. . . ."

Notice after I interrupt the text to think aloud, I often reread part of the text to help listeners get back into the flow of the reading. You may struggle with the logistics of this teaching. Are you holding a copy of the minilesson, or the book, or what? Many teachers insert Post-its into read-aloud books, using these as reminders of when and how to think aloud.

It was early morning and it looked like it might rain; it had been raining every day for almost two weeks. The sky was gray and the air was thick and still. Fog was hugging the ground. To Rob, it seemed as if the tiger was some magic trick, rising out of the mist. He was so astounded at his discovery, so amazed, that he stood and stared.

"I can see Rob's face." (My eyes popped open wide, my mouth gaped open and I hit my cheek in astonishment.) "But what if I saw that tiger! Man! I can only imagine." (I look to the ceiling as if pulling the image of a tiger out of the sky.) "I see that tiger." (I assume the role of the tiger, pacing back and forth in an imagined cage.)

Name what you were doing, helping children grasp that as you read, you pause often to put yourself into the character's shoes.

"Readers, did you see that when I read, I made a movie in my mind? It's sort of as if the words on the page are the script of the movie. I read them, then I project them into my mind. This way, as I read, I see what Rob is seeing, doing, remembering."

ACTIVE INVOLVEMENT

Continue reading, this time pausing often to prompt children to walk in the shoes of the character, seeing what he or she is seeing, thinking what he or she is thinking.

"I'm going to continue reading. As I read, become Rob. I'll call out reminders to help you keep the mental movie spinning in your mind. Let's try it.

It was early morning and it looked like it might rain; it had been raining every day for almost two weeks. The sky was gray . . .

"Picture the gray sky. See it in your mind.

The sky was gray and the air was thick and still. Fog was hugging the ground.

"Add the fog to your picture; puffy clouds around your feet.

In this instance, remember you are still shifting between leaning forward, book raised, to read aloud—for a few lines—and then sitting up, shifting back in the chair, to think aloud.

In this instance, instead of simply saying what it is that you visualize, you might act the scene out. You can act something out in a way that is so subtle that the kids hardly notice what you are doing. You can act out a tiger, pacing in its cage, without leaving your seat. Tiny gestures convey more than you might imagine. Of course, you may well decide to literally pace for a second as you depict (and imagine) the tiger.

In this minilesson, I introduce a couple of methods of learning that we'll return to often throughout the year. Instead of asking children to turn and talk, I ask them to stop and jot. The pace of this is very much like the pace of a turn and talk, and you'll see it used increasingly across the year. It's rare that a stop and jot time turns into a turn and share your jottings time, as happens in this minilesson, by the way. Your goal is merely to nudge children to do a particular bit of mind work.

There is one secret to success. You need to do whatever it is you are asking kids to do. So say the words "Picture the gray sky" as if you are giving yourself as well as the kids a prompt and then, sitting right in front of them, actually picture that sky. See it. Is it steel gray? Light gray? See it. Feel it. If you don't do what you ask children to do because you are consumed with worries about what you will say next and are thinking about your teaching and not the reading work you are advocating, the children will discern in a flash that you are merely giving orders, and the net effect will be astonishingly different.

To Rob, it seemed as if the tiger was some magic trick, rising out of the mist. He was so astounded at his discovery, so amazed, that he stood and stared.

"Stare at the tiger."

But only for a minute; he was afraid to look at the tiger for too long; afraid that the tiger would disappear. He stared, and then he turned and ran back into the woods, toward the Kentucky Star. And the whole way home, his brain doubted what he had seen, his heart beat out the truth to him. *Ti-ger. Ti-ger. Ti-ger.*

In the active involvement sections of minilessons, it is important for us to provide children with assisted practice doing what we have just demonstrated. In this instance, I know the active involvement stands a chance of being confusing, so I take extra steps to set children up and get them started, making it as likely as possible that they'll be able to do this work successfully—and in short order.

"Breathe hard, you've been running through the woods. You are sweaty. Your heart is beating like crazy over what you've seen. Ba-Bum, Ba-bum, Ba-bum.

"Readers, be Rob. Say it aloud. 'Ti-ger, Ti-ger, Ti-ger.'" They did and then I read on.

Teachers, be Rob yourselves. You have just seen a tiger in the woods. Think about it as you run. Ti-ger. Ti-ger. Ti-ger.

That was what Rob thought about as he stood beneath the Kentucky Star sign and waited for the bus. The tiger. He did not think about the rash on his legs, the itchy red blisters that snaked their way into his shoes. His father said that it would be less likely to itch if he didn't think about it.

"Partner 1, be Rob. You are waiting for the bus. Say aloud your thoughts as you look to your left for that bus, and as you try not to think about all these things. Say what you are thinking to Partner 2—and watch for the bus."

The room erupted into conversation as one member of each partnership assumed the role of Rob.

After a minute, I voiced over the role play, rereading a bit of the text and then reading on.

Stop talking. If you are like me, you'll find yourself a bit anxious over this and you will be apt to overtalk it. Give them a minute to do this. If you worry that there may not be enough in this passage for the kids to actually become Rob, you may be right. But what's the real risk here? So give them a minute. You'll find the invitation to dramatize is surprisingly powerful.

He did not think about the rash on his legs, the itchy red blisters that snaked their way into his shoes. His father said that it would be less likely to itch if he didn't think about it.

And he did not think about his mother. He hadn't thought about her since the morning of the funeral, the morning he couldn't stop crying the great heaving sobs that made his chest and stomach hurt. His father, watching him, standing beside him, had started to cry, too.

They were both dressed up in suits that day; his father's suit was too small. And when he slapped Rob to make him stop crying, he ripped a hole underneath the arm of his jacket.

"There ain't no point in crying," his father had said afterward. "Crying ain't going to bring her back."

It had been six months since that day, six months since he and his father had moved from Jacksonville to Lister, and Rob had not cried since, not once.

"Stop and jot in your notebook. What's the picture in your mind? Sketch what you are picturing, or use words." Jasmine jotted her thought down quickly, and beside her, Fallon wrote furiously. *[Figs. I-1 and I-2]*

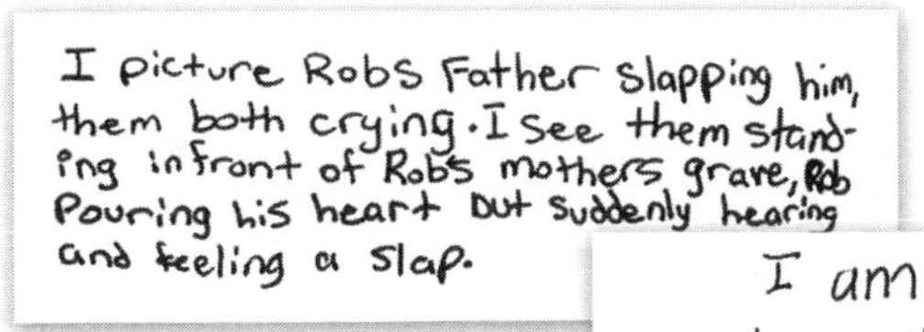

I picture Robs Father slapping him, them both crying. I See them standing in front of Robs mothers grave, Rob Pouring his heart out suddenly hearing and feeling a slap.

Figure I-1

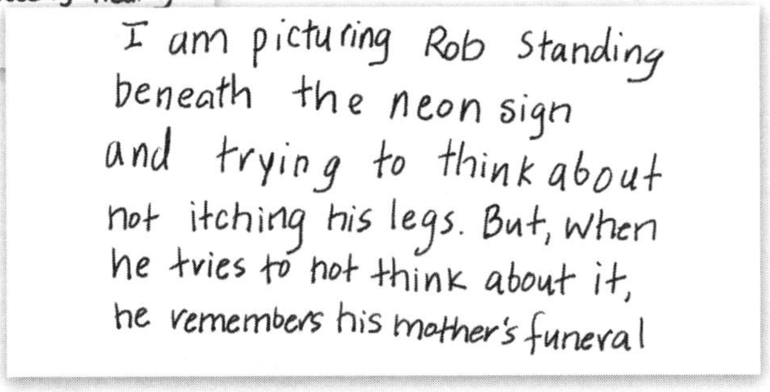

I am picturing Rob standing beneath the neon sign and trying to think about not itching his legs. But, when he tries to not think about it, he remembers his mother's funeral

Figure I-2
When Fallon is asked to picture the moment, she uses concrete, physical details to convey a complex welter of emotions.

After a moment, I said, "Readers, turn and talk to each other." The room erupted into conversation. I listened as Jack read what he'd jotted to Sarah, his partner. *[Fig. I-3]*

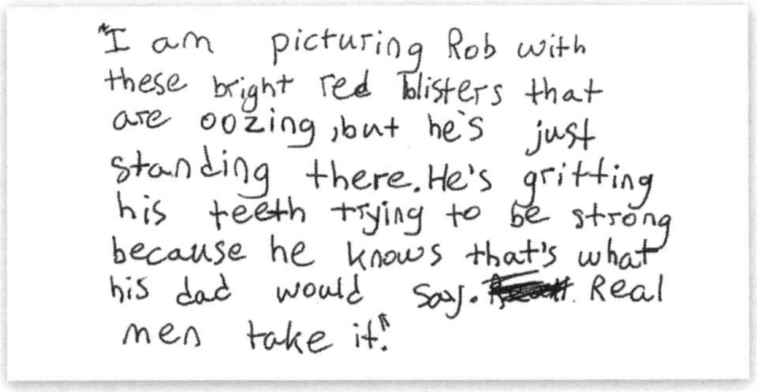

"I am picturing Rob with these bright red blisters that are oozing, but he's just standing there. He's gritting his teeth trying to be strong because he knows that's what his dad would say. Real men take it."

Figure I-3
Jake synthesized information gleaned from earlier in the text and from his personal response to the text and produced a sophisticated envisionment.

Sarah said, "Mine is sort of the same only less about Rob and more about his dad." She then read: "I picture Rob standing there all itchy but thinking about his father. Rob imagines his dad and that makes him scared and angry all at the same time. Rob is trying not to itch or think about his mother because his father scares him." *[See the CD-ROM for other examples.]*

LINK

Make it as likely as possible that when children disperse to read, they continue visualizing and almost dramatizing. Channel them to mark especially powerful passages as they read independently.

"Readers, move to your reading places, get out your independent reading books, and continue reading where you left off last night. And remember, whenever you are reading, make sure you are seeing the movie of the story in your mind and picturing yourself inside the scenes. You'll need to take a moment to fill out your log when you get to your reading spot, but then slip right back into the skin of your character."

A particular challenge for children on this day might be to infer, adding to what has been explicitly stated. If children are having a hard time adding to the mental movie, encourage them to act out what they imagine, showing how the character does the action, then naming their thinking. You might say, "Sometimes it's hard for us to say what we are seeing. Right now, show me how your character is doing this. Be the character and act it out."

There will be times when the transition between one unit and the next requires children to stop one kind of independent reading and begin another, but in this instance, there need not be any distinction. Readers can carry on with the same reading they've been doing, and you'll simply lift the level of their reading work.

CONFERRING AND SMALL-GROUP WORK

Rally Kids to Do the Work of the New Unit and Then Assess and Clarify Your Goals

Rally Readers to Envision and to Connect to Characters

For the first few days of any new unit, your conferences and small-group work will rally kids toward the work of the new unit. Today you will probably move quickly among lots of kids, hoping to mobilize their energy and enthusiasm for envisioning and for walking in the shoes of a character. This is not the time for you to fine-tune one reader's thinking or to tackle another reader's resistance. Both jobs will be important ones, but at the start of a new unit, you first need to mobilize and build enthusiasm around the new work of the unit. For now you will probably work with children who are likely to run with your instruction and to bring others along with them. You'll encourage as many kids as possible to tackle the work of this unit with energy, hoping that those early starters will then lure others into the work, so that very soon, there'll be a new buzz in the room.

Meanwhile, as you recruit children to make movies in their minds and to envision as they read, you will observe their efforts and use those observations to tailor your plans for the upcoming unit.

> ### MID-WORKSHOP TEACHING POINT
>
> #### Readers Envision Not Only the Character Engaged in a Sequence of Actions But Also the Setting
>
> Voicing over as the class continued to read, I said, "Readers, you don't need to stop yet. I can tell you've got that lost-in-a-book feeling. For the next few minutes, read on but be sure you are making a movie in your mind as you read. In a tiny bit, I'm going to ask you to sketch what you are seeing in your notebooks."
>
> After a minute I said, "Readers, right now, envision your main character in your mind (I paused). Now, see the place around your character (I paused). Quickly sketch that place." After they sketched for a minute, I coached in a voiceover, "In your mind's eye, look around and see what else is there. Remember, the book might not tell you all that is there, but if you put yourself right into the scene, in your character's shoes, you can notice things. Fill in details that you know from earlier in the book, and from having been to places like this one, details that aren't explicitly stated in the book."
>
> After about thirty seconds I said, "Now pick up your book and read on, but remember to continue seeing as you read. You'll be stopping to sketch again soon." After a few minutes, I stopped the readers and said, "Readers, either add to your sketch to show what else you pictured new, or make a new sketch. If you already drew what your character was doing, see if you have ideas
>
> *continued on next page*

At the start of the previous unit, you used nonverbal signals to settle children, touching one child's page to signal, "Eyes on the book," and making a "What's up?" gesture to direct another child to stop being disruptive. Back then, you were channeling children to read with volume and stamina. Use the start of this new unit (and of any new unit) as an opportunity to note which of the behaviors you taught earlier have become automatic for your children. When you disperse children from the meeting area, for example, notice whether children walk directly and swiftly to their seats. Notice, too, whether it is second nature for them to pull out their logs and fill in the starting time and page number. Has it become natural for children to scan upcoming pages, readying themselves for whatever they'll be reading? Are they able to settle themselves down fairly quickly so they do not lose many precious moments at the start of reading time? If these reading behaviors are not yet well established, you won't necessarily address your concerns just now, but you'll definitely make plans to address them within the next few days. For now, it may be more important for you to move among your readers, making sure that each one connects to his or her character, reading as if in the character's shoes.

I drew alongside Tyrell, whose head was bent in concentration over the first book in the series, *The Littles*. I noticed he was sitting on his hand, a habit he got into when I tried to help him break the habit of pointing as he read. "Oh! I just love this series. I love the way the family sticks together and doesn't give up. They are always stumbling into trouble, and yet they always find ways to use their teamwork and determination to push on. I sometimes remember *The Littles* when my family is in a tricky situation. You have a big family too—just like them! Maybe *The Littles* will come to your mind, too, when you're with your family. You're going to love this series!"

Then I spotted Grace, reading Patricia MacLachlan's beautiful book *Journey*, and immediately, I felt protective of the story itself. I worried that Grace would race through the book, bypassing all that it has to offer and consequently missing the opportunity to feel deeply as she reads. I knew that to deepen her connection to her reading (and in turn to make reading become something she views as a pleasure more than as an assignment), Grace needed to have plenty of experiences reading books that capture her heart and mind. I knew *Journey* had the potential to be one of those books for her, so I wanted to set her up to read it with her heart and mind. "Oh my gosh," I said. "I'm so glad that you are reading this. The characters are so complicated, aren't they? Take Journey. I find myself thinking so much about his relationships with everyone. With his mother—I keep wondering if he knows his mother at all, or if his relationship is with a figment of his imagination. With his grandfather—over and over, I notice ways the grandfather works to build

a bond. And I watch Journey building bonds, too, though it is hard, but he bonds not just with people but also with things—with the camera, the animals. Will you *definitely* keep track of your thoughts and feelings about Journey as you read, 'cause I am dying to talk with you about your ideas. And don't read it too fast because this is a book that needs to be savored."

These rallying conversations (book introductions, really) tend to be quick, encouraging, and warm. As Richard Allington says, it's impossible to overemphasize the value of kids having relationships with richly literate adults who wear our love of reading—and, in this instance, of characters—on our sleeves. When we say to children, "Don't you love how . . . ?" or "Isn't that so cool when . . . ?" or "One thing I do when I'm reading and that happens is . . . ," we are inviting kids to live shoulder to shoulder with us inside the richly literate world of our classroom. There is little that matters more at the start of a new unit than the fact that we offer kids a generous invitation to join us in the heady work of the upcoming unit.

MID-WORKSHOP TEACHING POINT

continued from previous page

about the weather or the mood in that scene. Can you capture it in your sketch? You may need to add some words to show what your character is thinking or feeling."

Isaac, who was reading *School Story*, had sketched a character lying in bed. He added posters on the wall and a desk in the room. I whispered to Isaac, "What's the mood in this part, and how can you capture it?" Isaac said, "He is upset because he cheated."

I prompted, "Show that in the character's face." Isaac picked up his pencil and changed the character's facial expression. He made the character's smile into a zigzag and his eyes tiny and squinty. Then he made his hand into a fist.

Izzy, meanwhile, had sketched Sally, the protagonist of *Starring Sally Freedman*, lashing out against adults. Her thought bubbles read, "I don't want to!" and "Don't give me a hard time." *[See the CD-ROM for examples.]*

"Readers, will you resume reading? As you read, continue making movies in your mind, and remember, you create those mental movies by drawing on everything you read earlier and on everything that relates from real life. If the character walks into the school, you can insert the front steps of our school into the movie you are making in your mind, unless the book tells you that school is different. When you get to spots in your book where you are envisioning like crazy, for today jot or sketch what you see onto a Post-it so you can talk about your envisionments later.

"Readers, I also want you as you are reading, to look for intense parts of your book, parts that fill you up with big, strong emotions—maybe fear or hope—and put a Post-it note on those parts. We will be working with them during the teaching share today."

Assess Readers' Abilities with the Skill You Aim to Teach—Envisionment—Then Plan and Record a Trajectory of Development

If you have decided that during the first bend in the road of the character unit, you are aiming to teach children to envision as they read, making mental movies by drawing both on the details of the text and also on their own similar experiences, then you'll want to be in touch with why and what it means to do it well. For now, it will help if you realize that teaching envisionment means teaching toward that lost-in-a-book feeling that is too often regarded as something so magical that it's only accessible to a very few readers.

I often return to the wise words of Poet Laureate (MD 1979–1985) Lucille Clifton, who once said, "You cannot create what you cannot imagine." To move kids toward good work, it is crucially important for you to have a crystal clear image of what is entailed in that good work. If you are clear about what many of your readers currently do with that skill, and clear also about your goal, then you are on your way.

In the assessment section that follows this session, we suggest some ways you can collect baseline comprehension data and some informal assessment tools you can create for your own use. One way to create an informal assessment tool is to insert prompts into a text that you read aloud. The teachers who piloted the first draft of these units of study read aloud Eve Bunting's *One Green Apple*, pausing in carefully selected places to prompt students in several ways, including "Jot what you are picturing." They did this assessment at the start of the year.

To conduct a similar assessment at the start of the year, you'll want to read aloud a short story or a picture book, inserting prompts into the text that nudge students to demonstrate their abilities to use the skills of envisioning, predicting, and monitoring for sense within the context of the story. Specifically, in the assessment section, you'll learn how we did this with the short texts *Abby Takes a Shot* and *One Green Apple*. Once you've collected a jotted response from all your prompts from all your students, we suggest you sort the children's jotted envisionments and predictions into a continuum of piles representing ascending skill level. When the teachers who piloted these units sorted children's envisionments into piles, we started with gross categories: less skilled and more skilled at envisioning, less skilled and more skilled at predicting. We then tried to crystallize the differences between the novice and skilled work.

This day, I had the children write after hearing a section of *One Green Apple*, in which the main character, Farah, arrives at her new American school and climbs into a hay wagon with her new classmates. We regarded Max's envisionment as less skilled. *[Fig. I-4]* Aly and Emma, on the other hand, had written strong envisionments. *[Figs. I-5 and I-6]*

> I'm picturing a girl who misses her dog.

Figure I-4
Max doesn't fill in the setting or the specifics yet.

> A small covered wagon pulled by a tractor with all the kids facing in except for 1 girl facing out looking at the field.

Figure I-5
Aly draws on what the text says to fill in details it does not say.

> I am picturing kids staring at her, and one kid trying to communicate with Farah, with trees, cows, and a few dogs in front of them.

Figure I-6
Emma shows her ability to determine importance and to use visual details to convey emotions.

After studying the differences between less and more proficient envisionment and discussing these with our Teachers College Reading and Writing Project (TCRWP) colleagues, we created a list of how strong envisioners go about creating mental movies as they read.

Novice envisioners struggled to do much of this work. Intermediate envisioners fell somewhere in between the novice and the proficient envisioners. You can find the lists we've created differentiating the levels of envisioning we uncovered in the assessment section at the end of this book.

You needn't adopt our descriptions of what a strong envisioner does. Instead, I strongly encourage you to read a text aloud, interspersing prompts including "Picture what is happening now. Describe what's happening now, including as many characters as you can," and then sort your readers' efforts, as we did, and name what separates the least from the most developed work. In this way, you can develop your own list of what it is you hope your readers will do when they envision.

Strong Envisioners Are Apt to . . .

- Create a mental movie as he or she reads. When asked to do so, the reader can convey that to others.

- Monitor for sense by recognizing when the reader stops being able to imagine the story. The reader knows that by rereading, he or she can usually resume the mental movie.

- Generate a mental movie that draws on earlier sections of the text for specifics that flesh out the characters and setting.

- Create a mental movie that draws also on the reader's knowledge of the world, of other texts, and of similar settings, feelings, and situations. That is, readers infer to fill in gaps in the text.

- Picture not only the dominant character but also secondary characters.

- Derive a rich sensory experience from words on the page, picturing sounds, sights, and details and noticing the tone or atmosphere when appropriate.

- Determine importance so that his or her mental movie features significant parts of the scene.

Once you have in mind the signs you can look for to suggest whether your children are more or less proficient at this particular skill, you'll quickly be able to cluster your readers into levels of envisioners and begin to imagine some of the specific strategies that you can teach the different groups of readers. You'll want to think, "When I work with novice envisioners, what skills and strategies will be especially appropriate and within reach for them?" And then you'll want to turn your short list of goals into a dense, abbreviated list of prompts that you can put onto the record-keeping sheets you use as you work one-on-one or in small groups with these children. Perhaps you'll type these prompts for novice,

intermediate, and proficient envisioners onto mailing labels so that you can easily take notes in one spot, then separate the notes into the children's folders, affixing these onto record-keeping sheets to use as cue cards. You can see some examples of these in the assessment section at the end of this book.

One way or another, you'll want to turn your list of what skilled envisioners do into teaching plans. If you say to a child like Gabe who needs practice with envisioning, "Can you tell me what you are picturing in your mind as you read this page?" and Gabe's mental picture has no detail at all (perhaps he pictures a boy of indeterminate age, race, personality, appearance, and so on), then your list of what proficient envisioners do will keep you from feeling empty-handed. You'll know, for example, that one option for your conference will be to help Gabe fill in more specific information. On the other hand, had Gabe envisioned with elaborate detail but cited many details that seemed extraneous to the main gist of the story, then you would have known that one option for your conference would be to teach him to determine importance, letting a knowledge of what's important to the story guide him as he envisions. In the conferring sections of the next few sessions, you'll have a chance to eavesdrop on conferences and small-group work which helps readers envision well. Notice how the characteristics of a strong envisioner become a resource for teaching.

TEACHING SHARE

Readers Sometimes Share Especially Intense Passages—Reenacting and Discussing Those Passages with Friends

Ask readers to fill out their logs and join you in the meeting area.

"Readers, may I stop you? Fill out your logs, and then join me on the rug." As the children worked on their logs, I spot-checked those logs, giving children quick compliments and suggestions. "Kobe, I see you are close to the end of your book. Don't you love endings?" Kobe nodded slightly, and I was happy to see him beginning to express a love for books, even if it was just for the endings of books. "You better bring another book home tonight because I bet you'll finish this one and have time to start another."

Then I sat in my seat at the front of the meeting area, welcoming children as they convened. Speaking loudly to the stragglers, I said, "Readers, by now you should be making your way to the rug. Please bring your books and sit next to your reading partner."

I gestured to the chart we'd made during Unit 1 titled "Ways You and Another Reader Can Talk About Your Books." I said, "Let's go, readers. You should all be here, rereading this chart."

Remind children of the class chart of ways to share books with a partner, and tell them you have another way to add to the chart. Add the idea that readers can read a favorite part and act it out.

Once most children were with me, I began. "Readers, last month you thought up great ways of sharing books with your partners. Today I want to suggest one more way that partners can share our books.

"What I love to do when I'm talking about books with my friends is to say, 'Here's one *really* intense part . . . ,' and then we talk just about that one part, and how it goes with the whole story. But here's the cool thing. Instead of simply *talking* about those parts, we often actually read them aloud as if we are in a play, with each person taking on a role. You willing to try? For example, if you had read *Stone Fox* during independent reading time, you might tell your partner that the race at the end was an intense part, and then your partner might assume the role of Stone Fox and you might be Willy, and then you might reread the ending—just a page of it—aloud, with each person reading the words that he or she would say, and one of you reading the rest, too.

COACHING TIPS

Pay attention to the use of time in your classroom. As I visit classrooms, I am struck by how utterly differently people handle transitions to and from the meeting area. In some classrooms, it may require well over five minutes for children to fill in their logs and assemble on the carpet. Watching youngsters in those classrooms, it seems as if they are moving in slow motion through space. Each child slowly, slowly, reaches for his or her log. Each child's log gets retrieved from its hiding place and put front and center on the child's desk, and then one child after another stares open mouthed at a log, perhaps thinking, "How many minutes did I read?" and hoping the answer will descend from outer space. Eventually, the child records a number to represent the time he or she spent reading, and now (at long last) the child begins the long process of moving to the meeting area.

If you must, start the meeting before every child has joined you to speed up any stragglers. You may need to develop a plan for the child who is chronically late to the meeting area. Perhaps that child needs to participate in the minilessons from a remote location—his or her workspace. Or that child's desk needs to be especially close to the meeting area so the youngster has less ground to traverse.

Describe, step by step, how children could share a book this way, and then ask them to try it.

"Most of you are not reading the same book as your partner, but you can still share an intense part. Fill your partner in by starting with a 'previously in,' summarizing the book up to the part that you want to share.

"So put the book between you. Decide on the section you'll read (keep it very short) and the roles each of you will play. And read the passage, taking on roles as if you *are* the characters (you can leave out the 'he said' and 'she said' tags).

Tim Rasinski argues that all readers need opportunities to cultivate their read-aloud voices, and struggling readers especially need this. As you'll see, this particular teaching share session ends up channeling children to reread important sections of text several times, and Rasinski emphasizes that providing meaningful opportunities for repeated reading is important. He writes, "I also wish to express a strong concern that the aim of repeated reading should be meaningful and expressive oral interpretation or performance of text, not faster reading. To that end, certain texts lend themselves to oral interpretive reading." He recommends that oral rereadings work well in "partner time" and have a "positive impact on students' reading development."

Ways You and Another Reader Can Talk About Your Books

- Share passages that especially drew you in—parts that made you feel a strong emotion or exciting parts that had you on the edge of your seat.

- Share parts in which you really pictured what is happening, perhaps parts where you felt like you were in a 3-D movie—one with surround sound.

- Show each other parts of your books where the mental movie you made as you read got blurry, places where you thought "Huh?" and then talk about those parts, discussing what's going on in them.

- Figure out a tricky word by discussing what the word might mean and by using words you **can** read to figure out how to say this unfamiliar word.

- Tell the big things that happened to the main character so far, either by reaching back and starting at the beginning, perhaps saying "Previously in . . . ," or by starting with now and tucking in past events.

"Here is the best part, though. *After* you read the scene, talk about what you've read so you understand each character more. What was that one character thinking? Feeling? Then you can *reread* one more time, this time adding gestures and intonation so you really make the scene come alive. Some partners go so far as to put the book down and use their own words to act out what they think is really happening.

"Let's do this together for now. Partner 2, think of a passage you read in your independent reading book that is important to the story. (It's helpful if you choose a part that has lots of dialogue.) Take just a second to find a section.

"Okay, now do a quick 'previously in' to catch your partner up on what's already happened. Remember to take big gigantic steps as you retell. (Partner 1, if Partner 2 is not moving in big steps but is instead retelling in teeny tiny steps, say, 'What's the next big thing that happened?' or use your hand to signal, 'Move it along.')"

I voiced over, "Readers, put the book between you and glance ahead at the selected scene. It should be about a page in length. Decide quickly who will take which roles. Then begin reading aloud, taking parts."

Teachers, this dramatic interpretation work is electrifying. It helps kids get lost in their stories. Don't be afraid of it. Don't bypass it or you will miss out on something that is a surefire hit, and incredibly good for readers' fluency and comprehension. You'll find, too, that the drama can lead kids into heady conversations about what's really happening in the scene and can help children dig into an analysis of the characters. The conversations that this sparks are as important as the drama itself.

Teachers, don't give the children more than a minute to find a passage. Remember, you already set them up to find an intense place in their books during the mid-workshop teaching point. You will have to move them along quickly or this will take too long.

Teachers, you'll see that we often suggest you help one partner coach another. You and your children can invent hand signals that function as prompts. One signal can suggest, "Go on, say more." Another can suggest, "Cut to the chase. What are you really saying?" A listener can point to his or her mouth to signal, "Read the speaking parts as if someone is saying them." A listener can pat his or her heart to signal, "Read it with feeling." Touching an ear can signal, "Louder!" Although I'm suggesting motions and ascribing meaning to them, you'll want your kids to invent their own. In any way possible, encourage your youngsters to coauthor the rituals of your classroom.

Coach children as they try this, lifting the level of their fluency.

As children read aloud, I moved among them, assessing fluency, especially. I coached one reader by saying, "Put your words closer together as you read." To another I said, "Read that again. This time sound like you are talking." To others, I said, "Don't forget to leave off the 'he said,' and 'she said' tags. You are the character!"

In a voiceover to the entire class, I said, "Partners, when you're done rereading, move on to the next step. Discuss what the characters are feeling, then reread again, and this time be sure your rereading shows these feelings. I'll give you a few more minutes."

As partners continued, I coached one listening partner to use a "Come-on, continue, keep it going" hand gesture. I encouraged another listener to question the reader's interpretation of the character's affect. ("Was she *really* bored? Could she have been more confused than bored?").

Celebrate one partnership's work in a way that recaps what you hope all the children have learned.

After a bit, I intervened to conclude this teaching share. "Readers, I watched you *become* the characters in your book—right in front of my eyes! What I loved best were the conversations you had after you reenacted a scene because I watched you actually grow ideas about characters. For example, at first, Rosa and Gabe just thought Amber Brown was a pretty annoying kid. But then as they pushed themselves to keep talking, they decided that maybe she was only *acting* annoying because that was the only way she could get both of her parents' attention. Gabe and Rosa had the idea that maybe if her mom and dad, and even her mom's boyfriend, paid her more attention, Amber Brown wouldn't seem so bratty. Our goal needs to be to understand characters more deeply because of this work.

"Today, we tried out a new way to share the flagged parts in our books. We reenacted particular passages with a partner!" I added "Share a passage you flagged because it is especially well-written, intense, funny, and so on. Then perform the passage, talking about how best to interpret it" to our chart of ways readers can share books.

Rebecca reflected on the experience of acting out a scene. Her writing shows all she did to climb into Jean Little's world.

Some teachers do informal surveys of their classes, asking for partners to raise their hands to indicate which option they have chosen. This allows you to see if your class tends toward certain options and yet never chooses other options. This will tell you if you need to do some more teaching and demonstrating of the less popular options.

Developing Concrete, Obtainable Reading Goals

What a wonderful month October is for teaching and learning. You will definitely want to continue conducting the formative assessments you began last month and to use these, plus everything else you are coming to know about your individual readers, to establish and communicate concrete and obtainable goals for readers. You'll want to begin giving individuals targeted feedback to help them see where they are going, how they are doing, and what the next steps might be. This month in our teaching and assessing, we emulate the coaching an Olympic athlete might receive!

So far, you've begun immersing your students in a learning community that is imbued with high standards, and you've begun modeling a love of reading for them. Now it will be important for you to develop learning pathways for readers. You'll need to do everything you can to be sure that each of your students senses that he is traveling toward important goals, and that he can, with hard work, make dramatic progress toward those goals. To create these learning pathways, tailored to specific individuals, you'll need to draw on two things: formative assessments and your knowledge of the specific challenges your readers will confront as they work with the texts they're reading now and those they will be reading soon. For more about the latter, you can turn to the next assessment section of this volume, at the back of the book. For now, we'll turn to formative assessments.

Creating Assessments that Give Kids a Sense of Personal Power

To being this work, you'll want to continue showing readers ways in which growth in reading can be turned into tangible goals. Let me take a detour for a moment. I have a coach who helps me train my very ebullient puppy (who has been growing up as I write this series!). Early on,

the coach announced that we were going to work on teaching Emma not to clamber out of the car after me, but to instead wait in a dignified, restrained fashion until I signal that it is time for her to join me. I protested. Of all the possible goals, the goal of teaching Emma to get out of the car properly was low on my list. "How about, instead, teaching her to come when I call?" I suggested.

My coach was firm. "No, we're going to teach her to remain in the car until you signal it's time for her to follow you," she said. "And this is the reason we're teaching Emma this lesson: It's easy to teach. Every time she starts to follow prematurely, you can simply slam the door in her face. In no time, she learns."

"But who cares if she learns that particular lesson?" I grouched.

"You are missing the point. You need to teach Emma something that you can teach and she can learn because by doing this, you will be teaching her that she can learn, and she can be successful at learning. You need to teach her to get into the habit of learning from you."

I do not mean to suggest that kids are like puppies (although yes, I admit I sometimes see the parallels), but I do think that early in the year, one reason to conduct formative assessments is that this provides you with a tool for showing kids that you can teach and they can learn this all-important skill called reading. Too often, I think, kids grow up feeling that reading well is one of those God-given gifts that some people have and others don't. Kids who read well don't seem to work at it. Instead, they seem to have emerged *ex nihilo* as good readers. And kids who don't read well often enter our classrooms feeling like this is just "who I am." "I'm a bad reader," they say. "Sometimes the words are too hard," they tell us.

In contrast, kids will say, "I started playing trombone, but then I quit it, so I can't really play good at all," or "I didn't really get to play any baseball last summer, so I'm not playing my best anymore," or "I'm not sure I want to go out for baseball this year—it takes so much time and all," as if they believe that being skillful at playing an instrument or a sport is a matter of choice and within their control. But many kids don't feel as if becoming a good reader is a matter of choice, something that is within their control.

It is important to change this. Malcolm Gladwell has shown (in his book about successful people, *Outliers*) that people who are successful at anything are people who are willing to work at that thing, to put in the time. Surely that is true for success in reading. And in any case, as Peter Johnston says in *Choice Words*, "If nothing else, children should leave school with a sense that if they act, and act strategically, they can accomplish their goals. I call this feeling a sense of agency" (p. 29). We need to help our children to develop this sense of agency—in reading and in life.

In this section, I will describe several important ways you can invite kids to join you in making proficiency in reading into concrete, observable, objective skills. I can see some of you wincing at those words, and yes, I understand that publishing programs and administrators have sometimes used the language of "concrete, objective skills" to reduce reading instruction into a regimen of skill-and-drill work, but I urge you to remember that the terms can be taken back and used by any educator who thinks there is value in providing kids with explicit instruction in the habits, skills, and strategies that proficient readers use. I have come to believe that to enable all kids to progress steadily forward in their skills, it is helpful to take the risk of actually detailing, with as much honesty and integrity and specificity as possible, what good work entails. After all, who among us was not mystified by the teachers of our childhood who used to extol us to "think symbolically" and to explicate the ways an author used imagery and figurative language to advance a theme? I remember thinking, "Huh?" and wanting to ask, "What exactly do you mean?" I'm convinced that often when we urge kids to predict, envision, grow theories about character, infer, interpret, read critically, determine importance, or do a host of other intellectual work, many of our kids are echoing the question I used to ask. "Huh?" they are thinking. "What exactly do you mean?"

There will be a homespun quality to the assessments I describe in this section. They're formative assessments, made by hand—unlike the more systematized running records and text levels with which we've

been working. Later, in the second volume of this unit of study, we'll revisit the assessment system that involves matching kids to levels of text difficulty and tracking their progress up this gradient of difficulty; we are not leaving that kind of assessment behind! We turn now to other forms of assessment because every assessment tool has limitations. For example, imagine someone wanted to glean a quick indicator of your skills as a teacher to track the progression of your teaching skills across time. Say this person devised a way to take a five-minute sampling of your teaching and then to analyze that sampling for patterns that revealed your strengths and your needs. Presumably such an assessment could illuminate aspects of your teaching, but one would hope that the assessor would bear in mind that the assessments were based on a teensy bit of data and would be eager to look between the findings from that assessment and those from other assessments.

There will never be The Right Way to assess a young reader. Learning to read well, like learning to teach well, is a complex enterprise. Every mind and person is different, and no single tool will do the whole job. The best we can do is to use multiple tools to assess our readers and their learning and regard all of our findings as fallible, keeping all our conclusions about children as works in progress, drafts to be revised.

This assessment section, then, will move away from running records and matching readers to text levels and instead suggest ways formative assessments can help you and your students fix your eyes on concrete, obtainable goals—goals that are especially aligned to the curriculum of this upcoming unit of study. This section will help you use a steady flow of data to ensure that everyone's learning (your own as well as the kids') stays on a productive course.

Help Kids Translate the Data in Reading Logs into Goals for Themselves

Earlier, I emphasized that a treasure trove of information is available in students' reading logs, if only we help students maintain these records with vigilance. The best way to do this is to show children how to become researchers of their own reading habits, poring over their own and each other's reading logs to deduce patterns. Encourage readers to count up the pages read or the minutes spent reading in one week and contrast that with data from the next week, and eventually to do the same for one month, contrasting with the next month.

Of course, the reason to notice patterns in one's own data is to learn from those patterns. If a child notices that she reads almost twice as much one week than another week, the important question is, Why? What explains the sudden rise in her reading volume? How can she continue to create those conditions for herself? These questions are especially important because the data collected on a reading log is amenable to change. The child can at any point resolve to read longer and more. This matters. Just as it is important for you and me to feel as if we can draw a line in the sand right now, starting today, and resolve to change our ways, so too it is important for kids to realize this.

Let Kids In on the Research that Can Help Them Analyze Their Data

I think it is wise to share research findings with youngsters, asking them to join you in figuring out whether those findings have relevance for their lives.

Reading Rate

For example, you could recruit kids to join you in researching their reading rates, and then, once each child has established his or her words per minute, you can share guidelines from the research for evaluating that rate. That is, without telling children your purpose, you could set them up to mark the starting place in their book and then to read, stopping after two minutes, and you could use this dipstick to help them to calculate their words per minute. Then you could show children Harris and Sipay's (1990) guidelines for thinking about reading rate based on levels of text difficulty. These researchers suggest:

C–I: 60–90 words per minute

J–L: 85–120 words per minute

L–O: 115–140 words per minute

P–R: 140–170 words per minute

S–U: 170–195 words per minute

T–V: 195–220 words per minute

V–W: 215–245 words per minute

If some of your youngsters are reading much more slowly than the research suggests is advisable, you may want to assess their fluency, which includes not just the speed with which a child can read but also their expression, prosody, and parsing. For example, you might make a list of students whose reading rates are slow and check to see whether they are reading in very brief phrases. You could listen to them read and check off whether they are reading in two-word phrases or in three-word phrases. You could also note which of these readers attend to punctuation and which do not. Of course, as you do this, you'll probably end up reconsidering whether in fact you have established just-right reading levels for these readers, because one of the preconditions for a level being just right is that this is a level at which the child can read with fluency (which includes an attention to punctuation and phrasing).

If you've decided that fluency or reading rate is holding a reader back, you will want to let the reader see the data that you've collected, contrasting it with what research indicates would be data the readers could aim to achieve. You could let them know tips that researchers say can help. For example, sometimes when children are reading slowly, they are running a finger or a bookmark under the words, or mouthing the words as they read—all habits that slow down a reader's rate and that can be set aside. Many children who read really slowly are in fact doing constant little check-backs as they proceed down the page, rereading often a score of times while reading even just a single page of print, as if worried that some name, some detail, might get past them. These children need to be encouraged to read on, unless something is really confusing, and to trust that the important things that the reader needs to hold onto will usually recur anyhow. Many children who read too slowly need help phrasing and can be encouraged to reach for larger chunks of words, taking in longer and more meaningful phrases at a time. It can help to reread a familiar text aloud multiple times, with tremendous attention to the meaning of the text, trying to read it in ways that allow the meaning to really shine through.

My point, right now, is not to summarize methods for supporting a child's fluency so much as to suggest that we benefit from letting children join us in collecting data on their reading and join us also in working with resolve to strengthen their muscles as readers. And the good news is that after working for a few weeks, children can collect more data and look for indications of growth. If a child's data suggests that child is growing, then it is critically important to use that data to help the learner develop a self-concept of "I'm on my way as a reader. I keep growing and growing. This year looks like it'll be one of those growth spurt years."

Reading Volume

You could also share the data (Gentry) that suggests that children who are reading books at particular levels will generally complete those books within predictable lengths of time. Allington points out that many level M books, including the *Magic Tree House* series, contain approximately 6,000 words. Readers who can handle level M books will tend to be reading at least 100 words per minute, suggesting that one of these books should require no more than an hour of reading. If children are reading an hour or two a day, that suggests that a child reading level M books will read at least seven books a week. Meanwhile, many level R books are closer to 50,000 words, the word-count for Paulsen's *Hatchet.** Readers who can read this level of text difficulty will tend to be reading at least 150 words per minute, suggesting that they'll tend to be able to read one of their level R books in six hours—suggesting that certainly readers will complete these books within a week. The important thing to realize is that children reading at lower levels of text difficulty need to read closer to a book a day than a chapter a day!

It is entirely likely that you will find that some of your readers are creeping through books, reading exponentially more slowly than these figures suggest. I strongly suggest you talk to these kids about what you notice. Say, "I want to talk to the two of you because I'm noticing that you both have been reading something like sixteen pages a day in school, and a bit less at home, and I need you to know that some scientists have studied what kids need to flourish as readers, and they're suggesting that kids need to read at least twice as many pages a day as you are reading. They're suggesting that a reader like you should be aiming to read close to thirty pages a day in school, and the same amount at home. I know that must sound crazy to you. It is so much more reading than you are doing, but I am wondering if there is any chance you'd be game to try for this. I mean, these researchers—these scientists—have studied thousands of kids, and they are really sure that the amount of reading you're doing just isn't enough. Would you be willing to really push yourself, and see what's possible? We could talk tomorrow about what you discover." When I've talked like that to kids, it has often happened that the next day, the kids gallop into the classroom, calling, "We did it! We did it!"

Of course, it is not a small thing to help kids ramp up the amount of reading they're doing, and you and the youngsters may need to talk about how this could be possible. One way to do this is to interview the youngsters who are getting a lot of reading done (ideally there will be some readers who do not read especially challenging text levels but who do make time for lots of reading, so these children can become famous for their time on task). You can help youngsters learn that the way to get a lot of reading done is to carry books everywhere, using stolen moments to read. It means making time during the prime time of the day for reading and not just relegating reading to those weary moments before bed. It means disciplining oneself to not watch TV or play video games or talk on the phone constantly, and perhaps even asking parents or caregivers for help establishing boundaries. You'll also want to be sure that you don't teach as if the goal is a measured increment of time each day for reading. Be stunned when a child never reads for three times the required length of time. "I'm so surprised. Don't you ever get so drawn into your book that you can't put it down and you read way on and on?"

These are just general guidelines, but the powerful thing about them is that they highlight some of the most important aspects of teaching reading well, and again, the data can reveal patterns that are easily shared with kids and easily addressed. So often, the term "data-based instruction" has been used to pull young people away from reading toward text-prep exercises, but in fact, data-based instruction can rally kids to exponentially increase the time they spend reading.

Help Kids Understand What It Means to Comprehend Well—and More Specifically to Envision and Predict Well, to Adopt Concrete Goals that Allow Them to Travel Along Trajectories of Skill Development

The running records you will have taken include a minimal check on children's comprehension of 250-word passages. However, asking children to retell or to answer a couple of literal and inferential questions can't be the sum total of your tools for assessing the comprehension skills needed to read full-length novels. We need more information.

To collect more information, you and your students will notice and name the distinctive patterns in each other's responses to texts—in Post-its, entries, and contributions to discussions—and at the end of this section, I'll address the value of studying these responses. For now, let me suggest that there is something especially startling and informative that can be learned when you ask every reader to respond at the same time and in the same way to the same text (or to the same questions, planted in similar places within similar texts of varying difficulty).

The start of the year is a crazy time for teachers, with everything feeling especially urgent, so I hesitate to suggest that along with everything else you use a formative assessment tool such as the one I describe in this section. I do, however, suggest you push yourself to do this, even if you simply read a text aloud, stopping at the appointed spots to call out a question and to ask children to write their responses to that question before you continue reading. Even if you do not have time at the start of this unit to analyze deeply what children do, taking the time to collect baseline data will be enormously powerful later on in the unit when you want to show children and their caregivers the progress they've made in even just a few weeks' time. Johnston reminds us that it is crucial to help children tell stories about their performance in which their engagement and motivation yields achievement. "Children with a strong belief in their own agency work harder, focus their attention better, are more interested in their studies, and are less likely to give up when they encounter difficulties than children with a weaker sense of agency" (Skinner, Zimmer, Gembeck, and Connell, 1998).

Insert Questions into Texts that Call for the Reading Skills You Plan to Teach and Therefore Want to Study

It is impossible to emphasize enough how illuminating it has been for my colleagues and me to use an assessment tool that I will describe for you in this section, and that I will include in detail on the CD-ROM. I heartily encourage you to devise your own variation of this assessment tool. It is infinitely variable. But a word of caution: The tool looks deceptively simple. It actually took ten Teachers College Reading and Writing Project staff developers, working together with Kathleen Tolan, Mary Ehrenworth, and me, one full morning a week for almost two months to devise this tool and analyze the data it yielded. It required countless pilot trials to tweak the wording and placement of questions so that it elicited what kids can do in ways that revealed telling differences among kids rather than showing kids' varied understandings of the task. It was even more challenging to analyze the data we collected to describe ways that skilled answers differed from less skilled answers!

For starters, we selected texts at two distinct text levels—one a level K and one a level R text—and then inserted carefully constructed questions at points in the texts where we felt that any reader who was comprehending the text would need to be using the particular reading skill of the question or prompt. We asked each reader to read one story or the other, making sure the story was easy enough for each to read and to jot answers to the questions as they read. To facilitate this, we formatted each of the two texts so that as a reader progressed through the text, he or she would encounter a question and a large space for a written response just at the point where we wanted the reader to stop and answer that question. After the space for the response, the story would resume. And so on with a few other questions or prompts.

The questions were designed to reveal what children can do with a handful of skills that we felt were essential for reading fiction and that were important to us during the earliest portion of our year-long reading workshop. Specifically, we wanted to understand how children develope theories about characters and revise them in light of new information. We wanted to understand the ways children predict, envision, and interpret.

The first of the stories is "Abby Takes Her Shot" by Susan Dyckman. (See the *Resources for Teaching Reading* CD-ROM.) Abby is a fifth-grade bench-warmer on a middle school basketball team. Because she is cheering herself hoarse, and because her brother teases her by calling her "a cheerleader in a basketball uniform," a reader might at first think Abby is a cheerleader, not a team member, but as the text unfolds, it becomes clear that she is on the team, though she rarely plays in actual games. Any reader who has begun the text with the misconception that Abby is a cheerleader will need to revise that understanding. The two questions we've inserted in the text, "What have you learned about Abby?" and later, "What more have you learned about Abby?" are meant to reveal to us the ways different readers are developing and revising theories about the protagonist as they read.

As the story continues, Abby's brother teases her for never playing, and she fights back tears over never getting to play. Then she goes home to practice basketball with great determination into the late evening. Her mother, helping her, says she's proud of Abby for hanging in there and assures her, "Your time will come." Then her mother asks, "What time is your game on Saturday?"

At this moment in the story, we've inserted a question, "What do you think will happen in the rest of the story? What makes you think this?" This question is designed to help us see what children do when they are asked to predict.

Later, when the game is under way, another player is knocked to the floor and does not get up. The gym quiets as the coach checks on the hurt player. At this point, we've inserted a prompt, "Picture what is happening right now. Describe it, including as many characters as you can." This prompt is designed to help us understand the ways and depths at which children are envisioning.

Sort Responses into Categories from Not Proficient to Very Proficient

Across hundreds of Teachers College Reading and Writing Project schools, teachers gave readers either the story described above or an easier story, with similar questions inserted into it, making sure that every reader could read the text that he or she was given, and asked readers to do this work during class time, alongside each other but working alone. Some teachers altered this plan by reading aloud the text rather than asking children to read it on their own, allowing them to use the same text for all children and making this a listening assessment. Others adapted the questions to another text, placing them into that text with care. This is what we did in our most recent pilot of the Units of Study, inserting the questions into Eve Bunting's picture book *One Green Apple*, which we read aloud. Children's responses to some of those questions are included in Session I's conferring and small-group section.

Working with the participating teachers, we then sorted children's responses to each question (that is, their work on each skill the question or prompt was meant to hone in on) into three piles: not proficient, competent, and very proficient. Then we set out to pinpoint what the concrete, objective differences were between the three categories. Not surprisingly, it was easier to describe and differentiate the not proficient and very proficient work. The work that fell between these extremes could fall between in a host of different ways.

Examine the Gradient of Student Envisionments

Let's look at the differences in children's responses to the question inserted into "Abby Takes Her Shot" that we hoped would reveal children's ability to envision. Remember, the teammate has fallen to the floor in the midst of the basketball game, the game at which Abby is desperately hoping to play. Readers are prompted to picture what is happening, describing it with reference to as many characters as possible.

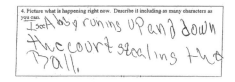

Those two examples were not idiosyncratic. There were countless readers whose work resembled the two examples I've shown, as well as, of course, many whose work fell in between those extremes. Answers to other questions were equally revealing.

Examine the Gradient of Student Predictions

You will recall that after Abby's struggles to somehow get some playing time, and after her resolute efforts to practice her shots late into the night, her mother reassures her that her time will come and asks when the next game will be. At that moment, we've asked readers, "What will happen in the rest of the story? How do you know?" There were, once again, dramatic differences in readers' responses to this question.

Student Examples of Prediction

Highly Proficient at Prediction

> 3. What do you think will happen in the rest of the story? What makes you think this?
> Well, the title is "Abby Takes Her Shot." I think something will happen in the game (maybe a star player gets hurt) and Abby will get to take maybe a game deciding foul shot. The kind of set you up for it by Abby barely ever getting to play and her being so determined and keeping her commitment to the team.

Not Yet Proficient at Prediction

> 3. What do you think will happen in the rest of the story? What makes you think this?
> That Abby won't know how to play Basketball anymore. I think this because when she shoot the ball she hit the rim and missed.

Analyze Responses To Extrapolate Descriptors of More and Less Proficient Work with Each Skill, Making Sure These Could Apply to Any Reader, Any Text

It would *not* have been helpful if we simply noted that in the more proficient envisionments—mental movies—readers included not only the characters who had just been described (Kathy, the coach) but also other characters (Abby, the fans). We can't go through life teaching readers that to comprehend well, it is important to envision Abby! Instead, the challenge was to describe what more proficient envisioners did that the less proficient envisioners did not do, using terms that were transferable to another day, another text, and another reader. This work of standing back to name what one person has done in ways that are broadly applicable is something that reading and writing workshop teachers must do constantly: We name what we will do and did do in the teaching sections of our minilessons; we use the work that a particular learner did during mid-workshop teaching points; we use teaching shares and small-group work to show pathways that others can follow.

Draw Conclusions About Envisioning with Skill

In Session I's conferring and small-group work section, I include the complete list of descriptors we developed for highly proficient envisionments.

Even just a quick look at the two samples I provided above will reveal to you that highly skilled envisioners create mental movies that draw on precise information about characters, incorporating details that aren't specified from the text but are instead drawn from the reader's prior knowledge of similar situations, that these envisioners can imagine what characters are doing who are off stage at the specific moment, and that their envisionments reflect an ability to determine importance and to do so in part by relying on a sense of how stories tend to go and in part by ascertaining the main idea of the story.

Draw Conclusions About Predicting with Skill

We also analyzed what readers did, exactly, who were highly skilled at prediction, distinguishing what they did from what the less skilled predictors did, and in a similar fashion, devised a list of qualities of skilled predictions (see Session VI's conferring and small-group section.)

For example, we found that the better predictors drew upon not only the immediate text but also relevant details from previous parts of the story to speculate about the upcoming story line. That is, in this instance, a more skilled prediction might mention that when the time for the game arrives, Abby "takes her usual place on the bench," or it might mention that her brother and mother attend the game or that she will be called upon to make a jump shot—the very shot she'd practiced so successfully the evening before.

We found, too, that the more proficient predictors demonstrated an ability to predict about events that were apt to be important to the narrative curve, and to do so, they relied on the title, the sequence of events, and their knowledge of how stories are apt to go. That is, a reader might reasonably suggest that after practicing basketball outside while the daylight ebbs, after her mother asks when tomorrow's game will start, the next event in the story could be that Abby comes inside, gets a snack, and watches her favorite show. A more experienced reader would draw on a sense of how stories go and on an accompanying ability to determine importance and would not produce such a response. There is more than one prediction a skilled reader could make. It would be feasible to suggest that the brother sees her coming in from practicing her shots and again ribs her, for example, but most readers who have a sense for narrative structure can predict Abby will be given an opportunity to take her shot.

I have described our work with two of the questions on this assessment tool and two of the skills we aimed to teach—prediction and envisionment—but of course we also assessed readers' abilities to develop theories about characters, revising those in light of new information, and to interpret. Assessments of interpretation will be a focus of the assessment section in the unit of study on reading historical fiction, *Tackling Complex Texts*.

Use This Assessment Tool to Help Readers Self-Assess and Work with Efficacy Toward Achievable Goals

If you collected baseline data on your children's abilities to do any of the skills that you are especially highlighting in this unit, then you and your students will be in especially good positions to watch for progress and to hold yourselves accountable. Teachers, the most important accountability will be your own. You will absolutely want to make sure that your children progress in dramatic ways. In early October, you can't watch, right then and there, to see if all your children can perform well on a standardized test, but if you have a sense of learning trajectories that kids follow en route to learning to envision, predict, and grow theories about characters with increasing sophistication, then you should most certainly be able to hold yourself accountable for teaching in such a way that every one of your kids progresses along those trajectories. And the important thing is that a reader can be reading a level J book or a level Z book and can still progress along those trajectories. It won't be the case that your teaching is applicable only to a few of your readers.

My point is that if we hope to teach a skill, then we need to be willing to try to convey with precision and clarity what good work with that skill entails. If we can say to a child that a skilled predictor thinks, "What happened much earlier in the story, not just in this immediate spot, that can help me imagine what might happen next?" then we can also help readers improve their predictions by suggesting they take a minute to scan back over the initial part of a text, looking for details from that early section of the text that can play a role in their predictions. That is, if we know what it means, exactly, to do any skill well, then we can help readers do exactly that, demythologizing for the learner what it is that is entailed in good work. In Sessions II, III, V, and VI, I show ways in which this knowledge can inform our conferring and small-group work.

We can also engage children in self-evaluation. "Readers," we can say, "will you reread your Post-its from today and locate one in which you did what you think of as your best predicting work?" If we'd like, we can remind children of characteristics of skilled predictions they've already been taught so they can compare and contrast their work against that standard. Then we can go a step farther and say, "Will you and your partner link up with another partnership and all four of you share the prediction Post-it you selected as your best? And then determine, as a group, which one of your prediction Post-its represents the group's prediction work at its best." After children locate the best example of prediction, it's easy to take this a step farther either by suggesting the group work together to take their good work and make it even stronger, if possible, or by suggesting the group join forces and revise each other's work so that the entire group's collection of prediction Post-its represents the group's best efforts. We can also say, "Let's keep these excellent predictions near us as we read on, and today, let's push ourselves to predict as we read, and more than that, to make our predictions draw on everything we know about predicting really, really well."

The assessments I've just described—which are created by inserting questions into texts and then studying students' written responses to those questions—are one of several ways we have devised for tracking students' growing abilities to envision, predict, grow theories about characters, and demonstrate other similar sorts of reading skills. The tool has been miraculous in its ability to shed light on skills that at one time seemed nebulous and ill-defined to us.

Help Kids Learn to Study Their Responses to Texts to Create Concrete Goals for Either Becoming Specialists or Widening Their Repertoire of Responses

Of course, looking at what children do when they are asked to perform a given task is revealing, but it is also revealing to look at how children respond to texts when they are not questioned or prompted—times when their reading responses are theirs to author. Although you and your children will want to devise some formative assessments such as the one I've detailed above, don't forget that the work you do together, day in and day out, always revolves around assessments. Your work in every conference and every small group begins with assessment, and as you adapt, revise, reject, and invent minilessons, you'll do so in ways that are grounded in assessment.

For example, you'll want to pay special attention to the ideas that children record on Post-its and in their reading notebooks and those they express as they talk about texts. Study all this evidence—this data—to learn about the thinking your children do (and don't do) as they read. Invite them to join you in this study.

If you look across the collection of jotted thoughts that each child accumulates during a week or two of reading, you'll quickly see that most readers have patterns in the ways they respond to texts. One reader's Post-its will contain lots of empathetic responses—comments such as "I'd be so mad . . ." or "I bet she . . ." or "I'm so worried about her . . ." or "Oh no! She's going to get hurt." Another reader will generate all sorts of questions, especially questions about why the author wrote in this particular way. Those two youngsters—the empathizer and the critic—read differently, and their Post-its and reading logs reveal these differences. Children too can notice and name these patterns when they lay out their responses over time. In your conferences and small groups, you and your students can engage in reader studies in which you notice and name patterns of responses to reading.

Any reading skill that a reader tends to do a lot—whether it's predicting, questioning, envisioning, inferring, empathizing, theorizing, monitoring for sense, synthesizing one part of the text with other parts, drawing on a knowledge of other texts or of story structure, drawing on a knowledge of the world, reading critically, and so forth—is a potential talent of the child's that can be named, celebrated, and developed. "You've got this knack; if you develop this, you could become quite an expert! You could teach this way of reading to the rest of the class or to your partner." In addition to deepening their areas of reading expertise, we can also encourage readers to expand their repertoire of ways of responding to texts. They can simply give themselves assignments to try certain other ways of responding, or they could mentor a classmate who tends to respond in ways different from their own.

What is crucial for us all to remember is that we must never rely on just one form of assessment to form a picture of a child. Certainly, we will use our systematic assessments, our running records with their helpful formulas and corresponding text levels. We will also invent our own formative assessments, based on prompts and questions and texts and situations we devise to help us shed light on our readers and the ways they think and the skills they have and the strategies they use. We must also find ways to assess and learn from what the children give us—the responses they invent, and the ideas they create and lay before us, unprompted, un-asked for, and freely given.

Living in the World of a Story

IN THIS SESSION,

you will teach students that readers monitor our own levels of engagement with texts, and if we find ourselves drifting, we work to bring the story to life by envisioning our characters' worlds.

Teachers, here is the important question. Have you been reading differently because of your teaching? When you lay in bed last night, reading your novel, did you let it take you to another world? Were *you* there, in the scene of the story, taking in the sounds, feeling that air on your arm?

A year from now, when you gather a whole new class of children close around you and suggest that each child might make a timeline of his or her history as a reader, and when you proceed to pull out the timeline of *your* reading life, will this unit of study be one of those turning points on your timeline? It could be, if you let your teaching be a course of study for you, and not just for your kids. And it's not just your timeline that would be different as a result. Your life as

a person, a reader, and a teacher could be changed in big and important ways, too. So today, I want to encourage you to say to yourself, "I'm going to let this unit of study be for me, not just for the kids."

You might be thinking, "What?" You might want to tell me, "Frankly, Lucy, I learned to read when I was six. Reading is no big deal for me anymore—I actually do it effortlessly." But you and I learned to write at six, too. And yet when we teach writing, we *do* let writing be not only for the kids but also for us.

Today, I want to suggest that if you think that learning to read is somehow "kid stuff," if working on your own reading is beneath you, then your teaching of reading will inevitably be wooden. I want to suggest, too, that the kids

GETTING READY

- You will have finished rereading Chapter 1 of *The Tiger Rising* prior to today's minilesson.

- Find a place in your read-aloud where you can model what you'll describe as "reading yourself awake." If you are using *The Tiger Rising*, the beginning of Chapter 2 works beautifully.

- The session begins with a personal story about a time when you lived as if on autopilot and then someone helped you "wake up" and truly experience life. Your minilesson will be immeasurably stronger if you bring your own story to it.

- Today might be a time to review the charts you and your class made during the previous unit, which should continue to be displayed prominently and which should be archived.

- Before Session 3, you will want to have completed Chapter 2 of *The Tiger Rising*.

really, really need you to live among them as a great reader, as a "famous reader." In a reading workshop, it's even more important than in a writing workshop for us to be willing to be mentors. After all, in a writing workshop, we can tell kids stories about great writers. We can tell them that Maurice Sendak's wild things were patterned after his Jewish relatives who'd visit every Saturday, leaning their big faces down toward him, pinching his cheeks and saying, "Oh I could eat you up!" The world doesn't contain many stories of famous readers. But most of our children don't have

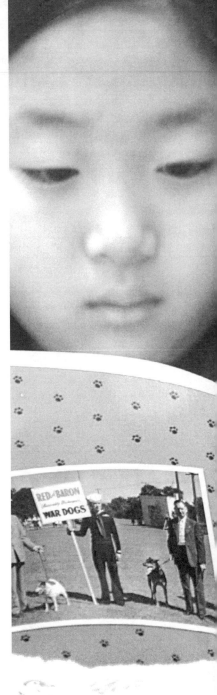

> *If our kids are going to have reading mentors, then we need to be their famous readers.*

famous *readers* in their lives. If our kids are going to have reading mentors, then *we* need to be their famous readers.

I suggest you start by personally exploring the thin line between reading and drama. At last summer's reading institute at Teachers College, the teachers in my section all tried their hand at selecting a scene that they regarded as a turn-ing point in their book, then reading the scene aloud to a partner, not just once, but over and over again. The teachers and I deliberately worked on reading as if we were the character, on using our hands, our facial expressions, our posture to capture the unfolding story. We even progressed from reading aloud that one section to putting our books down and improvising the section. We held conversations in between the readings and the enactments. Our conversations went like this: "Do you *really* think his voice has a snide tone like that? Isn't he also. . . ." The work lasted all of five or six minutes. It was just a tiny pocket of drama. But every teacher came in the next morning and said, "Oh my golly. I read so differently last night. It was almost like I was acting out as I read!"

So teachers, try this. Find a scene in a book you are reading. It could be a picture book that you and a colleague both read to your kids. Choose a scene in this book where emotions run high. Try not only reading that scene aloud, taking on roles and reading with expression, but also try talking with your friend about each character's tone and about changes in tone. Talk about the actions that are occurring, including the small ones, and including those the author doesn't specify. Then read the passage again, adding gestures. Really use your shoulders, your hands, and your voice—above all, your voice.

I think your teaching will take on new power. Better yet, so will your reading.

MINILESSON

Living in the World of a Story

CONNECTION

As an analogy for reading oneself awake, story-tell a time when you lived on auto-pilot until someone helped you to wake up, to pay attention.

"Readers, I won't forget the first time I drove through the Rocky Mountains. My friend had convinced me that I couldn't live another year without experiencing the mountains. We drove through a mountain pass. I looked out the car window at the snow-capped peaks surrounding us, and the blue, blue sky on all sides. 'How do you like it?' my friend asked.

" 'It's so beautiful,' I said. 'Like a postcard, a calendar.'

"Then, suddenly, for no reason, we were stopping. My friend got out of the car. Befuddled, I wondered, 'What's going on?' But there was no one to ask because my friend had just started walking out onto the rocky plain that stretched before us. He didn't wait for me, didn't explain, he just walked off.

There are lots of sections such as this in these units of study where I take a few minutes of the minilesson not only to teach but also to preach. I think miniature keynotes are important ways to teach from the heart and that it is as important to teach why we do things as readers as it is to teach how we do these things.

If you decide to borrow this exact story instead of writing a personal moment from your own life that illustrates the same point, be sure that you dramatize the moment on top of that mountain rather than simply reading the words. If you haven't ever been to a mountain top, then you'll be doing what readers do all the time, letting language lead you into new worlds.

As you tell this story, you need to picture yourself getting out of the car, dazed and confused. You do not literally need to stand up, to walk, but you might. You do need to use your shoulders, your hands, your gaze to suggest that you are reliving the moment while story-telling it.

"So I made my way after him, thinking, 'This is crazy.' (You've got to understand that I wasn't walking into one of those meadows that you read about in *Heidi*. There were no cascading streams, no meadows of wildflowers. There was just a flat stretch of rocky rubble.) I walked and walked. Finally, I sat myself down on a little boulder to wait until my friend finished whatever he was doing.

"For a bit, I just sat there. Then I noticed some tiny Alpine flowers growing in the crevices between the rocks. 'So tiny, so perfect,' I thought, and when I looked up again, something was different. This time I took in the world. The sky was everywhere, a giant dome. The air, cold and wet, rose up from below. The world stretched out before me, a rolling sea of clouds and mountain peaks. I felt like a little blip on the mountainside, with a giant forever sky on all sides of me. And I realized that so often, I pass by books almost like I almost passed by that mountaintop world."

Name your teaching point. Specifically, teach children that readers need to monitor not only for sense but also for complacency, and to have fix-up strategies to wake ourselves up, reminding ourselves to envision as we read.

"Today I want to teach you that when we read, *you and I* need to be the ones to notice if we are just gazing out at the text, thinking only surface-level thoughts: 'It's as pretty as a postcard.' *We* need to notice times when we are reading on emotional autopilot—maybe understanding the text, but not taking it in. And we need to say, 'Stop the car. Pause the reading.' When we read, we need to see not just *words*, but also the *world* of the story through the eyes of the character. There is a rap on the door, and we hear it. Even before the character calls, 'Come in,' we practically call out a greeting ourselves.

"John Ciardi has said, 'If you love a poem, you never have to study it. You live your way into it.' That's what I hope we learn today and this year."

As the story unfurls, you need to picture yourself sitting on that tiny boulder in the middle of a flat field of rubble. Progress from a feeling of "Humpff. Why am I here?" to, bit by bit, one of wonder and awe. Picture that blue, blue sky, an endless dome above you. Picture the view—mountaintops and clouds, rolling out on all sides like a field of wheat. Feel the air from the valley below—distinctly cold, wet air. Even on this summer day, you draw your sweater close and fold your arms around you. Above all, experience that sense of smallness, that sure knowledge that you are but a blip.

Be sure your voice changes. And your posture. Show that you went from being a curmudgeon to taking in the scene as if it was gold.

You'll notice that when I do give a little keynote address within a minilesson, this usually entails going away from reading to make my point and then suggesting, finally, "Isn't that true for us as readers as well?" You can try this process. Jot powerful, emotionally intense moments from your own life. They needn't have the slightest connection to reading. Then take one of those moments and say to yourself, "I know this has a ton of parallels with reading. This has huge implications for readers." Say that even if you really don't think the moment is linked to reading in any way at all. Pretend it is. Then, after approaching the vignette with a spirit of "Of course this has implications for reading," try listing some of the possible links to reading that surface for you, and you will be well on your way to writing your own metaphor for reading.

It is helpful if you can keep in mind ways in which the various teaching points in your unit of study overlap, one with another, because children will never be able to remember them all if each is utterly separate from the others. This teaching point should remind you of the minilesson in which you taught kids that we can read as curmudgeons, or we can read like the text is gold. It should also remind you of minilessons in which you have taught children that sometimes we read as if on autopilot, not really taking in the words at all, and that we need to monitor for sense. Your larger point is that it is easy to slip into patterns of reading in ways that don't represent our best work, and we need to have ways to catch ourselves when we do that, and to alter our own ways of reading.

Teaching

Remind children of a story in which the character crosses a threshold to an imagined world, and suggest that all readers must cross a threshold of sorts, entering the world of the story.

"Do you remember that in *The Lion, the Witch and the Wardrobe*, Lucy and Edmund and Susan and Peter find a wardrobe, a closet, and they go into it, and they push past the furry coats, going deeper and deeper into the closet, and suddenly Lucy feels cold air, and something cold brushes against her arm? She looks down and sees that it is a tree bough, covered with snow. Ahead a lamp burns in the forest. And Lucy realizes that she has entered another world, the world of Narnia.

"When any one of us reads a story, when we read fiction, we need to be a bit like Lucy and her brothers and sister. We need to let whatever book we are reading take us through our own magic wardrobe, so that we go from reading words on the page to suddenly feeling as if we have entered another world. It might not be a fantasy world, like Narnia—but it is the world of the story. We read, and we see that world through the eyes of the main character."

Your children may not have read this book, but many of them probably saw the movie, so they may grasp the reference. But even if they do not recall the story, if you tell this well, they can grasp your point. You are inviting children to let words on a page be the wardrobe or the yellow brick road or the garden door that leads them into an alternate universe.

You could decide that this minilesson has too many stories, one overlaid against another, and you could easily delete the mountain top or The Lion, the Witch and the Wardrobe. Become accustomed to seeing ways in which these minilessons can be thinned without losing much, and then go at it!

Notice this is a brief teaching section. That is because the active involvement section is longer than usual. Notice that what's missing from the teaching component is the actual teaching. You tell readers what to do, but don't convey how to do it. Your minilessons won't always follow the template, and that's fine, but it helps if you are aware when of the minilesson diverges from the pattern.

ACTIVE INVOLVEMENT

Read aloud an upcoming section of the read-aloud book, asking children to listen as if they are living within the scene. Direct partners to assume different roles.

"So let's continue to read *The Tiger Rising*, and as I read, you can be in the world of the story. Listen as if you are Rob, so that later, we'll be able to reenact this moment.

> Chapter 2
> "Looky here," said Norton Threemonger as soon as Rob stepped onto the school bus. "It's the Kentucky Star. How's it feel to be a star?" Norton stood in the center of the aisle, blocking Rob's path.
>
> Rob shrugged.

"Readers, you are being Rob, so I should see you shrug. You're standing in the aisle of the bus and Norton is in front of you.

> "Oh, he don't know," Norton called to his brother. "Hey, Billy, he don't know what it's like to be a star."
>
> Rob slipped past Norton. (I turned my shoulders sideways as if I was Rob.) He walked all the way to the back of the bus and sat down in the last seat.
>
> "Hey," said Billy Threemonger, "you know what? This ain't Kentucky. This is Florida."
>
> He followed Rob and sat down right next to him. He pushed his face so close that Rob could smell his breath. (I moved my face back, and as I did this, I turned it away from Billy's glare and his bad breath, crinkled my nose a bit in distaste.) It was bad breath. It smelled metallic and rotten. "You ain't no Kentucky Star," Billy said, his eyes glowing under the brim of his John Deere cap. "And you sure ain't a star here in Florida. You ain't a star nowhere."
>
> "Okay," said Rob. (I looked passively at the ground.)
>
> Billy shoved him hard. (I backed up, as if recovering from a big shove.) And then Norton came swaggering back and leaned over Billy and grabbed hold of Rob's hair with one hand, and with the other hand, ground his knuckles into Rob's scalp. (I felt him grinding his knuckles into my head, and I sat frozen.)
>
> Rob sat there and took it.

Your reading of the text is meant to set children up to reenact the text, improvising. You can help them feel successful if your reading leans toward being dramatic interpretation. So when you read Norton's opening line, puff up your chest and move a fraction to the right so as to stand in Rob's way. And when you read that Rob shrugs, become Rob, and shrug as you believe he would. Is he cowering from Norton? Just standing silently?

This active involvement portion of the minilesson provides children with scaffolding as they try a new strategy of acting like a character. You'll notice that I don't just assign the work; instead, I guide kids step-by-step through the process of using this strategy. In a few minutes, they will try the strategy again, this time without scaffolding.

Read this passage carefully because the children will revisit it time and again during this unit of study. Because bullying is a struggle many children face, this passage will resonate for many readers.

Raise the stakes. Reread the excerpt again, and this time set readers up to actually act out the passage as you read it aloud.

"Readers, let's reread that tiny section, but this time, Partner 1, you be the bullies. You be Norton and Billy combined. And Partner 2, you're Rob, trying to make your way safely to the back of the bus. I'm going to read it first, and I just want you to use your body postures, facial expressions, and gestures to live into the part. Then I'm going to ask you to make a tiny play out of this, with each of you improvising whatever lines you think your character might be saying (you don't need to stick to the exact words of the story). Partner 1s, get ready. Turn toward Partner 2, toward Rob, and be ready to gesture, to dramatize."

Chapter 2

"Looky here," said Norton Threemonger as soon as Rob stepped onto the school bus. "It's the Kentucky Star. How's it feel to be a star?" Norton stood in the center of the aisle, blocking Rob's path.

Rob shrugged.

"Oh, he don't know," Norton called to his brother. "Hey, Billy, he don't know what it's like to be a star."

Rob slipped past Norton. He walked all the way to the back of the bus and sat down in the last seat.

"Hey," said Billy Threemonger, "you know what? This ain't Kentucky. This is Florida."

He [Billy] followed Rob and sat down right next to him. He pushed his face so close that Rob could smell his breath. It was bad breath. It smelled metallic and rotten. "You ain't no Kentucky Star," Billy said, his eyes glowing under the brim of his John Deere cap. "And you sure ain't a star here in Florida. You ain't a star nowhere."

"Okay," said Rob.

Billy shoved him hard. And then Norton came swaggering back and leaned over Billy and grabbed hold of Rob's hair with one hand, and with the other hand, ground his knuckles into Rob's scalp.
Rob sat there and took it.

Reading researcher Tim Rasinski emphasizes that it is important for a teacher to find authentic, natural reasons for children to reread texts repeatedly, with expression, because this supports the development of fluency. Some people erroneously believe that fluency is synonymous with reading rate, but actually fluency refers to a reader's rate, phrasing, and expression combined. All of us have heard children who read aloud robotically. Those children's inner voices, as readers, are also robotic and it. is. hard to. understand. someone. who. reads. like a. robot—even if that someone is you.

"Now, partners, try acting this out without my reading. Start with the bullies, Partner 1, saying, 'Looky here,' and blocking Rob's way. Make up what the people probably say. Act out as you sit there, though if you want to stand up, you may. Go."

LINK

Send children off, after rallying them to read their independent books as actively as they've been experiencing the read-aloud.

"Today, try to read your book like we've been reading *The Tiger Rising*. Try to practically turn it into a play. Try to *be* the main character. Don't worry about Post-it notes or anything (except the log). From now on, as you read books, try to make the stories come to life. Read as if it is all happening, act it out if you need to, as if you've pushed past the coats and entered into the world of your story."

The teachers who piloted these minilessons found their children were enthralled with the invitation to act. Some won't get into the acting out, of course, but there will be plenty of action for them to watch and absorb. In any case, this endeavor lasts only about two minutes. You'll revisit this work often, and over time, more and more of your children will become comfortable with it. Soon children will read and act out favorite parts of their books in partnership conversations (see the DVD video of a partnership talk about Old Yeller). Best of all, your children will read differently because of the dramatization.

Think about it: The entire reading workshop is based on the premise that we help readers be successful at progressively more challenging work. They begin reading level A books, and only when they can do that well do they progress to level B books. Similarly, you should notice that between yesterday's minilesson and teaching share and today's minilesson, and then again across today's session, children have been carried along a progression of work with drama. What you ask readers to do today involves lots more actual drama than the work you asked them to do yesterday. You can notice a dozen similar sequences across these units of study.

CONFERRING AND SMALL-GROUP WORK

Plan Predictable Ways You'll Support Children As They Progress along a Trajectory of Skill Development

When you confer, you teach on your toes in response to what your children say and do. And your children never fail to surprise you—which is what makes teaching so enthralling. Recently a little boy was stuck on a word and looked up in the air as if reaching into the clouds to decode the troublesome word. My colleague, Randy Bomer, said to him, "You know, usually it helps to look at the word."

The youngster bent close to Randy and whispered, "Sometimes God tells me the word."

There was nothing Randy could have done to prepare himself for that child's curveball. One researcher described the responsive nature of conferring by saying, "You never step in the same river twice." Of course, many of the curveballs that children send our way are a bit less unpredictable!

Because conferences are invented on the spot in response to the surprising things that children say and do, it is especially important for us, as teachers, to approach a day of conferring with possibilities (but not plans) in mind. You will want to consider the content of the day's minilesson, the skills you are supporting in the unit of study, and the work the readers' books ask the readers to do, and imagine possible conferences and small groups that you might lead in the upcoming days.

MID-WORKSHOP TEACHING POINT

Readers Keep Offstage Characters in Our Peripheral Vision

In a voiceover, while children continued to read, I said, "Readers, don't stop reading. But within the next few minutes, find a part of the story where there's a lot of action happening, and a lot of emotion too. I'll stop you in a couple of minutes and ask you to do something with that scene, so be looking for it as you read on."

A couple of minutes later, I said, "Readers, grab a Post-it note and quickly sketch what's going on in that scene of your book." They did this *[Figs. II-1 and II-2.]* "Now will you think, 'Who is in the scene I just drew? Who is missing?' Then think, 'Where might the other people in the story be? Those missing people may not have been discussed recently. They may be offstage, but as a reader, you should know where you think they are and what you think they are doing. You know you can be watching the main character or event—say, watching the action around the ball at a basketball game—and still, out of the corner of your eye, be aware that the father sitting beside you on the bleachers is acting like a ten year old? You're seeing that father with your peripheral vision—and you are aware of offstage characters in just the same way. Sketch the offstage characters as well."

Then I said, "Instead of talking with a partner, right now see if you can act out the main interaction in your scene. Use your hands as puppets. One hand can be one character, and the other, another character or two. Try letting your two hands interact—say what one character is saying and say what the other is saying."

After a minute or two, I said, "The work you've just done should give you a goal for the reading you're going to do for the rest of this workshop. Will you read with peripheral vision? Will you almost dramatize as you read? You decide."

continued on next page

Throughout this series, I have been suggesting that you develop a record-keeping system that will help you be sure that when you draw alongside a child as he or she reads, asking, "What are you working on as a reader?" you will be able to follow that question with more specific inquiries. If you carry historical records and glance at them as you enter a conference, then when the child doesn't immediately orient to your conference and provide a clear direction for the interaction, you won't feel as if you are left to pull your teaching points out of thin air. The historical records can help you recall what you have already taught this particular reader so you can check in on how he is doing with whatever work you positioned him to tackle.

The historical records are especially important because while the work that a child has been doing often relates to the work of the whole-class unit of study, that work will be tempered by the child's specific history and combined with other long-term on-going agendas.

That is, if you found at the start of the year that a child needed to work more on using context clues to help discern possible meanings for unfamiliar words, that child will presumably still need you to support that work. The fact that this is a unit of study on character and that the minilesson spotlights envisionment doesn't mean you won't continue to help this child work with context clues. Your historical records will remind you to continue to check in on and support this skill in whatever books the child has been reading.

But you will also want to help many of the children in the class try their hand at the work you have decided to spotlight within the unit of study, and again, your record keeping can be a resource that helps you feel ready to do this teaching. You'll recall that I suggested earlier that your records will be especially valuable to you if you have thought about the handful of skills that you will be particularly advancing within any one unit of study (the work with any skill will probably, of course, prevail across units) and if you've thought about what a trajectory of development might look like for each of those skills.

In Session I's conferring and small-group work section, we helped you get a sense for what a reader is apt to do that might suggest she is more novice or more proficient in her growth line as someone who envisions. This should help you read the signals that a

continued from previous page

Figure II-1
Many readers would have overloooked this scene altogether!

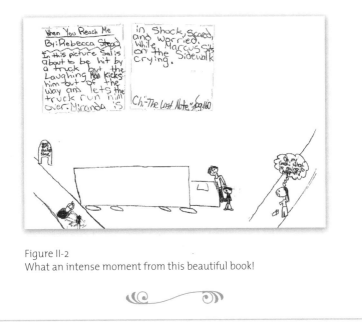

Figure II-2
What an intense moment from this beautiful book!

reader gives you. This session's conferring and small-group write-up and ones that follow, along with the assessment sections in this book, will help you develop a repertoire of ideas for teaching readers at different stages in their development as envisioners. You and your colleagues will want to spend more time working together to cumulate ideas about how you can help readers at every stage in this developmental journey.

As I mentioned earlier, you will probably want to create abbreviated notes about your teaching plans for specific readers, adding those notes to your record-keeping sheets. This will mean that your record-keeping forms can whisper suggestions to you as you confer. (A few days from now, your minilessons will spotlight prediction, and then you'll want to add yet more notes to your record keeping. See *A Guide to the Reading Workshop* for more about record keeping.)

Support Novice Envisioners: Teach Readers to Picture Not Only Who Is Doing What But Also How the Character Does that Thing

Whenever possible, I work first with readers who seem more novice at a skill, launching them into a progression of work that I know will take a bit of time. Before I drew my chair alongside Malik and asked him to tell me about the work he'd been doing, I anticipated that his envisioning would not be well developed. Together,

Malik and I reread the jottings he'd made as he read his independent reading book. I noticed he tended to write the main facts—who is doing what—in an objective observer sort of way. One Post-it note said, "Peter is a good basketball player," another said, "Peter is walking home," and a third, "Peter and Billy are friends."

Because I had my record-keeping sheet close at hand with reminders that I wanted to teach readers to draw on specific information from earlier in the text to create mental movies as they read, and because I knew Malik was far enough along in the book that what might reasonably start as outline-only sketches of the characters should by now have been filled in with some specific, precise information, I immediately spotted what he was not doing and felt ready to impart my wisdom. Over the years, however, I have trained myself to resist the common tendency to see only what a person is *not* yet doing and to teach from that deficit view. I therefore reined myself in, saying to myself, "Think about what he *is* doing, and *start* by supporting that. Then you can impart your wisdom."

It is not always easy to arrive at what the child has done that can be complimented. Remember, all Malik had recorded on his Post-its were the bare facts: "Peter is walking home," "Peter is a good basketball player." What was there to say?

I took a big breath and dove in. "Malik, I can tell that as you read, you *notice* the characters and you pause to think, 'What are they doing?' I see that you use Post-it notes to keep that stuff straight in your mind. It's helpful to grasp the main action of the story—who the characters are and what they are doing."

He glowed, and visibly puffed up a bit. "Malik, 'cause you are good at thinking, 'Who are the characters? What are they doing?' I think you are ready to graduate. Can I teach you a tip that will make your reading a ton stronger?" He was game.

"It's this. Once you know the bare bones of a story—who the characters are, what the main events are—then you can pay attention to fleshing out those bare bones. One way to do that is to add *details* to your picture, paying attention not only to *who* is doing *what* but also to *how* the person is doing that thing. Details are interesting because they reveal so much about the characters. Let me show you what that looks like when you watch a character closely, noticing not just *what* the character is doing but *how* she is doing it."

"For example, let's watch Aly right now (I gestured across the room to where Aly worked). Let's just watch her in a bare bones way, saying *who* we see and *what* she is doing, like you did when you jotted, 'Peter is walking home.' What do you see?"

"Aly is reading and . . . ."

"Oops," I said. "If you are seeing in a bare bones way, you'll only notice *who is doing what*. That is it: Aly is reading."

Then I said, "But you saw a lot more, didn't you? This time, describe what you see—only tell not just *who* is doing something, but also tell details that show *how* she is doing that thing."

"Aly is reading a huge, fat book and her head is practically in it and she doesn't even hear us talking about her."

"That's it! You just graduated. You used to tell *who* is doing *what*—Peter is playing basketball, Aly is reading—and now you are seeing not only *who* is doing *what* but *how* the person does that thing, and you are seeing details. Here's the thing: Based on what you now have seen, you and I can grow some ideas about Aly, can't we? We couldn't really grow any ideas about her when you just said, 'Aly is reading.'

"Now, go back and try to redo the Post-it notes you've just collected about your book. Like this one: 'Peter is a good basketball player.' What can you add about how he plays basketball? What details can you provide that help someone know Peter?"

Malik said, "He passes the ball to Billy all the time. He's like, like, nice? 'Cause he passes the ball to Billy?"

I ignored the question intonation in Malik's voice and the use of the generic term *nice* and simply responded to the content he had finally produced. "That's so interesting. You're saying that Peter plays basketball in a specific way. He passes the ball a lot." I pressed to learn how Malik knew this and heard the information came from earlier in the story. I repeated what Malik had said—"Peter passed the ball a lot"—and added, "That says a lot about him, doesn't it? Now we know he's generous, not selfish, with the ball. You've given me a more nuanced, more specific, vision of Peter than simply saying, 'He is a good basketball player.'"

Teachers, I knew Malik's work wasn't perfect. When working to mobilize readers who are at the beginning stages of work with a particular skill, our goal can't be perfection. Our goal needs to be to invite the reader to begin approximating whatever it is we hope the reader will eventually be able to do.

Continuing in my conference, I tried to extrapolate my larger point for Malik. I said, "So Malik, I'm hoping you always remember that whenever you are reading, it helps to keep track of who is doing what, as you have been doing. You have a flair for that, and it is important." I try to make a habit of returning to the compliment when a conference ends, because I want to be sure that I help the reader fashion an identity of himself or herself based in part on that compliment. I want the reader to leave our interaction thinking, "I am the kind of person who. . . ."

Then, I also said to Malik, "But you are also ready for the next step. You are ready to graduate. And you will find that your ideas about a book become much more interesting if you bring more details to the picture that you make of your character. You will want to not only notice who is doing what—like 'Malik is writing Post-it notes'—but to notice details— 'Malik is zealously working, collecting three Post-it notes on even just one page of his book, and then revising those Post-it notes to make them state-of-the-art.' You'll want to think about not only *what* a character is doing, but also *how* the character is doing something, and to draw on information from earlier in the book as you did today. Can you remember to push yourself, after this, to envision with more detail?"

Support Novice Envisioners: Teach Children that Readers Enrich Understandings of a Text by Drawing on Memories of Similar Life Experiences

As I pulled my chair alongside Gabe, whose long arms were folded under his chin as he read, I said, "Gabe, may I look at your thoughts?" I knew I was equating his Post-it notes with his thoughts. "I'm researching envisionment," I said as I scanned his Post-it notes. He had quite a few of them, grubby with pencil smudges and sticking out of his book at odd angles. It did not take me more than a second to see that like Malik, Gabe also recorded only the essential facts of the story. I didn't even glance at my record-keeping sheet for ideas about what I might teach, although I did think to myself that it is helpful when we, as teachers, cluster readers together in our minds and think, "This child's work with envisionment is not all that different from that other child's work."

As I mentioned earlier, once I have developed a theory about what a reader *can't* yet do, I make a point of trying to do a bit of further investigation. I know that I need to try to understand what the reader *can* do as well as what the reader can't yet do in relation to the particular skill I'm investigating. In this instance, I was quite sure that I couldn't draw conclusions from Gabe's written responses alone. What was he thinking? What might he *say* rather than *write*?

"Can you tell me a bit about this story?" I asked, anxious to learn if he had been attending to far more than he'd recorded. He sat up, unfolding his arms, and gave what seemed to me to be a remarkably cursory, under-developed although sequential retelling of his independent reading book. At one point I probed a bit for details, and although my probing produced more, it still seemed to me that Gabe had taken a level M book and reduced it to a book that resembled those at a far easier level.

For a second, I thought that there might be other children in the class who would resemble Gabe and Malik. Based on the *One Green Apple* assessment, I already had a short list of children who seemed to me to be novice envisioners. I considered convening those in need of the same sort of coaching, teaching them as a group. But the other children on my list of novice envisioners seemed engrossed in what they were doing, and I was not entirely sure I'd done enough one-to-one conferring to know how to help a small group anyhow. Conferring allows me to develop teaching ideas that I later use in small groups or in whole-class instruction.

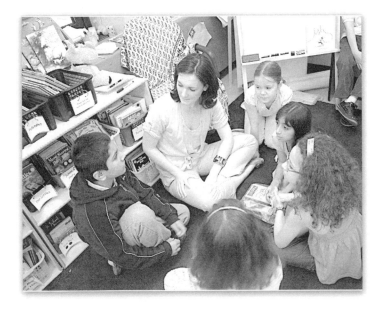

I recalled the compliment I'd given Malik, tweaking it to also fit Gabe. I also wanted to compliment Gabe on some of the work he'd done in an earlier conference. "Gabe, I can see from your Post-it notes that you're keeping track of the characters and the action in the story as you read. It makes the story clear, doesn't it! And you also seem to be reading more quickly—perhaps you can do that because you are keeping track of who does what. Keep this up!" Gabe grinned slightly and nodded.

"I have one tip to teach you. When readers envision the story and characters, we try to make movies in our minds that are in brilliant colors—actually, movies that have not only colors but also sounds and sometimes even smells. Our sense of the place, the people, the actions, becomes richer when we think, 'Have I ever been in a place like that? When have I ever done stuff like that?' and then let our own memories add to all that the author spells out for us.

"Let me show you what I mean." I opened *The Tiger Rising* to an early passage (one I had already read to the class) where Rob, standing at the bus stop, recalled his mother's funeral. Gabe leaned toward me and the opened text as I read a line or two. Then I said, "Hmm, Rob is remembering being at the funeral. I'm having some trouble picturing it. The author doesn't tell me what to picture at the funeral."

I paused long enough that I hoped in the interval, Gabe would begin solving my dilemma in his own mind, and then I continued. "Oh, wait, I *did* go to *my* grandpa's funeral. Maybe I should think back to what I remember about that funeral and let my grandpa's funeral help me picture what Rob experienced." Then I added, "'Cause I remember every single thing about my grandpa's funeral." I paused, then pointed out to Gabe, "See what I'm doing to help myself envision what Rob's experiencing?"

"Yeah. I remember my grandfather's funeral, too. He and my grandma lived in Montana, but he died last summer," Gabe uncharacteristically confided.

I said, "I'm so sorry to hear that, Gabe. It must be really different without him. I know you spend a lot of time there." He nodded but didn't seem to want to add anything, so I continued.

"So, let me see if I can bring any of the stuff I remember to the picture in my mind of the funeral that Rob and his dad went to. You could try it too. I'm picturing that they are at a funeral. I see that they're standing . . .

where? I think they are in a small church, and there are lots of people crying around them. (That's how it was at Grandpa's funeral, so I'm using that to fill in the gaps in my mental movie.) Rob's crying and wearing all black, and he's standing next to a casket, and there's a framed picture of his mom propped on top of it. (We had that picture at Grandpa's funeral and I remember it almost made me cry.)"

Stepping out of the role of the reader, I named what I'd just done in a way that I hope made the work transferable to other days, other texts. "It helps, doesn't it? When I had a hard time picturing what I was reading, I thought back to a similar experience from my life and then let that experience help me fill in missing stuff.

"Let's try the same thing with the book you're reading. Let's go back to the Post-it notes where you wrote, 'He's excited about the game.' Reread that part of your book out loud for a moment." Gabe read a paragraph or two. I was glad to see he seemed to recall conversations we'd had about letting the punctuation help him read smoothly. "That was so smooth, Gabe!" I tucked in. "So what can you add to your Post-it?"

"He's excited about his game . . . *because it's the championship*? He wants to win."

"The author doesn't really tell us much more about what the character is thinking and doing, does he?" I said. "So this is a good example of a time when it will really help to think about a similar time in your own

life, and to see if doing that helps you imagine how your character feels. Have you ever been in a similar situation?"

Gabe shrugged. "No." As I kept looking expectantly at him, he added, "Well, I do have a big baseball game in two days and, um, five hours."

"Great! Use that to help you picture the character, the events."

"Well, I'm excited about it. And kind of nervous. And I can't stop thinking about the game. I'm sort of not paying attention to other stuff."

"Like if your friend asks you a question, you just nod like this?" (I modeled an inattentive facial expression and then a lazy nod.)

"Yeah."

"So how can all of that help you imagine what might be going on for your character?"

Then he said, "I guess my character's probably excited too. Maybe he can't eat 'cause he's nervous, so when it's dinner, he doesn't really eat a lot because his stomach feels funny. He's, like, 'no thanks,' to his mom's food even if it's his favorite."

"Wow, Gabe, you did that beautifully! You used your own baseball experience to help you guess what your character is probably feeling. And look at how many more details you've added! After this, remember that one way to picture what a character is going through is to think, 'Have I lived through something like that? Has someone I know?, We can let our experiences help us fill in stuff. Keep it up, Gabe." I moved on, noting that the teaching I'd given to Gabe could probably serve well as a whole-class minilesson (see Session III).

TEACHING SHARE

Readers Reflect on Our Reading Lives and Establish Goals for Ourselves

Gather children and ask how the day's reading work went. Ask them to study their logs and set reading goals for themselves, based on their logs.

"Readers, it's time for us to stop today. Show me with a thumbs up or thumbs down whether you think you were able to read yourself awake today." Most of the children signaled with thumbs up. Some wavered, their thumbs rocking back and forth. I took in the data and seemed to fashion plans for the teaching share based on what they were telling me. "You are going to fill out your log in just a minute, but before you do that, let's talk more about goals. Remember that often this year I have said to you, 'You are the authors of your reading lives.' Each of you, as the author of your own reading life, will want to make sure that you continue to reflect on your life as a reader and that you set and work toward new goals for yourself.

"I'm going to give you a few minutes to look over your logs, your Post-it notes, and the charts in this room so that you can select a reading goal or two for yourself. Think about how many pages you tend to read during our forty minutes or so of reading at school. Are you reading just about that much at home? Could you set yourself a realistic, challenging goal for the number of pages you want to read each night?"

As children work, coach them to lift the level of what they are doing.

After children had reread their logs and thought to themselves for a few minutes, I did a bit more voicing over. "Think also about the reading work you think you should aim to be doing. What reading muscles do you need to develop? If you want muscles, you can't just tell your arm to grow and then, poof! You have bigger muscles. No! You need to spend time lifting weights every day, and then your muscles begin getting bigger and stronger. It's

COACHING TIPS FROM LUCY CALKINS

Early in a new unit, it is especially important for your teaching to harken back to earlier work. Lots of kids have become accustomed to teachers teaching a unit of study, then finishing that unit, wrapping it up in a bow—and leaving it behind. Workshop teaching, instead, aims for teaching to accumulate. You will see that throughout this series, you will need to continually remind children of the tips you've imparted during the first month of your teaching. This will be especially true when the reading workshop takes whole new turns, as when readers begin reading nonfiction instead of fiction (for example, at that point choosing just-right books will again become huge) or when readers begin to work in reading clubs in which they progress in sync with other children through multiple copies of books (then volume will become huge.) In any case, it will be important to show your children that the charts, rituals, and learning from the first unit continue to matter, and that as the year unfolds, one unit of study builds upon another.

Notice how I coach all the readers as they are working by inserting voiceovers into the work the children are doing. This is a way to provide support for all of the children, not just the few that I can reach as I move among them, coaching into what they are doing.

no different with reading muscles, so think what your goals will be for the time you spend reading, for the number of pages read, and for the reading work you want to get better at doing."

Again I gave them a minute to read and to think, and then voiced over, saying, "Jot your goals on a Post-it note and place the Post-it on your reading log. In a few minutes, you'll have a chance to share your goals with your reading partner." After a bit, I channeled children to read their goals aloud.

Celebrate the work of some children to help all children remember how to do this work.

After a minute, I did a voiceover, reading aloud a few of the children's goals. I read these Post-its: *Figs. II-3, II-4, II-5, and II-6. [See CD-ROM for other examples.]*

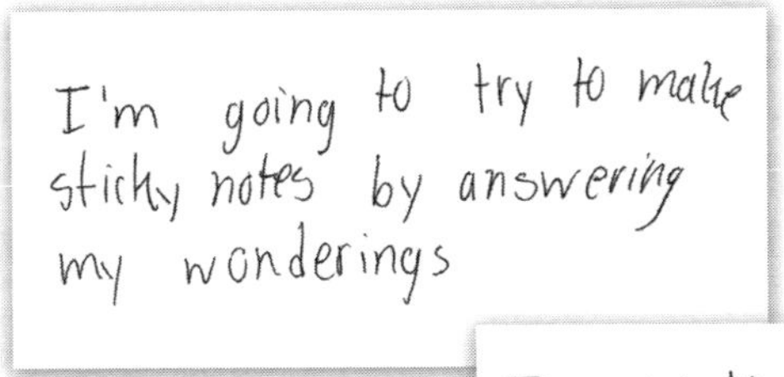

> I'm going to try to make sticky notes by answering my wonderings

Figure II-3

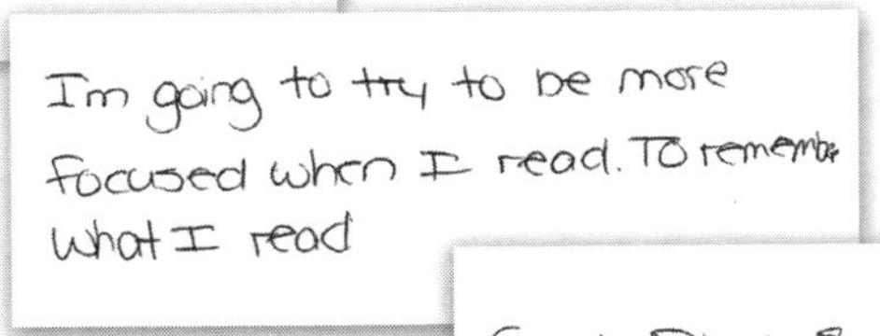

> I'm going to try to be more focused when I read. To remember what I read

Figure II-4

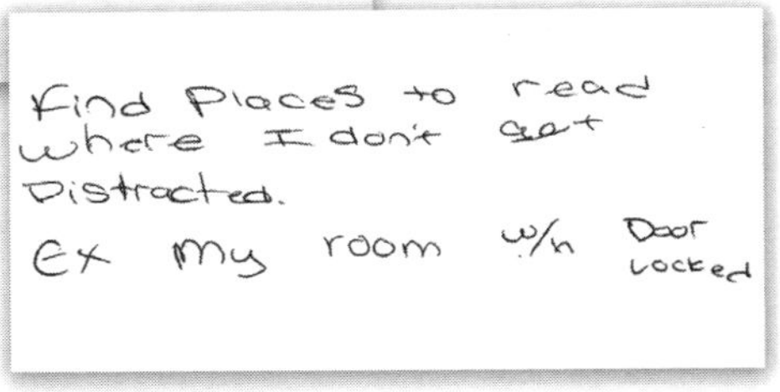

> Find Places to read where I don't get Distracted.
> Ex my room w/n Door Locked

Figure II-5

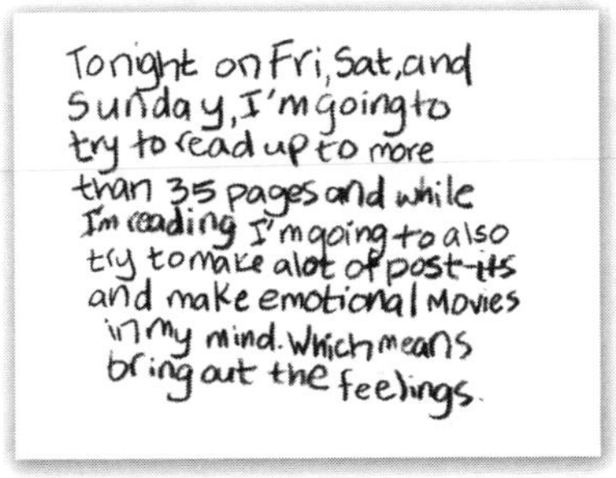

> Tonight on Fri, Sat, and Sunday, I'm going to try to read up to more than 35 pages and while I'm reading I'm going to also try to make a lot of post-its and make emotional Movies in my mind. Which means bring out the feelings.

Figure II-6
Juan invented a phrase. He'll make "emotional movies" as he reads.

Here I have done something that is a stand-by for share sessions. I have taken a bit of a child's work and thought, "What actions has this reader taken that others could emulate?" Then I talk about the work in ways that allow the work to set the standard for the class.

Stirring Our Empathy Through Personal Response

IN THIS SESSION,
you will teach students that readers empathize deeply with characters by making connections between characters' experiences or feelings and our own.

e've been talking about how important it is to learn that we can walk in the shoes of another person. This is crucial not only for reading but also for life. The poet and novelist Naomi Shihab Nye has said, "When I love someone who is very different from me, I become bigger, my sense of self becomes more encompassing."

I've been loving my mother lately, and she is showing me the truth in Naomi Shihab Nye's words. I mean—I have always loved my mother, but lately, she is becoming different from me. Lately, my tough, stoic mother has been growing old and vulnerable. Last year's spinal problems left her feet numb, and her hip has dislocated dozens of times, each time causing unbearable pain. Last week a neighbor found her collapsed in agony on the floor of the horse's stall, unable to crawl away from the horse's hoofs. I hear this story and I am on the barn floor, watching the hind legs of the horse, praying someone will notice that I'm taking too long doing the barn chores.

I'm living in my mother's shoes, seeing through her eyes, not only when I am with her, and not only when I am hearing the stories of her traumas. I also walk through life seeing the world through her eyes. The other day, flying back to New York City after a visit with my mum, I got off

GETTING READY

- Bring your class read-aloud to today's lesson. Identify a section of your read-aloud book that will easily allow children to make a connection to their own lives. If you are using *The Tiger Rising*, you'll find that rereading the same passage you read in Session II during works well.

- Share a classroom chart titled "Strategies Readers Use to Grow Ideas About Characters" and prepare to unveil this chart during the minilesson.

- For today's teaching share, you may want to create a chart entitled "Acting Out an Important Scene" that will provide a concrete physical scaffold for children who need it. If you decide to make such a chart, you'll uncover it during the teaching share.

- Be sure you conveniently display the chart you referenced in Session I titled "Ways You and Another Reader Can Talk About Your Books." You will add to this chart during the teaching share.

- Before Session IV, you will want to have completed Chapter 3 of *The Tiger Rising*, and have helped children envision Sistine as a shy girl wearing a fancy pink dress. In Session IV, you will be reading the beginning of Chapter 4 for the first time and you'll help children revise their initial image as they read on and learn more about Sistine.

the airplane at La Guardia and walked along the ramp, down the hall. It all seemed interminably, hip-achingly long. An elderly couple whooshed along on a cart, beep beeping down the hallway, and I imagined my proud, stoic

> *When we truly empathize, we not only experience the story as it is written on the page, but we also become bigger, more encompassing.*

mother sitting beside that couple and knew she would be horrified when that cart beeped, saying "Look at me." I passed the X-ray scanner and saw an elderly woman approach the machine. I saw her gingerly take one plastic tray from the stack and put it before her, and then watched her stand beside that tray, clutching her purse, shifting her weight from one foot to the other. I knew she was thinking, "How do I take my shoes off?" I knew she had already scanned the room, looking for a place to sit, worrying that she couldn't balance on one leg, stork-like, while removing a shoe. I mouthed to the security guard, "Is there a chair?" and smiled as the woman took advantage of the chair he pulled into place.

Loving my mother as she becomes different from me gives me new eyes. This changes even how I walk from the airplane to the parking lot.

It's easy to say the words "It is important to walk in the shoes of another person," but actually doing so is a very big deal. When we truly empathize as we read, we do much more than look up and announce, "I made a text-to-self connection." When we *truly* empathize, we not only experience the story as it is written on the page, but we also become bigger, more encompassing, for when we love someone who is different from us, we take on a new dimension.

MINILESSON

Stirring Our Empathy Through Personal Response

CONNECTION

Recall a scene that you and the class read previously and envisioned, a scene you will revisit later in the minilesson to illustrate the contribution empathy can make to responsive reading.

"Yesterday, we sat on that school bus, staring ahead, not looking at Billy Threemonger with his bad breath. We smelled that bad breath—metallic and rotten—but we didn't turn away; we didn't walk away. We just sat and took it. We sat there and took it, too, when Norton stood above us, when he reached down to grind his knuckles in, giving us a headache. When Norton pointed at our legs, hooting at them, we wanted to channel his eyes elsewhere but we were too paralyzed, unable even to pull our legs back under the seat."

Name your teaching point. Specifically, teach children that readers not only envision what's happening in the story, but we also empathize with the characters.

"Today I want to teach you that when we read ourselves awake, really envisioning what's happening in the story so that we are almost in the character's shoes, we often find ourselves remembering times in our lives when we lived through something similar, and we then bring feelings and insights from those experiences to bear on our understanding of whatever we are reading."

TEACHING

Tell children that readers are apt to approach a text with our baggage tucked away. But we can nudge ourselves to respond personally as we read.

"I think that for some of us, we resist opening ourselves to reading in such a way that we think, 'Hey—I've lived through stuff like that.' You know how Rob, in *The Tiger*

Hopefully it makes sense for you to say, "Yesterday, we sat on that school bus. . . ." I'm trying to suggest that yesterday we lived through Rob's ride on the bus. Sometimes our teaching can become so artsy it isn't clear. If that's the case here or elsewhere, make it clear!

When teaching reading, we're wise to let the authors of our books become coteachers. Here, I'm leaning on Kate DiCamillo's talents, letting her give children a sense of what it means to read.

You may squirm uncomfortably over the fact that I am asking children to fill in details that are not there in the story, but I am totally convinced that all good readers do this. An active reader doesn't wait until all the information has been amassed before creating mental pictures. I want children to experience a text deeply and fully. Later, I will also want children to hold the text at arm's length and to think about the messages in it, rereading in ways that lead them to cite sections of the text to defend ideas.

I love this point. It strikes me as deeply true. Of course, this message harkens back to the message in many of these minilessons. They're variations of the same theme.

Rising, keeps his feelings and his memories of his mother stuffed into his suitcase, under lock and key? I think I sometimes approach a book with my own life and feelings stuffed in a suitcase, out of sight. It can take some doing before I'm ready to read with my suitcase, my life, open and accessible.

"But it doesn't need to be that way. Because I'm trying to teach you to read well, I try to read extra well myself. Last night, I tried giving myself a self-assignment. I said to myself, 'Lucy, reread that part about the bus, and this time, let it spark memories of episodes in your life when similar stuff happened to you.' An assignment like that might not always work, but I was bowled over by how easy it was for me to reread, this time remembering similar experiences. And I was bowled over, too, by how much deeper my thoughts and feelings were about this passage after I did that.

"I could show you what I did and thought, but I'd rather you try this."

Active Involvement

Channel readers to let the scene you've been discussing spark memories of times they've experienced something similar, jotting their associations and then talking about how their personal response illuminates the passage for them.

"You ready? I'm going to reread just a bit of that bus scene, and I want you to let it jar memories of one time in your life when you were wronged and felt like you couldn't cry out. After I read this, just stop and jot, writing as quickly as you can, a scene when something similar happened to you. You can start it, 'I remember the time when. . . . It started with. . . .'"

I reread the scene:

> "Looky here," said Norton Threemonger as soon as Rob stepped onto the school bus. "It's the Kentucky Star. How's it feel to be a star?" Norton stood in the center of the aisle, blocking Rob's path.
>
> Rob shrugged.

This again is a short teaching section, and you should know without reading that a short teaching point signals the active involvement section of the minilesson will be especially well developed. The reason the teaching section is abbreviated and the active involvement section is long is that instead of teaching through demonstration, I teach through guided practice (which requires active involvement).

You'll want to select a scene from a book that is familiar to the children and a scene that you're pretty certain will provoke feelings of "I've been there" for most of your children. I selected the bus scene from The Tiger Rising *because I know most children have been bullied, many even during bus rides.*

One of the interesting things to realize is that actually, when a reader reads a text and thinks, "The same thing has happened to me," then the reader essentially generates a parallel text—the reader's own version of the event. Now the intellectual work that the reader does is not unlike the work done when the reader compares and contrasts two related texts. "This is like my life in some ways," the reader thinks and explores these similarities as well as the differences. The technical term for this is intertextuality.

"Oh, he don't know," Norton called to his brother. "Hey, Billy, he don't know what it's like to be a star."

Rob slipped past Norton. He walked all the way to the back of the bus and sat down in the last seat.

"Hey," said Billy Threemonger, "You know what? This ain't Kentucky. This is Florida."

He followed Rob and sat down right next to him. He pushed his face so close that Rob could smell his breath. It was bad breath. It smelled metallic and rotten. "You ain't a Kentucky star," Billy said, his eyes glowing under the brim of his John Deere cap. "And you sure ain't a star here in Florida. You ain't a star nowhere."

"Okay," said Rob.

Billy shoved him hard. And then Norton came swaggering back and grabbed hold of Rob's hair with one hand and, with the other hand, ground his knuckles into Rob's scalp.

Rob sat there and took it.

"When has something similar happened to you? Stop and jot, recording your memories." [Figs. III-1, III-2, III-3, and III-4; see *the CD-ROM for more stop and jots*]

Help children name what it is they have done that can transfer to their work another day with another text.

After a few minutes, I said, "Now, I have an important question. How does the memory of your own experience help you realize stuff about what Rob was probably thinking, feeling, going through? Think about that for a moment and give me a thumbs up when you have some ideas to share." I waited until two thirds of the class seemed ready to share and then said, "Turn and tell your partner what you are thinking."

As the children talked, I moved among them. After a bit I intervened. "Readers, may I have your eyes?" Then I said, "I just overheard Izzy and Emma's conversation. Emma remembered a time she'd been taunted, and she pointed out that even though Rob didn't cry, he probably wanted to. She used her personal experience to relate to what the character feels and she said, 'I know from what happened to me that he was trying really hard to keep the tears in.'

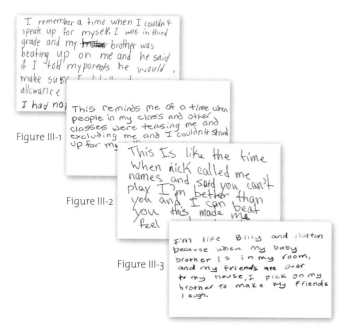

Figure III-1

Figure III-2

Figure III-3

Figure III-4

Although jotting can take a bit longer than turning and talking, it is something I chose to sprinkle throughout the minilessons. Varying our methods in our minilessons keeps children engaged and on their toes. Also, writing their thoughts holds children accountable for their thinking and allows me to research, studying what each one is thinking.

As I moved among children, I coached a few things to consider. "Why do you think you responded differently than Rob?" and "Have you ever felt like Rob is feeling?" That is, personal response can spark intellectual work whether or not the reader identifies with the character. Feelings of "not me" can be as provocative as feelings of "me, too."

LINK

Send readers off, reminding them of the cumulative work of the unit. Encourage them to empathize with the main character as they read independently and, for now, to use Post-it notes to mark places in the text that prompt such work.

"So, readers, whenever you read now, I know you'll keep an eye on yourself and make sure you read yourself awake, really taking in the words and imagining the story. And I know this won't just mean that you *see* more. It will also mean that you *feel* more.

"We'll want to talk about the way that picturing stuff and remembering stuff helps your reading, so leave Post-it notes on the places where you are truly, actually, picturing whatever is happening in the story and also on places that spark memories or associations." I unveiled a chart I'd created earlier, "Strategies Readers Use to Grow Ideas About Characters," that I hope captured much of the work we had done so far. "This chart will help us keep track of our learning as we work through this unit."

Strategies Readers Use to Grow Ideas About Characters

- We make a movie in our minds, drawing on the text to envision (or become) the character.

- We use our own experiences to help us walk in the character's shoes, inferring what the character is thinking, feeling, experiencing.

Usually you will have made (or added to) a chart before the minilesson so that children needn't sit and watch as you squeak your marker pen along the chart paper, writing your teaching point into a bullet point or two. There are two kinds of charts. One, sometimes referred to as an anchor chart, will thread through a great deal of a unit of study, with the teaching points from many minilessons or teaching shares becoming bullets on the chart. Those charts last not only for the unit of study but also across the year and are often referred to and expanded during later units of study. There are other charts that are more temporary, transient charts, such as a chart that lists the four or five steps that you hope readers take on one particular day. These charts are meant to help readers hold onto what you have said on that one occasion, but they do not tend to last across a great many days. "Strategies Readers Use to Grow Ideas About Characters" is a chart that will weave through only today, not tomorrow, so it is not an anchor chart for the entire unit.

As often as possible, I try to use the link as a time to reference and revitalize classroom charts that spell out strategies I've taught earlier in the unit and in the year.

An effective chart has a title that captures a goal that has become important to the class and then lists optional strategies for achieving the goal.

ONFERRING AND SMALL-GROUP WORK

Weave Your Ongoing Skill Development into the New Work

Donald Murray, the Pulitzer Prize–winning writer who pioneered the idea of teaching writing as a process within writing workshops, once said, "If I am going to write about a topic, I must first find in that topic some echoing chord of my own being." Murray's words pertain not only to those who write but also to those who teach. We might say, "If I am going to teach a content well, I must first find in the content that I'm teaching some echoing chord of my own being."

To Confer Well, We Need the Content We Teach to Resonate within Us

In your conferences over the past few days, you have been helping readers develop their ability to envision. Among other things, you have helped readers who picture characters as pen and ink drawings begin to flesh out those characters.

As a teacher of reading, you have a choice; you can reduce reading to something small or you can help readers participate in work that is deeply significant. Instead of cranking out a million little conferences, all designed to help readers envision more, pause and reflect on why this teaching is worthy of your attention and that of your class. Make sure that you can feel,

---

MID-WORKSHOP TEACHING POINT

Readers Make Connections between a Text and Our Lives to Become More Insightful

While children continued to read, I said in a voiceover, "Readers, don't stop reading. But within the next few minutes, find a place where you can press the pause button on your reading and think back over what you've read, seeing if the text can spark memories of times you've experienced (like we've been talking about). And when you reach one or two of these moments, pick up your pen and jot, 'This reminds me of when. . . .' Record the memory and then let it help you, realize something about the character. So go from jotting, 'This reminds me of . . . ,' to jotting 'This makes me realize that . . .' Your memories can help you walk in the character's shoes."

After children read on and paused to jot, I intervened again. "Readers, will you pause in your reading for a quick minute? A wise man once said, 'It takes two to read a book,' and for me it is true that the books that matter the most to me are those that I share. We've been working today on remembering times in our lives when we lived through something that is similar to what occurs in the story. We've been using the feelings and insights from our own lives to understand our characters better. You are going to have time to talk in a minute. I want you to try to talk not only about *the book* but also about *how the book is affecting you*—about what it's making you remember and feel."

continued on next page

---

welling up in your chest, the infinite depth and significance of that which you have chosen to teach.

Take today's minilesson. In it you have taught children that when reading themselves awake, really envisioning what's happening in the story, it helps to remember times when they have lived through something similar so that they can bring feelings and insights from their own experience to bear on what they are reading.

If you imagine that perhaps half or a third of your conferences today will advance that principle, then you'd be well advised to take in your own words, letting them strike some echoing chord within you. For example, I think about what it must be like for Willy of *Stone Fox* to suddenly find that his grandfather is no longer the source of strength in that family. All of a sudden I think about how my mother, who has always been the Rock of Gibraltar in my family, is now frail and needs us kids to prop her up. In a flash, I realize that the way my relationship with my mom has changed is not unlike the way Willie's relationship with his grandfather has changed. And suddenly, that little teaching point doesn't seem little at all. I know, then, from the deepest recesses of my heart, that this connection building is crucial to understanding stories. Once you've reminded yourself that the content you intend to teach is hugely important, then you can move among children, teaching in ways that will make a difference.

To Teach Children to Care and Envision, We Need to Ensure that They Are Carrying the World of the Story from Chapter to Chapter and across the Text

Although the skills we are highlighting in this session are empathizing and envisioning, it may be wise to take a moment to work with your strugglers on basic comprehension work. Both Max and Gabe were now reading level N texts. I'd been noticing that as they retold their stories, neither of them had a strong sense of which details were important enough to carry along with them to the next chapter. When they'd been reading level M texts, their stories tended to be comprised of a single trajectory, with the main character encountering and then solving a problem. The titles of those books had often highlighted the problem-solution trajectory. Now the plot lines in their books were a bit more complex, with often more than one factor contributing to a story's development. Characters' motivations in books within the N–Q band of text difficulty tend to be less concrete and more emotional. I knew that both Max and Gabe would profit from help holding onto important information across chapters in order to construct a coherent storyline. If students have trouble carrying information and details across the text as they read, they will no doubt have trouble creating and carrying pictures in their minds across it. Powerful envisionment work depends upon readers' ability to add lay-

This Reminds me of my own life because just like Fern who doesn't like to see an animal hurt or dying especially Wilbur I don't like seeing Animals Suffering or hurt either. This Makes me realize That Fern is a very Caring Person and is stubborn when it comes to something she Can do to help an Animal.

Aly has captured a dynamic tension in Fern, who is caring and also fiercely stubborn. Characters come alive when their traits are in tension with each other.

ers and details to the world of the story as they read from chapter to chapter. To set readers up to hold onto the mental movie in their minds, adding in details from the text or their own lives and revising their pictures as they read, we must ensure that they can hold onto the important details inside each chapter and carry those details forward.

The texts Gabe and Max were reading were substantially more challenging than those they'd read at the start of the year. I decided to convene a small group with the boys, along with Kadija and Malik. Although Kadija and Malik were reading more difficult books than Gabe's and Max's, I knew they would profit from similar help, because Kadija's very literal retellings didn't always carry forward the most important details, and Malik needed help deepening his thinking.

I'd chosen a short text, an *A-Z Mystery*, that would make the strategy really clear. Mysteries are great for this purpose because successful navigation of them requires noticing and holding onto details to piece together clues.*The Bald Bandit*, level N, was right on target for both Gabe and Max and slightly easy for the others. I knew the children could all finish the book in a day and an evening, returning soon to the books in their bins.

After sending the rest of the class off, I asked Gabe, Max, Kadija, and Malik to stay on the rug with me for a moment. I told them that I'd noticed they were becoming strong at paying attention to the important details as they read, and that today we were going to practice the next step: holding onto those important details across chapters. I had a copy of the book for each of the kids (though photocopied selections would suffice). Since none of them had read this text before, I began by asking the group to look at the cover and read the blurb on the back. *A-Z Mysteries* all begin with a prologue, so they read that as well. "When you read the packaging around the story," I said, "let it give you some hints about the main storyline because that'll help you know which details are important enough to carry with you as you read."

Max read sitting bolt upright, collar tucked neatly into his sweater vest. Gabe sprawled out floppily. Kadija leaned slightly back against a bookshelf and started reading immediately, eyebrows drawn together as she concentrated. Malik mouthed something that made Kobe giggle, but started reading after a slight shake of the head from me.

When the kids had finished reading the prologue, I said, "So what do you think? What do you need to carry with you in your mind so that the story makes sense and so that you can stay focused on solving the mystery?" The students agreed right away that the book would probably be about an unknown man robbing a bank. I jotted that onto a list of important details. They suggested other details, which I added to the list.

"We should remember that the kid has the video of him," said Malik. I added that to our list.

"And Dink and Josh and Ruth Rose (the gang) meet the detective," said Max.

"The bandit ran away dropping money. I wonder where he dropped it," said Gabe. "I wish I would've been following him!"

"Do you all think that the fact that the money was dropped is something we need to keep in our minds as we go on?" I asked. Of course, money being dropped on the street engaged Gabe's imagination, but in this particular story, it did not seem to be a crucial detail. I wanted to help Gabe focus on the details that were especially integral to the story, and I

know that children who struggle with accumulating the text have a hard time deciding what matters and what is extraneous.

"I don't think so," said Kadija. "I don't think that's what the main mystery is going to be about. But I would've followed him, too!" she grinned at Gabe.

"And he offered them a reward to help get the kid that took the video!" finished Malik.

I reread the list I'd made of their ideas, trying to consolidate what each child had contributed so all the readers could recall these bits of information.

"So, given these important details that we'll be keeping in our minds as we read on, what information do you think we'll need to look for as we read?"

"How they find that kid and get the video," said Malik.

"Yeah, and their reward money!" said Gabe.

I said, "I bet we'll start learning about things as we read on. We'll also learn more aspects of the story that will be important to follow. Read Chapter 1, and then I'll be back so we can talk."

MID-WORKSHOP TEACHING POINT

continued from previous page

> • I feel bad for Rhianna because I can relate to her I hate getting in trouble while someone is watching. Its really embaresing. (47)

Sophie has zoned in on the particular quality of Rhianna's distress. When a reader uses many words to describe a character's feeling, it usually pays off.

Important Details from The Bald Bandit

• A bald bandit robs bank.

• The kid has video of him.

• The detective finds the gang (i.e., Josh, Dink, and Ruth Rose).

• The detective offers them reward to find kid and get video.

As the group read, I made my way around the room, resettling kids, doing a quick conference, answering a question. When I saw Malik trying to get Kobe's attention and Kadija looking quietly around the room with her finger holding her place in the book, I rejoined the group on the rug. "So, what new information did you find that relates to the details you carried forward from the prologue?" I asked.

Malik replied, "The boy with the video has red hair."

Kadija countered, "No, that's not new. It says he has red hair on the back of the book. We knew that already."

Before Malik got disheartened, I replied, "That's great, guys! You're really listening to each other and thinking about which details are new and which details you already knew. You're right, Malik, that we need to know more about this kid with the video. And Kadija, you're right that the back tells us he has red hair."

Max continued, "Yes, there could be lots of red-headed kids in their town. They need to know something else about him, besides his hair. Or, or, or . . . they won't find him."

"Right, Max." I continued, "So, everyone, what new information did you find about the kid as you read Chapter 1?"

Max and Kadija added that the kid is tall and skinny and possibly a high school kid. Definitely a boy, put in Malik, because the detective called him "he." I jotted the new information onto our list.

Since Gabe hadn't jumped in yet, I prompted him to check the top of page 7. He scanned the page for a moment and then said, "Well, we know he was older than the kids in the gang," pointing to the sentence reading, "No, the kid was a lot older than you." The strategy of prompting a reader to look at a particular page is one that Peter Johnston suggests in his important book, *Choice Words*. When I coached Gabe to look at page 7 without pointing out the exact words that answered the question, I was giving him a scaffold. Then I celebrated his expertise. This kind of teaching builds a reader's self-concept. Since he'd been working hard on understanding pronoun reference, I did a quick check, asking him who the word *you* meant in that sentence.

"It means the gang, of course—what are their names?" he said as he scanned. "Dink and Josh and Ruth Rose." His stated "of course" as he swung his bangs out of his eyes was encouraging. Not only was he understanding pronoun reference, but he was beginning to internalize it enough when he read to regard my question as obvious. I asked Gabe about pronoun reference to highlight his emerging control over that. Learning theory calls reviewing known information in this way "maintenance learning."

"Great," I said. "You added some important details." Then I asked the students whether all their details were ones they'd carry on to the next chapter. I suggested they read to a stopping point halfway through the book, accumulating important details onto a list. As I sent them off to their independent reading, I reminded them that the work we'd done with this book was work they could do with any book. I suggested that they add *The Bald Bandit* to their book bins if they were hooked and wanted to find out what happened.

When We Teach Readers to Envision and to Empathize, We Are Teaching Them to Care, to Understand, and to Comprehend

I pulled up alongside Tyrell, who was reading *Molly's Pilgrim*. I was glad to see he had branched out in his book choices while still reading a book well within his reach. "So Tyrell, what sorts of things are you doing in your mind as you read?"

Tyrell smiled as he gripped his book. "I like acting like the people."

"You do?" I said. "That is so interesting to me. Did you do that with this last book?" Tyrell nodded. "I ask because the books you are reading now are a lot more challenging than the ones you were reading earlier in the year, right?" Using intonation to show that I was impressed, I said, "And yet you are *still* able to read them so well that you practically pretend to be that character?"

Tyrell nodded. "I'm kind of like this when I read," he said, and gripped his book tightly, peered intently at the text. He made out a few expressive faces that indicated he was feeling worried, excited, shocked.

Clearly he wanted me to know that the books were getting through to him and that he was seeing the close line between reading and drama. "Wow!" I said. "I bet when you listen to me read *The Tiger Rising*, you are right there inside the story and you can actually see that tiger. Am I right?" Tyrell nodded and did a bit more acting to show that his eyes popped out and his hair stood on end when he encountered the tiger. I joined in the dramatization, agreeing that I, too, could feel the mighty creature pacing back and forth in front of me.

I glanced at my records for a moment, mulling over what to teach Tyrell. I wanted to be sure to build on the work he was already doing as a reader rather than simply pulling him off course to try something new.

"Tyrell," I said. "I'm thinking about ways I can imagine you continuing your reading growth. It's making me realize how far you have already traveled as a reader—you've already challenged yourself to take on harder books, and you've already begun reading as if you are in this intense sort of a drama, like a play. So I am thinking, 'What is next for this reader who keeps taking on more and more challenges?' I have an idea. Want to hear it?"

"Okay! Sure," Tyrell said.

"When readers read in such a way that we are in the character's shoes, when we are living through the character's life, this can help us grow huge, deep ideas about the whole character, the whole book, and about our lives even, too," I said. "Let me show you what I mean by that." Tyrell nodded.

Picking up *Stone Fox* I said, "When we were reading *Stone Fox,* I didn't just *picture* Little Willy racing down the hill on his way to Doc for the prescription. I tried to practically *be* Little Willy—just like you do. I felt the moonlight giving Willy almost a glow, the air so cold it was slicing his face. I was right there, in the story. Then I took myself out of the scene for a second, and I thought, 'Okay, how does this help me understand the story better? What ideas does this give me about what the character must be living through?'"

"Then I went back to the scene and put myself in Willy's shoes, racing in the night, and this time, it occurred to me that Little Willy must feel like he can do anything. There must be something in him, like a force that makes him do more than a kid usually can do. Because in the scene, I'm becoming him and I feel like maybe I'm becoming taller, and it's like I am flying through the night. I had never thought of Willy like that before."

Tyrell nodded. "It's like he believes in himself?"

"Exactly," I added. "Like the light is not only *on* him but *in* him. There's a force inside of him. When you read this way, so intensely pres-

ent in the story, you challenge yourself to focus that empathy you are feeling, the intensity of your connection to that character—to really understand him. You can use this focus to think big important thoughts about the character, or the moment, or the book, or your life."

"Do you think you could try this in your book, and in all your reading? Could you return to a part of your book that mattered to you and read it again, really picturing it in your mind, practically being the character? And when you find that passage and you have read it, will you signal to me?"

Tyrell picked up *Molly's Pilgrim* and began reading while I circulated through the room. After a bit he signaled me with his book saying, "Got it!" Then he pointed. "Right here, I see Molly is walking into her classroom, holding her pilgrim doll. She's standing there, really nervous because her doll is strange looking."

"Really picture the whole scene, not just Molly," I coached.

"And the kids are staring at her and then at her doll and then back at her," Tyrell added. "I think, maybe, she's embarrassed."

"Great. Now reread the passage, and as you do so, put yourself in Molly's shoes, so you are almost dramatizing that scene. And catch the ideas that come to you. Let them fill up your mind."

Tyrell did this, reading quietly. Then he said, "Maybe she realizes that she *is* different and it doesn't feel the best, but maybe it's not the worst. She doesn't have to be embarrassed."

"Tyrell, do you see what you just did? By pretending to be Molly, you figured out what might be at the heart of her. You didn't just try to see the details of the scene. You tried to understand the whole depth of the character—what makes her tick and what is holding her together? That effort really paid off, didn't it? Do you think you can try this work some more on your own?"

"Okay!" Tyrell grinned.

"It might mean doing a bit more writing as you read. If your mind can't hold your ideas and your Post-its aren't big enough, you could use your reading notebook," I said.

TEACHING SHARE

Readers Put Ourselves in the Shoes of Characters, Nearly Dramatizing as We Read

Gather readers. Name the steps involved in reenacting an important part of the text and then ask them to do so.

"Readers, let's gather on the rug, sitting next to your partner. Yesterday we learned that readers read, imagining ourselves in the shoes of a character. A famous writer, Joyce Carol Oates, once said, "Reading is the sole means by which we slip, involuntarily, often helplessly, into another's skin, another's voice, another's soul.

"Let's again reread and reenact a scene or two that feels important. Let me remind you of the steps we took yesterday. They're probably becoming second nature to you now. First, (I put one finger up) you found a scene that matters, preferably one with lots of dialogue. Then (I put a second finger up) you did a 'Previously in . . .' to catch the listener up with what was going on before now. Then (I put up a third finger) you put the book, open to the selected scene, between the two of you and decided who would assume which part. Next (fourth finger) you read and talked about the scene so that you could understand the characters better. And finally, you reread the scene, this time adding more gestures and intonation so you really brought the scene to life. So, encore! Do it again."

Coach children as they try it, lifting the level of their work. Celebrate the work of one group of children in a way that helps cement the learning for them all.

As I moved among the kids, I sometimes coached them on to the next step in this progression, saying things like, "Remember, the book needs to be held between the two of you so you can both look over the scene and select roles.

After a few minutes, I reconvened the class. "Readers, I noticed some incredible things as I listened just now. Kobe realized that Brian, the character in *The River*, might not be a grumpy person so much as a sad one. Kobe decided he is revising his ideas in reading, just as he revises his drafts in writing. So he then read Brian's dialogue differently and found that changing Brian's tone of voice ended up changing other things too!

"Watching you act out scenes in your books and then overhearing the kinds of conversations those dramatizations inspired was really exciting. I heard many of you even change your minds about your characters as a result.

COACHING TIPS

You'll notice that today's share matches yesterday's. The goal is for kids to dramatize often enough that they feel at home doing this and, even more importantly, that their dramatization affects the ways in which they read.

Teachers, you may have these steps written on a chart. This will provide extra support for your readers who struggle. The chart may go something like this:

Acting Out an Important Scene

- *Find a scene that matters, preferable one with lots of dialogue.*
- *Give your partner a "previously in . . ." to catch them up on what has happened up until that point.*
- *Open the book to the scene you will act out and leave it open between the two of you. Decide who will take which part.*
- *Act it out!*
- *Talk about the scene and how you are coming to understand the characters better.*
- *Act one more time, using all you've realized about the characters to add more gestures and intonation. Bring it to life!*

Teachers, you may want to suggest that children spread out just a bit as they act out scenes. Some children may opt to swing their arms, shuffle their feet, make grand entrances or exits. On the other hand, you can ask kids to act in place if that makes you feel more comfortable.

It's hard to emphasize enough the importance of this work. Langer argues that reading must "enter an envisionment" to experience text. Enciso (1992) describes engagement in reading as "our entry into the world of the story and the intense involvement we feel as we imagine and interpret the characters, setting, events, and many possibilities of literary text."

Letting the Text Revise Our Image of the Character

hen we consider the characteristics of strong readers, most of us would agree that strong readers read a variety of genres with engagement, stamina, fluency, and comprehension, and they choose to spend lots of time reading. While these characteristics certainly suggest reading strength and can be quantified through running records, reading logs, and standardized tests, there are other important characteristics of strong readers that are not so easily quantifiable.

For example, we know that a strong reader is flexible and agile. When a strong reader encounters difficulty either on a word level or a comprehension level, she tends to move

GETTING READY

- Bring your class read-aloud to today's lesson. Identify a part of the book to read that spotlights how new details from a text often make readers change their initial envisionments. If you are using *The Tiger Rising*, you will find the beginning of Chapter 4 works well. This passage is read aloud during the teaching and active involvement of this session.

- If you would like to provide scaffolds for your readers, prepare to give each Partner 1 a copy of pages 11 and 12 of *The Tiger Rising* (2006 Paperback Edition, published by Candlewick). These pages will be referred to during the active involvement. If you find your readers need extended practice, you may also copy pages 8 and 9.

- If you are using another read-aloud, you will want to make sure that prior to this session, you've been able to help children make a picture in their minds that will, in this session, be revised as you read ahead. If you can't find a place in your read-aloud to support this, many picture books, including *Dancing in the Wings* by Debbie Allen, can easily be used to demonstrate this.

- In the minilesson, you will be adding to the chart, "Strategies Readers Use to Grow Ideas About Characters."

- In the teaching share section, you'll channel partners to choose their own ways to share reading, drawing from the options listed on the charts, "Ways You and Another Reader Can Talk About Your Reading Lives" and "Ways You and Another Reader Can Talk About Your Books." that you created in previous sessions.

- During Session V's minilesson, you'll read the rest of Chapter 4. That will need to be the first time you read it to the class, as you will use it to teach prediction. It is important to refrain from finishing this chapter today! If you do finish Chapter 4, you'll need to read from a later excerpt tomorrow, chosen because it is appropriate for teaching prediction.

automatically and efficiently to call up the strategies that will be most helpful in dealing with the challenge. These agile readers are able to make adjustments on the run without losing hold of comprehension. Although reading agility and flexibility are invisible and hard to assess, it's worth our while to support children in becoming the kinds of readers who are nimble, both as word solvers and meaning makers. In other words, we want children to be the kinds of readers who can move from strategy to strategy in a flash when they are figuring out words and who can envision and then revision the story as they move through it, taking in all the twists and turns.

> ## Agile readers are able to make adjustments on the run without losing hold of comprehension.

In this lesson, we will provide readers with support for becoming agile envisioners, the kinds of readers who constantly take in new information and adjust their mental images. The idea for this lesson arises from our observation that many readers often carry forward something they've envisioned even if, as they read further, the text contradicts that mental image and requires that they revise what they've pictured. For example, several years ago, my colleague Donna Santman shared a story of conferring with a reader who was under the impression that the main character in her book had survived a fire. Although Donna hadn't read that particular young adult novel, she knew enough about the story to be surprised with the student's impression.

Donna said, "Can you show me the part where the character talks about surviving the fire? That sounds like it would be a part where we'd learn a ton about the character, how she handles such a frightening situation." The reader flipped back a half dozen or so pages to show the part with the fire, and Donna discovered that it was a brief scene where the character and her friends were at a beach bonfire. The child may not have understood the meaning of bonfire and consequently pictured a full-blown fire. That sort of misunderstanding is bound to occur when reading. But the significant thing to note is that the reader held doggedly to her erroneous impression in the face of growing evidence that should have signaled to her that she'd misunderstood something. Her inflexibility blocked her from taking in the information that would have created a more accurate mental image of the scene.

In books, as in life, it is important that people are willing to revise our first impressions. As we see more, hear more, learn more, we adjust the impressions we made in a flash. When we began this unit and started reading aloud *The Tiger Rising*, children were likely to have a one-sided and unambivalent impression of Sistine. We hope that as they learn more about her, listening to her words and watching her deal with a variety of situations, they will develop a more nuanced and mature image of her, one that allows for the continued streaming information that Kate DiCamillo provides us, and we hope they do likewise in their independent reading books—now and forevermore. To become the kind of readers who adjust their mental images and envisioning by taking in the story information, children will need to know that it's a powerful reader who reads along and can say, "Oops, let me think about that again," or "Wait a minute. That doesn't match what I've been picturing." This is the point of the following lesson.

# MINILESSON

Letting the Text Revise Our Image of the Character

CONNECTION

Recall that readers walk in the shoes of main characters. Tell them that today, and always, they'll continue to do this.

"During reading time yesterday, I know each of you *was* a character in your book. When your character got furious, you probably found yourself clenching your fists, kicking at the ground, scowling at your partner. When your character stopped and looked up, seeing that the clouds had parted and a ray of sunshine was shining through, you, no doubt, felt that sunshine on your face.

Be sure you use actions to accompany your language. When you say that you know readers shared their characters' fury, clenching fists, kicking at the ground, and scowling you'll want to do miniature versions of these actions. Help readers envision your words, and help them listen attentively.

"This is what John Gardner meant in that quote I read earlier this year. 'We read a few words at the beginning of the book and suddenly find ourselves seeing not words on a page but a train moving through Russia, an old Italian crying, a farmhouse battered by rain. We read on—dream on—not passively but actively, worrying about the choices that the characters have made.'

"Today I want to say, 'Encore.' That's what the audience at the theater cries out when the audience wants the actors to do it again. Encore, readers. Do it again. Today, read as if you were walking in your character's shoes—again. Remember to add in stuff from your own life—again. If the character goes to a park, recall the park right across from your house and fill in the details of your character's park. If the character walks up the front steps of a school, bring our huge cement steps—all ten of them—into your mental movie."

You'll notice that I often use vocabulary terms that will not be familiar to many children. Kids need to be immersed in rich nuanced language! But the language needs to be meaningful, and you'll see that I tend to weave a synonym into the text to help children grasp the meaning of a word such as encore, curmudgeon, peripheral vision, or autopilot.

Again and again, notice that minilessons need to help children accumulate and draw upon the entire repertoire of all you have taught, showing ways in which the new teaching extends and builds upon the old.

Name your teaching point. Teach children that readers revise our mental movies when new details in the text lead us to self-correct.

"And today I want to teach you that a reader not only sees, hears, imagines as if in the story, making a movie in the mind, but a reader also revises that mental movie. Often when we read on, the story provides details that nudge us to say, 'Oops, I'll have to change what I'm thinking.'"

TEACHING

Help readers crystallize an impression of a character from the read-aloud. Channel them to create an impression that will need to be revised after further reading.

"Let's for a second think back to Chapter 3 and remember the movie we made in our minds when the new character, Sistine, boarded Rob's bus, coming into the story."

Turning to Chapter 3 of the book, I said, "Remember that we pictured Sistine as a blond-haired, shy girl in a fancy pink party dress, nervously walking down the aisle of the bus. We thought she walked kind of like this?" I showed Sistine walking shyly onto the bus, looking down on the floor of the bus (it was her first day with these new kids). "The name Sistine, named after that beautiful painting that has angels in the clouds and God reaching out his hand to Adam, helped us form a picture of her, didn't it?

"We have that picture of Sistine in mind. As we read on, let's continue to imagine, filling in the details."

Chapter 4

Sistine was in Rob's sixth grade homeroom class. Mrs. Soames made her stand up and introduce herself.

"My name," she said in her gravelly voice (I read the word *gravelly* in a way which showed my puzzlement over this description of the tone of her voice, because I wouldn't have expected this girl in a pink dress to have a gravelly voice), "is Sistine Bailey." She stood at the front of the room, in her pink dress. And all the kids stared at her with open mouths as if she had just stepped off a spaceship from another planet.

Say these words as if they matter. They do. A doctoral student of mine has researched children who struggle to comprehend, and she's found that almost two thirds of them get themselves into trouble because they cling to their first 'read' of a story in face of all new evidence and end up with a chaotic hodgepodge of ideas instead of a coherent text.

You'll need to be a bit manipulative here. The point of the minilesson is that because our envisionments draw not only on the text but also on the reader's prior experiences, it is not uncommon for a reader to envision in ways that turn out to be wrong, and readers need to be nimble enough to revise those first envisionments. To convey this, you'll first envision (and get your class to do so, too) in ways that turn out to be problematic.

In planning a minilesson, we tend to look for portions of a text that will make it easy for readers to do the sort of work we're advocating. In constructing this minilesson, we first found two instances in the early chapters of The Tiger Rising *in which our initial impressions of characters were soon turned upside down by new information. Rob appeared at first to be a wimpy kid but then races bravely to Sistine's assistance. Sistine is introduced first as the new girl in a pink dress, but she eventually defies stereotypes. We used one of these passages in the minilesson, saving the other for small-group work.*

Notice, that although I have already figured out that Sistine turns out to defy our initial impression of her, I do not reveal this realization up front. Instead, I channel the kids to form the same initial impression of Sistine that I formed, so that then, after reading farther in the text, their first impression will be challenged.

Remember, you are still cultivating the shy-girl-in-the-pink-dress image that you know will be turned upside down soon.

I said, "Okay, so I picture her, standing in front of the whole class. I'm picturing a room like ours, with kids sitting at tables. Sistine is new so she looks out into a sea of new faces, each person with his or her mouth open and eyes wide, looking at Sistine as if she was an alien. She probably feels scared and shy."

Extract some overarching principles from the demonstration you've just given, emphasizing that readers use information from our own lives to fill in gaps in texts.

Shifting now into the role of teacher and looking kids directly in the eyes, I named what I hope they'd seen me do thus far. "Did you notice that I brought what I know of classrooms and of new kids into my picture? Readers do that. We draw on what we learned earlier in the book and draw also on what we know from our own lives to fill in the details of what we are imagining. But here's the important thing that I want you to notice. Sometimes when we bring in stuff from our own lives, we create pictures that when we read on, turn out to be wrong. As we read on, in those instances, we find ourselves saying 'Oops' and revising our picture."

Read on, encountering text that will challenge our envisionment of that character. Show that we revise our initial ideas.

Rob looked down at his desk. He knew not to stare at her. He started working on a drawing of the tiger.

"What a lovely name," said Mrs. Soames.

"Thank you," said Sistine.

Patrice Wilkins, who sat in front of Rob, snorted and then giggled and then covered her mouth. ("Oh, how horrible for Sistine.")

"I'm from Philadelphia, Pennsylvania," Sistine said, "home of the Liberty Bell, and I hate the South because the people in it are ignorant."

In reading workshop, minilessons often require the teacher to shift between reading aloud and thinking aloud. As I've mentioned earlier, it's easy for these two to become indistinguishable, something that creates confusion for the observing children. So remember that you'll want to rely upon a way to signal when you shift from reading aloud to thinking aloud. When you are thinking about the text rather than reading it, you'll probably want to lower the book and look up toward the sky: Don't hesitate to be a bit overly dramatic in ways that convey, "Now I'm not reading. I am, instead, musing over what I've just read."

So far you have demonstrated prior lessons in which you taught children that readers draw on their prior knowledge to fill in details of the text they're reading. But you haven't yet demonstrated today's teaching point, which is that when we read and find the text challenges our first envisionment, we often need to say "Oops" and revise these envisionments.

If it seems to you that we are creeping awfully slowly through the read-aloud book, know that Kathleen and I feel the same way. You will probably want to stay in sync with us nevertheless because if you zoom ahead in your reading aloud, this may make some of the upcoming minilessons harder, but know you are right to be chomping on the bit!

Putting the book down, I looked at the kids and said, "What??? That doesn't match our picture of Sistine, does it?" Then returning to the book, I said, "Let's read on."

> "And I'm not staying here in Lister. My father is coming to get me next week." She looked around the room defiantly.

I again lowered the book, signaling that I was thinking rather than continuing to read. "Hmm, . . . 'Sistine looked around the room *defiantly*,'" and I acted out that sort of look. "Boy does that change a lot for me! I was envisioning Sistine as shy and nervous, but now I need to revise my image, don't you?"

Set children up to talk in partners about how they need to revise their mental movies in light of new information. Then summarize what you hope they learned that is applicable to another text, another day.

"Turn and tell your partner what words you once used—and now use—to describe Sistine." The class erupted into conversation.

Convening the children, I summarized. "Readers, I heard you say that you used to think of Sistine as shy, quiet, girly, worried, and now you think of her as rude, snotty, angry, a snob. I hope you have learned not only about Sistine but also about reading. When we encounter new information, we, as readers, often need to change our minds."

ACTIVE INVOLVEMENT

Invite children to revisit a section of the text they read earlier, this time showing their new sense of the character.

"This makes me wonder if maybe we misread that bus scene from earlier, when Norton and Billy made fun of Sistine. Now I'm remembering how she said to them, 'It's not my fault you don't have good clothes,' and how she said to Rob, 'What are you looking at?' I'm realizing I was so consumed with the image of this shy girl with blond hair, wearing a pink dress that I didn't notice all the clues that suggested she never did fit my image of a girl in a pink dress.

Teachers, you'll notice that for the demonstration portion of this minilesson, we read aloud a part of Chapter 4, and then for the next part of the active involvement, we will return to Chapter 3. We often return to text that the kids have previously heard during a minilesson.

If the upcoming section feels a bit too ambitious for you—the amount of drama required—you can always think of the partner talk (above) as the active involvement section of the minilesson and shift from that work, above, directly to the link.

"Let's reread and reenact that earlier scene. Partner 1s, you be Sistine. And Partner 2s, you again be both Norton *and* Billy. I'll reread the scene from earlier in the book, and then you reenact the dialogue, making sure you bring out the tone of each character." I read from the beginning of Chapter 3.

> "Hey," Norton called, "this is a school bus."
>
> "I know it," the girl said. Her voice was gravelly and deep, and the words sounded clipped and strange, like she was stamping each one of them out with a cookie cutter.
>
> "You're all dressed up to go to a party," Billy said. "This ain't the party bus." He elbowed Rob in the ribs.
>
> The girl stood in the center of the aisle, swaying with the movement of the bus. She stared at them. "It's not my fault you don't have good clothes," she said finally. She sat down and put her back to them.

At this part a few of the kids called out, "Oooh" and "What a dis!" while others giggled.

> "Hey," said Norton. "We're sorry. We didn't mean nothing. Hey," he said again. "What's your name?"
>
> The girl turned and looked at them. She had a sharp nose and a sharp chin and black, black eyes.
>
> "Sistine," she said.
>
> "Sistine," hooted Billy. "What kind of stupid name is that?"

Again giggles resounded around the carpet. Max leaned forward on his knees, shaking his head. "I'd be mad," he whispered.

> "Like the chapel," she said slowly, making each word clear and strong.
>
> Rob stared at her, amazed.
>
> "What are you looking at?" she said to him.

"Partners turn and act out. You don't need to try to stick with the words of the book. Say whatever your character might have said. Start with Norton saying, 'This is a school bus. . . .'"

You can distribute a copy of this page to children or not. The presence of the page will, of course, lead them to reread rather than to improvise, but it'll also provide scaffolds. You may wait to see which partnerships seem at a loss without the page and distribute it only to those partnerships.

These reactions are comprehension monitors, showing the extent to which children are taking in the story.

Time and again you will notice that one of the most helpful things you can do for a reader is to get him or her started doing whatever it is you hope the reader will do.

As I moved among children, I watched two children role-play the scene on the bus, with the child who was role-playing the bullies saying, "This bus is going to school, not to a party," and "Why are you wearing that fancy dress?" The child role-playing a tough version of Sistine, retorted, "You gonna hate me because I have nice clothes and you don't?"

To one child, I said, "I want to caution you to not go over the top with the way you see Sistine. Remember we're thinking she's rude and tough. We didn't say she's brutal."

Name what you hope children have learned that they can carry with them to another text, another day.

After three minutes, I wrapped up this section of the minilesson by saying, "Look what you've done today! Readers envision, and then we learn new evidence about the character and so we *re*-vision. At the start of today, we thought Sistine was shy and nervous, but now we have revised our image, realizing she can also be arrogant and tough, and I know you'll do similar re-vision work whenever you read."

LINK

Remind children that reading involves not only envisioning but also re-visioning.

"Readers, whenever you read, let the words of the story into your mind. Envision. Be there. As you read on, the story will usually give you new details that will make you say, 'Oops' and that will make you revise that mental movie of yours. Remember, reading is not only a process of *envisioning*. It is also a process of *re-visioning*. As you read today, you'll be doing all that you have learned to do. (I pointed to our ongoing chart and added today's teaching point to it.)

"I know you'll be doing all this work as you read. For today, use a Post-it note to mark places where you revised your mental picture. I have a feeling those parts will be pretty important to your understanding of the characters in your book because authors want our ideas about characters to change, and when they do, those are important moments in a story. We'll talk and think more about them later.

Encourage readers to take on the role, to walk in the skin of the characters, using gestures and ad-libbing. Give them license to act as that fictional persona, adding in lines the characters could have said but didn't. Tell children that, of course, they will not have memorized the text, but they do know what Sistine is apt to say, what her responses would most likely be. It helps to ask children to put the photocopied page away and to ad-lib. Without the paper in their hands, they bring the text to life.

When I write minilessons, I draw on all I know about figurative language and literary technique in an effort to make my teaching memorable. It is no accident that I juxtapose the reference to readers envisioning with that of them re-visioning. I'm using parallel structure in hopes that my teaching will lodge into kids' minds.

Strategies Readers Use to Grow Ideas About Characters

- *We make a movie in our mind, drawing on the text to envision (or become) the character.*

- *We use our own experiences to help us walk in the character's shoes, inferring what the character is thinking, feeling, experiencing.*

- *We revise our mental movies as we read on, getting new details from the text.*

- *We revise our initial mental movie as we take in new information.*

"Remember—what do you do first when you get back to your desk?"

The children answered, "Fill out our logs."

"Those of you sitting toward the back get started." They dispersed. "The rest of you, don't forget your logs and don't forget that reading is all about imagining. Off you go."

Notice that over time, we lighten our explicit support for logs. On previous days, I told children to fill out their logs, now I nudge them to keep the logs in mind, but I don't specifically name this responsibility. Later, I'll pass even more responsibility on to them.

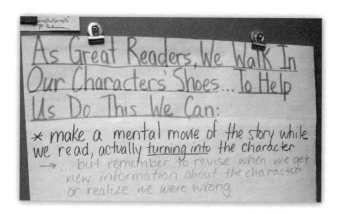

As Great Readers, We Walk In Our Characters' Shoes... To Help Us Do This We Can:

✱ make a mental movie of the story while we read, actually _turning into_ the character
→ ...but remember to revise when we get new information about the character or realize we were wrong

When you look at a chart, you should see that principles of outlining (or of boxes and bullets) have informed the structure of the chart. Here the stars are A-heads, the arrows B-heads. Note the extremely supportive title.

CONFERRING AND SMALL-GROUP WORK

By Observing an Effective Strategy Lesson, You Can Learn Replicable Methods for Teaching as Well as Ways to Support Envisionment

When writers want to get better at writing, we study the work of master writers, thinking, "What has this writer done that I could emulate?" We especially notice craft moves that the writer uses repeatedly, and think, "What does this particular move seem to accomplish?" and wonder, "How did the writer go about writing in this particular way?"

To get better as teachers, it is important for us to study effective *teaching* just as writers study effective *writing*. And we can look especially for moves that a mentor teacher has done repeatedly and ask, "What does this particular move seem to accomplish?" and "How did this teacher go about teaching in this particular way?"

In this session, we pull alongside Kathleen Tolan, who is leading a small-group strategy lesson, and we observe her teaching. I'm going to pretend that I'm accompanying you on this observation. From time to time, I'll suggest that instead of listening to Kathleen's instruction, we pull together to reflect on what we see her doing as a teacher, noting especially the moves she makes that might be worth repeating another day, with another group of readers.

Listening In on a Strategy Lesson

You'll notice from the start that although most reading conferences begin with a phase that we refer to as "research," when the teacher observes what children are already doing as readers and interviews them about their reading work, in this particular strategy lesson, the research has already been conducted. Often our teaching of reading is informed by research that we did a few days ago or even a week ago. When teachers confer or lead small-group work with *writers*, it is rare that they draw simply on research that occurred a day or a week earlier. As *writers* progress, they tend to shift from doing one kind of work to doing yet another kind. *Readers*, on the other hand, tend to do the same kind of work again and again, on any given day (with small shifts if they are reading a particular genre, or at the beginning, middle, or end of a book). So it is more likely that a teacher will bypass the research phase of a *reading* conference or small group, relying on prior assessments, than that the teacher will bypass the research phase of a *writing* conference or small group.

When we joined her, Kathleen had already gathered a group of six children in the meeting area of the classroom. She had asked them to bring their

---

> ## MID-WORKSHOP TEACHING POINT
>
> ### Readers Revise Our Mental Movies, Paying Attention to Details About the Main Character, Other Characters, and the Setting
>
> "Readers, may I stop you for a moment? Right now, find a place where you were able to see more in a part of your book—a place that changed the movie in your mind." I waited for children to find that place. "Go ahead and reread that part."
>
> As children read over their parts, I guided them to envision with prompts. "Perhaps you are seeing a character. Perhaps you are seeing that character's clothing or facial expressions or what that character is doing. Thumbs up if you are seeing your character." I scanned the room looking to see that most thumbs were up before I continued. "Now add to your picture. Who else do you see? Where are these characters exactly? Bring what you know about this place from earlier information from the book or from your life. Also, what are these characters doing? Add that to your pictures.
>
> "Readers, in a few seconds you are going to share with your partner what you are picturing. You'll need to first help your listener know the background, so you'll want to tell a 'previously in' summary. You may also find it helpful to read a bit of the text aloud to your partner and then tell what you are picturing. Watch me as I do that." I read:
>
> > Rob looked down at his desk. He knew not to stare at her. He started working on a drawing of the tiger.
>
> *continued on next page*

independent reading texts with them, which we notice, represent a variety of levels. This is a heterogeneous group. Sitting with the group in a close huddle, she said, "You have all been making movies in your mind as you read, and I think you've realized that it can be hard sometimes to actually get that mental movie going, am I right?" The children agreed. "So I thought we'd go back to this morning's read-aloud. I'm going to do a little coaching that can help you get a mental picture going. Let's first practice with a scene we know well from *The Tiger Rising*.

Kathleen turned to page 5 of Chapter 2 in *The Tiger Rising* and reread a scene the children had heard many times:

> "Looky here," said Norton Threemonger as soon as Rob stepped onto the school bus. "It's the Kentucky Star. How's it feel to be a star?" Norton stood in the center of the aisle, blocking Rob's path.
>
> Rob shrugged.
>
> "Oh, he don't know," Norton called to his brother. "Hey, Billy, he don't know what it's like to be a star."
>
> Rob slipped past Norton. He walked all the way to the back of the bus and sat down in the last seat.

MID-WORKSHOP TEACHING POINT

continued from previous page

I put down the book and said, "I picture Rob's eyes peering at Sistine for a brief second and then shifting downward, as Rob avoids looking at her. He's sitting in a small, old wooden desk that's lined up with others like it in rows. I see Rob lifting his pencil and closing his eyes briefly to remember exactly how the tiger looked before he begins to draw." I continued reading.

> "What a lovely name," said Mrs. Soames.

I looked up at the children and said, "Rob hears Mrs. Soames but keeps on drawing. And there's Mrs. Soames smiling encouragingly at Sistine who's standing in front of the class before a large, green chalkboard. Mrs. Soames's voice is soft and welcoming."

I named what I had just done. "Did you notice how I moved between the text and my mental picture? Adding the other characters and details about the classroom setting to my picture helped me imagine the whole scene.

"Okay, readers. Now it's your turn. Partner 2, you already read a part aloud. So why don't you start off and share what it makes you picture."

As partners shared, I listened in and coached.

José was reading to Kwami from *Crash*.

> My mother served the steaks.
> "Penn Webb's going out for cheerleading," I said.
> My dad is usually pretty cool, but this time his head jerked up like he got caught by an uppercut. "What? Who?"

continued on next page

Starting the Reading Work, But Letting Students Finish It

Kathleen paused and looked up from the text. She repeated the final words she'd just read: "Sat down in the last seat," and then said, "So I'm picturing Rob sitting there in silence, watching."

Notice that Kathleen wants her small group of readers to do a particular kind of reading work. Instead of explaining at some length what she wants them to do, she invites the children to do this work by getting started doing it herself, externalizing her thinking. For example, instead of saying, "Will you picture Rob, sitting on the bus . . . ," she simply said, "So I'm picturing Rob sitting there in silence, watching." That is, she gets students going on the work she hopes they will continue doing and then steps back, leaving the students to continue on their own. You no doubt do similar teaching when you begin some shared reading work with your children, at first taking a rather dominant role as reader with the other voices merely chiming in on your voice, and then pulling your voice back so that your children's voices take the lead. Of course, you are still right there, ready to become more dominant again if the readers flag and need your support.

Kathleen continued to read aloud and to think aloud.

Processing Your Demonstrations and Launching Children into Trying It

"Hey," said Billy Threemonger, "You know what? This ain't Kentucky. This is Florida."

"Okay, so I see Billy calling to Rob who is the back of the bus."

He followed Rob and sat down right next to him. He pushed his face so close that Rob could smell his breath. It was bad breath. It smelled metallic and rotten.

After reading a bit more of the passage aloud, Kathleen reiterated what the text said, saying the content in her own words. "Billy's face is this close to Rob like this." (Kathleen put her face inches from Rosa's face.) Looking at the children, she asked for confirmation. "Right? Can't you picture the scene? Huge Billy Threemonger breathing down on Rob with that stinky breath and Rob staring straight ahead not crying." In an aside, Kathleen said, as if parenthetically, "I'm bringing the not-crying detail from earlier in the book. That's what readers do."

For anyone wanting to emulate Kathleen's teaching, it is important to notice that she has just stepped back from what she was doing to process it for her observing children. She explicitly named what she'd done when she said, "I'm bringing the not-crying detail from earlier in the book."

Then she said, "See it in your mind, too. See Rob sitting in silence. See Billy's face so close to Rob's. See Rob's face as he breathes in Billy's bad breath. Do you see it? What do you think Rob's face looks like? Turn and tell the person sitting next to you."

You'll notice that Kathleen has launched the kids in doing the work she just talked about and demonstrated. Children worked in partners so they could all be engaged simultaneously, and Kathleen again sat in the middle of the circle, circulating among the children almost as if she was the hands of the clock and they, the numbers.

Kathleen listened in and heard Lily say to Emma, "He is mad but his face is frozen solid."

"Add on," Kathleen whispered to Emma.

"Like his eyes are squinting and his mouth is tight," Emma added, making the face herself.

"It's like his face is frozen solid! See all the characters," Kathleen responded, and then moved on to listen to and coach the next child.

MID-WORKSHOP TEACHING POINT

continued from previous page

José looked up and said, "I see the mom serving the steaks."

I coached, "Where is she and what, exactly, is she doing?"

José said, "I see the mom reaching across the kitchen table and putting a piece of steak on everyone's plate. Then Crash is smirking as he tells his dad about Penn wanting to be a cheerleader, and his dad is surprised."

"What exactly does the dad do?" I prompted.

José added, "His dad's head whipped around so fast and a look of shock and confusion crossed his face."

"Good job, José," I said. Then I reminded José and Kwami, "Remember, when you are envisioning a scene, you don't just picture *what* a person is doing. You also try to picture *how* that person is doing it." Then I moved on to another partnership and continued to coach.

After a few minutes I stopped the partners and named the reading work that the children had just practiced. "Readers, make sure that as you read, not just today but always, that you are not just re-envisioning your character but that you are also allowing your images of the other characters and the setting to be revised as well."

You'll notice that Kathleen coached with lean prompts, using as few words as possible and using very familiar phrases, all in hopes that with a few words, she could prompt readers to do things that she believed were right within their grasp. You'll also notice that after Kathleen coached, nudging readers to do something, she did not stay to observe whether the child followed her advice and certainly didn't go back and forth, working and reworking what the child did. Instead she coached one child, nudging that child to do something with another child. Then as the first child incorporated that advice, Kathleen moved to another partnership, then another, each time using lean prompts, inserted almost as voiceovers into the work that children were doing.

Setting Kids Up to Try the Work Again and Again, with Lean Prompts

The time Kathleen spent demonstrating, early on in this strategy lesson, was very brief, but it may not be her only demonstration. If there is a pie chart made of a strategy lesson, by far the biggest chunk of that pie chart is for children's own work, with a teacher coaching into that work. Still, the teacher may elect to do a second demonstration, this time showing children how to raise the level of their work. In this instance though, Kathleen simply sets children up to try again. "Okay, so now you're going to continue to envision, seeing the story in your mind. I'm going to read a little more to you, and again, try to see it."

"You ain't a Kentucky star," Billy said, his eyes glowing under the brim of his John Deere cap.

Kathleen continued to coach softly, "Add that to your picture."

And you sure ain't a star here in Florida. You ain't a star nowhere."

"Okay," said Rob.

Billy shoved him hard. And then Norton came swaggering back and grabbed hold of Rob's hair with one hand and with the other hand, ground his knuckles into Rob's scalp.

Rob sat there and took it.

"Picture being shoved and someone grabbing your hair and grinding his knuckles into your scalp. What would your face look like? Turn and talk."

Children turned and talked to each other, telling what they envisioned. Kathleen listened in, and again used lean prompts to coach one child, then another, to say more, to imagine what the character would say.

After a bit, Kathleen said, "Okay, so now will you pick up your own books and read? In a bit, I'll tap you, and then I want you to show me what you are picturing. You can show me on your face and act it out a little bit, or you can tell me what you see."

Emma was reading *Brother Below Zero.* Kathleen drew closer. "What do you envision?" Emma said, "I imagine he can't see. He's squinting." Kathleen coached Emma toward a more detailed mental picture.

"Why is he squinting?" Kathleen wondered aloud.

Emma paused, tilting her head to the side. "Because of the snow?"

"So it's hitting him in the eyes?"

"No, he's looking through a window," Emma answered decisively.

"Hmm, . . . he's squinting and looking out the window. What does he want to see?"

"He's trying to see if his brother is coming."

"Is he looking in a searching kind of way? Is it a serious situation, or a not so serious situation?" Kathleen asked.

"Serious," Emma decided.

"So it's serious. What's he probably thinking?"

Emma moved her head side to side in a searching sort of way, and said, "He's worrying and searching."

Kathleen nodded. "So keep reading, and as you read, add more to that picture. And remember that you don't want to picture just *what* a person is doing—like, 'he's searching.' You want to try to picture *how* he is doing it, *why* he is doing it." Kathleen is deliberately using the same words that she has used in previous teaching points. She doesn't want to use five different phrases to say one thing, but instead wants to attach words to experiences so that the words begin to take on real meaning. She worked for a minute with the next child, Lily, and the next.

Transcripts of reading strategy lessons are deceiving because if I included what Kathleen said to the next few children you would by then have heard what she said to one child, another, another, another, and so the transcript could lead you to believe that Kathleen is doing a lot of talking, that it is the teacher who is especially active. But in fact, in a reading strategy lesson, the children spend the bulk of the time reading and the teacher watches, then intervenes lightly to coach on the run, then moves to another child and again assesses and then coaches.

Helping Children Transfer Learning to Other Days, Other Texts

After coaching readers for five or six minutes, reaching several but not all the members of the small group, Kathleen knew it was time to move on to the rest of her class. Before the session could end, it was important for her to help readers understand that what she taught that day is not about working with this particular text, but that instead, it is transferable to any text, any day.

"So let's come back together for a second. Emma actually pretended to be a character and acted out the actions. And then she realized maybe she hadn't paid a lot of attention to the feelings of the character, so she figured out what those feelings were. Lily, meanwhile, had needed similar help. Lily knew what the character was doing. Right away, she jumped to her feet and acted out, 'She's just standing there,' but after we talked, Lily realized the character was perturbed, so the character was standing with an 'Awww, man' attitude, annoyed and angry, so she thought about how this would affect the character. This is all so smart! So when you keep reading, keep on making mental pictures as you read. Don't just let the text just pass you by."

# TEACHING SHARE

Readers Develop a Repertoire of Ways for Sharing Reading with Friends, and Draw from This Repertoire When We Have the Chance to Do So

Remind readers of all they know and invite them to call upon it when they need it.

"Readers, you are going to have time to talk with your partners now. Sometimes, I'll give you and your partner a specific way to share your reading, but today you can decide how to spend your time together. You can use the chart 'Ways You and Another Reader Can Talk About Your Reading Lives' or the chart, 'Ways You and Another Reader Can Talk About Your Books' to spark ideas, but before you choose, I want you to ask yourself, 'What do I need more support with?' You can use this time to strengthen your muscles as readers. You might not draw on the particular charts I mentioned, or on any chart at all. Perhaps you will think back to a conference or small group and recall something from one of those times that you could work on. So take a minute and make a mental short list of possibilities based on what you want to get better at doing. Thumbs up if you have an idea or two." I scanned the room and called on a few children.

Kadija said, "I was thinking that I need more practice in talking about what the book is making me remember and feel so I can really be in the character's shoes."

I pointed to Emma, who said, "I have been working on reading more at home, so my partner could look at my log and tell me how I'm doing."

"Readers, it's time for you and your partner to agree on what you'll do together and get started."

I quickly made my way from partnership to partnership and compared what each duo had chosen to work on with my conferring notes. I was curious to see how many of the children were working on things we'd concentrated on during conferring or small-group time.

COACHING TIPS

On a day such as today when the minilesson is lengthy, I usually have a briefer mid-workshop teaching point and teaching share so the children will get at least 30 minutes of reading time. We never want our whole-class teaching to take away from reading time.

Pay attention to the work readers assign themselves because this will show students' understanding of the unit of study and of themselves.

> My goal is to pick more thoughtful post-its to get more thoughtful and better partnership ~~conversation~~

> I would like to increase my reading stamina so my partner and I could push each other to read more. We could make goals together.

Spinning All We Know into Predictions

IN THIS SESSION,

you will teach students that readers use our empathy for our characters to help us make predictions based on what we imagine they might do, say, or feel.

ne day, my husband, John, and I were watching a mystery show on TV. In the show, some actors were making a movie. They had a camera crew there, and a woman actor came out carrying a fake gun. She raised the fake gun and pretended to shoot another actor. He fell down, pretending to be dead, and then the camera people yelled, "Retake." Before they filmed the episode a second time, the woman said, "I have to fix my makeup," and she went off to the dressing rooms. She was only gone a few seconds, and when she came out, they again got the cameras ready, again called, "Ready, set, go," and started filming, and again the woman pulled out her fake gun.

My husband, sitting beside me, muttered, "She's switched guns. It's gonna be a real gun." I shot a disparaging look at him. John's a psychotherapist, and psychotherapists see death everywhere. They think we're all struggling to deal with the fact that we'll someday die. "You and death," I said. "You should have gone into a different field!" Anyhow, the woman aimed her fake gun and pretended to shoot the guy. He fell down, pretending to be dead—only

GETTING READY

- Bring your class read-aloud to today's lesson. You will want to reread a bit of the chapter you last read and then read forward so readers can do some prediction work. If you've selected *The Tiger Rising*, you will find it works well to read aloud a part of Chapter 4 during the active involvement.

- Search your own classroom for a story of a child who was able to use his or her own life to imagine a character's feelings.

- You may want to have a supply of extra Post-it notes near the meeting area in case children may have forgotten to bring their reading materials with them to the minilesson.

- Make the chart "Strategies Readers Use When We Predict" so you can point to it during the mid-workshop teaching point.

- Hang the chart "Ways You and Another Reader Can Talk About Your Books" in a prominent place in the meeting area so that you can reference it during the teaching share.

- Prior to Session VI, you will want to have completed Chapter 7 of *The Tiger Rising*. If you've selected an alternative read-aloud for this unit, you will want to have read up to a part in the text that will be appropriate for teaching how to make strong predictions, so find a part that begs you to predict.

he didn't get up. He was actually dead. I looked at John. "How'd you know?" I said. "You watched this before, right?"

We need to channel children to read proactively, leaning forward to predict.

John rolled his eyes and said, "Luce, it was *obvious*." Then he added, "When you watch television shows, what are you *doing*?"

I answered, "I'm watching. I'm waiting to see what will happen," talking in that "duh" tone, as if my answer was the most obvious in the world. But since then, I've come to realize that when John watches television—and this might be true for you as well—he is doing something altogether different than I am doing. He's walking in the shoes of characters, thinking as they think, and he's imagining what's apt to come next, too, writing the story that has yet to be written. Then as the show unrolls, he watches, saying, "Yep, I was right!" or "Oh, I was wrong—that's surprising!"

And I'm struck by the fact that skilled readers, like skilled television watchers, are always proactive, always one step ahead of things. Drawing on all they know about the specific story, the genre, the language, and life itself, skilled readers read the words and then imagine the text that lies ahead. Then they read, thinking, "I was right!" "I knew it!" or "Huh? Where did that come from?"

Many of our students, though, read like I watch television. They sit passively, waiting for the story to come to them. This minilesson is the first of several that together aim to channel children to read proactively, leaning forward to predict.

MINILESSON

Spinning All We Know into Predictions

CONNECTION

Tell about a time in your life when, because you know a person well, you heard that the person was facing trouble and immediately did some envisioning and predicting how that person would probably rise to the challenge.

"I got a phone call last night. A friend of mine said, in a weak voice, 'I was taken to the emergency room last night. Turns out I'm really sick.' My mind raced. 'Have you been drinking that special green tea you love that is supposed to heal everything?' I asked. She said yes, and I knew what would come next. 'Is your mom coming down to take care of you?' Again, the answer was yes. Because I know my friend, I can imagine how issues unfold around her.

"That's how it goes in life. When we learn that a person we know has gotten into trouble, because we care about that person, we can sort of guess, or predict, what that person is likely to do, what resources the person will draw upon in the face of that trouble. That's what happens in reading, and it is what happens in life too. A character is sent to bed without his supper, and we're wondering whether he'll climb out the window, onto a tree branch, and make his way down for some food, or will a buddy slip him a sandwich?"

It's often very effective to begin your minilesson with some little bit of life news—something concrete, something newsy. All of us are hardwired to listen to each other's news. We're quickly drawn into whatever the person is telling us. So this sort of minilesson accomplishes the purpose of connecting with children, and if you end the news, the anecdote, by making a quick analogy to reading, you can bring home a big conceptual point without needing to talk a lot about concepts. This way, you can avoid a lot of abstract talk full of generalizations. That is, you can avoid connections that disconnect!

Name your teaching point. Specifically, tell children that readers go from empathizing to predicting, racing forward to anticipate things that are about to happen.

"One way readers read actively and wisely, then, is we empathize with the main character. We feel with the main character, in a way that leads us to anticipate what the character will do next."

Some teachers have altered the teaching point just a bit so that it says, "Our imagination not only helps us experience the book, but it helps us almost coauthor the book, anticipating the story that has not yet unfolded." These words, of course, harken back to the earlier notion that kids are authoring reading lives.

Teaching

Tell the story of a reader who identified with the character in a book and, to predict what would come next, drew on what the text said and also what he imagined the character probably felt.

"Readers, I want to tell you about this boy, Leo, that I taught one year. He was a teeny tiny boy; all his classmates towered over him, and I know he wished he was bigger. He loved reading about big strong animals, like gorillas. One day I sat beside him as he read this passage. Listen and try to imagine what Leo thought as he read this passage."

> Gorillas that have silver backs become the leaders of their tribe. They are not born with silver backs. Baby gorillas are born dark, but as they mature, some gorillas get a splash of silver on their backs. This silver signifies that this gorilla will become the tribe's leader.

I've watched kids miss the entire meaning of this section, so think about how you can talk and read in ways that accentuate the fact that Leo is what kids would refer to as a "shrimp."

Over the years, I've noticed that in the hands of one teacher, a minilesson will feel as if it is a read-aloud session, and in the hands of another teacher, the same minilesson will feel like a whole-class lecture. I very much prefer the former.

"Looking up from the book, Leo said, 'I bet every boy gorilla probably wakes up every morning and checks his butt to see if he's got any silver hairs on it yet. Then, one day, he's like, "Yes!"'"

Tell this well, with plenty of dramatizing, and your children will find it funny. Ideally, some of them will nod and think, "If I was that young gorilla, I'd definitely check my butt every day!" Notice that the language in the minilesson is colloquial. This is oral language and needs to have the ring of talk.

"I thought, 'Wow. Leo is using what the book says (that only the gorillas who get silver butts become the tribe's leader), and he is also using what he knows from his own life (as a shrimp) to allow himself to feel what his main character feels and to anticipate what the character will probably do. He predicts that young boy gorillas probably go through life, keeping an eye on their butts! Leo predicts that the book will soon say, "One day, when a young gorilla checks his butt, he sees silver hairs, and then he goes to other gorillas and says, 'Hey! Check out my butt!'" The book might not end up saying that is exactly what gorillas do, but Leo is doing smart work when he draws on what he would feel if *he* was one of those gorillas.'"

Your hope is that when the children hear that Leo reads that the young male gorillas who grow splashes of silver hairs on their backs end up becoming the tribe's leaders, the kids themselves will predict that Leo puts himself in the place of those gorillas, longing for that splash of silver to show up.

"I'm telling you this because today, I want to teach you that when we *read* as if we are in the skin, the voice, the soul of another, we feel for the character, and this sometimes leads us to *predict* as if we were the character, or as if the character was a person we know well. We see something bad coming and say, 'Oh, no.' We see a character wanting something, and we think, 'I know he's gonna go for that.'"

I reiterate the teaching point here, wording it just a bit differently. Notice that I often teach readers by using direct dialogue. You may wonder about this, asking, "Do you want to put words into their mouths?" The answer is yes, I do want to be putting words into kids' mouths, helping them carry on conversations in the mind. A good part of comprehension is the ability to talk over texts in one's mind.

Tell the story of one time when you watched TV and you were able to race ahead, predicting how the story would unfold. Then draw an analogy between watching TV and reading.

"Last night I watched this old movie, *Lilies of the Field,* on television. In it, Sidney Poitier is an unemployed construction worker heading out west to look for a job. He stops at a remote farm in the desert to get water when his car overheats. The farm is being worked by a group of nuns. The nuns circle him saying, 'Can you stay and help us build a church?' Sidney is intent on getting back on the road, so he keeps resisting their pleas. At one point, the car has been fixed, and he gets in it to drive away. He starts driving away, and all these nuns are watching him go, and calling out, 'Please don't go. Stay. Stay and help us.'

"On the screen, I watched the car driving down the long driveway, becoming smaller and smaller, and as I watched, I thought, 'He's going to turn around.' The car veered to the right and I thought, 'He's turning.' But then it straightened and drove on. Then just before it was out of view, the car turned and began making its way back to the nuns." Pausing in the midst of this story, I said to the children, "As I watched that show, I was predicting, like a weatherman predicts a storm. I was thinking of what was bound to happen next, and next, and next."

ACTIVE INVOLVEMENT

Invite children to listen to a scene of the read-aloud text as one might watch a TV show, thinking and then jotting what's going to happen next.

"So let's try reading *The Tiger Rising* in such a way that we feel what the characters feel, and anticipate what they'll do and say. You'll recall that previously in *The Tiger Rising,* Sistine had to stand and introduce herself in homeroom. When she said her name, another kid—Patrice Wilkins—giggled. Sistine responded,

> "I'm from Philadelphia, Pennsylvania," Sistine said, "home of the Liberty Bell, and I hate the South because the people in it are ignorant."
>
> "Well," said Mrs. Soames, "thank you very much for introducing yourself, Sistine Bailey. You may take your seat before you put your foot in your mouth any farther."

You have a zillion anecdotes to share that reveal ways prediction has played a part in your life. Draw on them. Do you make a point of never missing the first five minutes of the show Monk *because you know something will inevitably happen during the opening scene that unlocks the mystery? If so, you can use that fact as the basis for teaching readers that opening scenes are often important, or you could, alternatively, use it to teach readers that it helps to know how a series of books or a kind of text tends to go so you can use that knowledge to determine what is apt to be important.*

Teachers, you'll notice that this teaching section relies upon two different stories of prediction. First I tell the story of a little boy who read and predicted. It is a funny story, and I include it in part because it spices up the minilesson, because kids like to hear about other kids. But then I tell a more straightforward prediction story. You may decide to shorten the minilesson by eliminating one or the other. Of course, you'll draw on the television shows from your life, and the children from your prior classrooms, remaking the stories so they are yours.

The whole class laughed at that. Rob looked up just as Sistine sat down.

"Wow, Rob looked up as Sistine sat down. Hmm. My mind is leaping ahead in the story, isn't yours? I'm picturing Rob as he looks up, as he sees Sistine. And in my mind I'm almost writing the part of the story that'll happen next, aren't you? Stop and jot on a Post-it note, recording what *you* think Rob will do next."

I moved among the children, encouraging those who were sitting motionless to pick up their pens and think with them. "Sarah, pick up your pen and write, 'Rob is going to. . . .' Keep your pen moving. Don't stop."

Invite several children to read their predictions into the circle. You needn't discuss each one. Simply putting a few into the air accomplishes a lot.

"I'll be a conductor and point my baton to a few of you. If I point to you, instead of playing your instrument, share out what you wrote, okay?" I said. I began swinging my arms, as if to the whole symphony, then gestured toward Jack, who read his Post-it. [Fig. V-1]

Lily was next. I tipped my baton to her, then to Jasmine [Figs. V-2 and V-3].

Notice that when you want children to do some intellectual work, instead of just assigning that work, it helps to demonstrate the way that your reading of the text gets you started thinking in this way. By thinking aloud, doing the thinking you hope kids will do, you get them started, and then you simply pull back yourself, leaving them to do the work on their own.

Many of your children will probably write something such as, "Rob will stick his tongue out at her," which is the sort of action the reader himself or herself might have done at this point. You may want to coach kids, "What do you know about Rob that you can draw upon here? Sure he could have stuck his tongue back at her, but is that how Rob acts when people mistreat him? Think back to the scene in the bus."

In this lesson I'm using a teaching method I've introduced earlier in the year. I act like a conductor, using my baton to gesture for one reader and then another to read into the circle. I love watching conductors at the symphony, gesturing to the bassoon, the kettle drums, and I keep that image in mind. You can use a method such as this any time, across your curriculum. If your kids watch a movie on colonial America and you want to recreate what they learned, you can say, "What struck you as important from this film? I'll be the conductor and you be the symphony. Watch my baton. Recall the early bits first, and then think about the events that occurred later. Ready?"

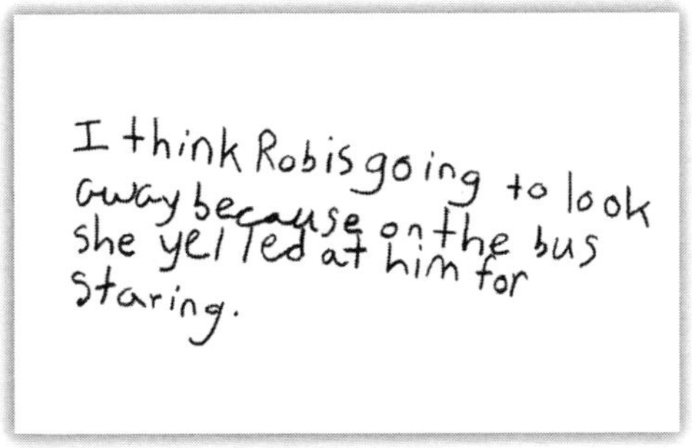

Figure V-1
Jack has wisely drawn on information from earlier in the text in order to predict what will happen next.

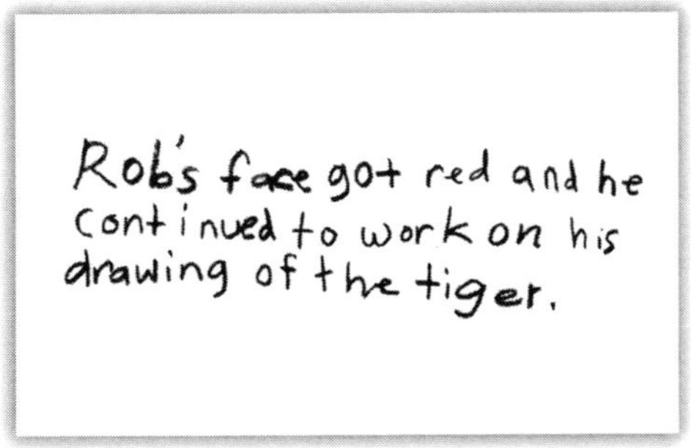

Figure V-2
Note the thin line between envisionment and prediction for Lily.

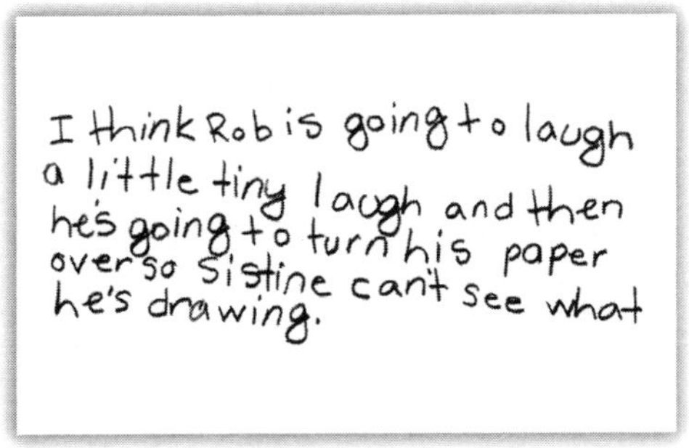

Figure V-3
Jasmine is emphathizing, walking in the shoes of her character, and uses this to engine her predictions.

Continue reading as a way to show children that readers carry predictions with us, looking for confirmation while also expecting to be surprised.

"Let's read on to see what *actually* happens. Sometimes an author will write the next part exactly as we expect, and sometimes authors throw a curve ball. I think you'll see that Kate DiCamillo goes where we expected her to go, and she also throws in a new spin. Let me back up a bit so we can get the picture back in our minds."

> "Well," said Mrs. Soames, "thank you very much for introducing yourself, Sistine Bailey. You may take your seat before you put your foot in your mouth any farther."
>
> The whole class laughed at that. Rob looked up just as Sistine sat down. She glared at him. Then she stuck her tongue out at him. Him! (I paused.) He shook his head and went back to his drawing.
>
> He sketched out the tiger. ("Thumbs up if you predicted he'd do something like that. Okay, here comes the new spin.")
>
> He sketched out the tiger, but what he wanted to do was whittle it in wood. (I inserted, "Oh!") His mother had shown him how to whittle, how to take a piece of wood and make it come alive. She taught him when she was sick. He sat on the edge of the bed and watched her tiny white hands closely.
>
> "Don't jiggle that bed," his father said. "Your mama's in a lot of pain."
>
> "He ain't hurting me, Robert," his mother said.
>
> "Don't get all tired out with that wood," his father said.
>
> "It's all right," his mother said. "I'm teaching Rob some things I know."
>
> But she said she didn't have to teach him much. His mother told him he already knew what to do. His hands knew; that's what she said.

Notice that I do not stop to discuss everything the kids suggested. It takes some discipline to leave hypotheses hanging there in the air that are wrong, but remember that that's exactly what happens during reading. A person reads, anticipates, leaves that hypothesis hanging in the air, and then reads on. The reading process does not include constant feedback from a teacher who tells you which of your ideas is right, and which, wrong.

Remember, when you say something like "The author might throw in a new spin," use your hands to help children know what you mean.

Teachers, notice that in The Tiger Rising, *readers continue to learn the backstory throughout most of the book. Less complex books are apt to include a big glob of backstory, all in one section of the text. Novels that are as complex as this one—generally those in the R-T or higher bands of text difficulty—often follow the pattern you are seeing in* The Tiger Rising. *You can use this text as a touchstone in conferences and small groups with readers who are working with texts that pose similar challenges.*

Debrief, reminding children that readers predict and that readers expect to be surprised.

> "I love predicting because when I predict, I can then be surprised. And I bet all of us were surprised that Rob went back to a memory of his mother teaching him to whittle. The story has taken a new turn, hasn't it? Now I have all these *new* predictions, don't you?"

Link

Impress upon readers the importance not only of walking in the characters' shoes but also of predicting what the characters will do next.

> "Readers, today and every day when we read, we want to be the kind of readers who read as if we are in the skin, the voice, the soul of another. When we read this way, it's just natural that we'll race ahead of the story, predicting and worrying about what will happen next."

> "I know you are dying to get started, so please be quick with your logs. *[Figs. V-4 and V-5]* Recording the time and page number should only take half a minute. While you sit here on the rug, take a minute to get yourselves ready for reading. Look back over what you've just read, giving *yourself* a 'previously in' summary to get yourself started. Then, while you sit here, begin reading. When I sense that you are beginning to get lost in your story, I'll send you back to your seat. You'll be aiming to read in great gulps, reading on and on and on.

Notice the aura in your minilesson. Are you sitting on a chair, leaning toward your children? Are they gathered as close as possible? Do you look directly into their eyes, and teach as if you are sharing stories, gossip, tips, secrets to success? You could, of course, vary that a bit by sometimes bursting from your seat to enact something, to make a point. But that sort of aura is absolutely different from the teacher who begins a minilesson by standing near the overhead projector or the white board, writing in a belabored fashion on the overhead or the board, expecting children to copy what the teacher has written. These teachers tend to use traditional teaching methods in an effort to make the minilesson stick. They write on the board, they pepper kids with questions, they elicit from kids rather than talking to them. My sense is that their efforts to make their teachings stick backfire. I recommend that you think of a minilesson as reading around the campfire, or as a huddle among teammates. Make your teaching intimate, intense, immediate, and urgent.

Notice that good teaching cumulates. So very often, just before you send kids off to work, you'll want to recollect earlier teaching points that have special relevance to today's work. Keep alive the work you taught yesterday, last week, and last month.

"I am pretty sure there will be places in the story where you find yourself predicting, imagining what might happen next. You'll no doubt envision as you read—that's great. But today make a special point to also predict. Put a Post-it note into the places where the text seems to make you predict (and there will be some) and jot your predictions so that later we can talk about them." I then moved among the readers, noting their jottings. [Figs. V-6 and V-7]

Figure V-4
Celebrate that this reader not only asks questions but also speculates responses to these questions.

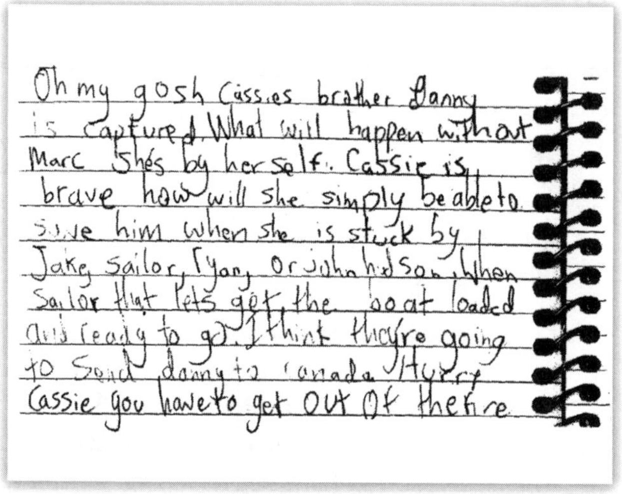

Figure V-6
Max's prediction is based on textual evidence but doesn't reflect a strong ability to determine importance.

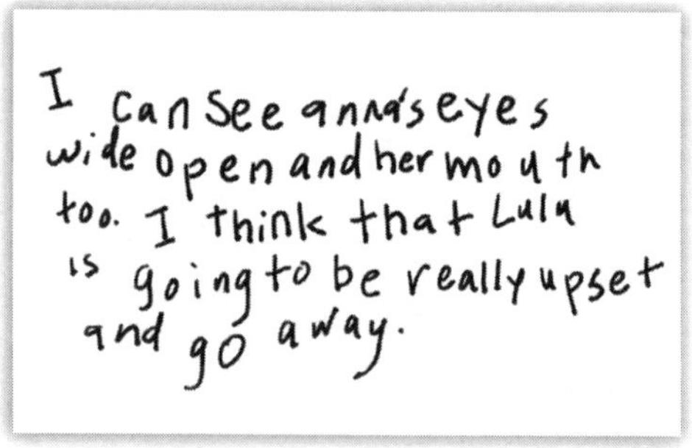

Figure V-7
You might encourage this reader to develop her envisionment in order to make a richer prediction.

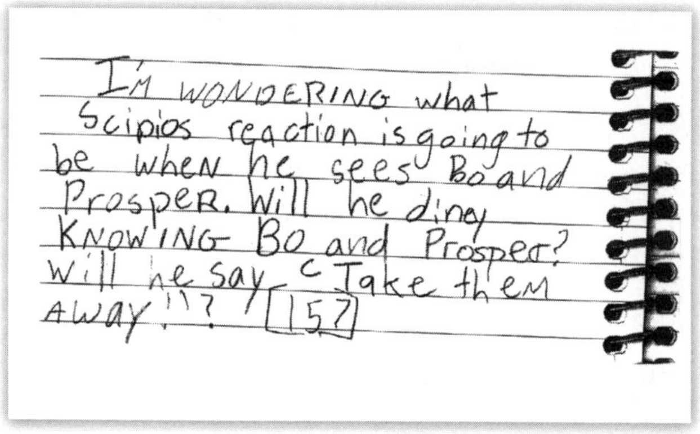

Figure V-5
You may notice that the decision to jot responses in reading notebooks, not on Post-its, is accompanied by a big step forward in thoughtfulness.

CONFERRING AND SMALL-GROUP WORK

Anticipating the Conferring and Small-Group Work You'll Do to Extend Children's Predictions

Because today's session channeled students to spotlight the prediction work that they do as they read, you'll want to approach the session having prepared yourself to assess what your students can do as predictors and to tailor your teaching to take into account your assessments. You'll probably find that the work you do to support prediction has an especially large payoff because prediction is one of those things that any engaged reader does almost naturally. There will be other reading skills that that require a reader to put on the brakes while reading and to momentarily disengage from the story, stepping back from the text to gain perspective on the entire story. But prediction is something readers can do as we zoom through the pages of any gripping story.

Assess Your Readers' Abilities with the Main Skill You Aim to Teach—Prediction—and Then Plan a Trajectory of Skill Development

To prepare for teaching prediction, you and your colleagues will probably want to think about a trajectory of prediction development, just as you have already thought about a trajectory of envisionment work. In Session I, I described the way Kathleen, a think tank of teachers, and I sorted children's written envisionments, done in re-

sponse to Eve Bunting's *One Green Apple*. When we had read that book aloud, we paused in carefully selected places to prompt students to jot what they were thinking; one of those prompts supported prediction ("What will happen next?"). Just as Kathleen, the teachers, and I sorted the children's envisionments into a continuum representing ascending skill level, so, too, we did this with prediction. Then, working with colleagues from the Teachers College Reading and Writing Project as a whole, we used this analysis of student work to help us become more concrete and specific about what constitutes a skilled prediction.

You'll want to engage in similar work and to try, as we did, to list differences between less and more proficient predictors and to see children who are clustered at different points along your trajectory.

Earlier you will have made a similar list containing descriptions of strong envisionment. Now this list pertaining to prediction, like that one, can inform your record-keeping notes, becoming a portable coach for the teaching you do on the run as you work with individuals and small groups. (See *A Guide to the Reading Workshop* for more detailed information.)

MID-WORKSHOP TEACHING POINT

Readers Lift the Level of Our Predictions By Drawing on a Knowledge of Characters and Ourselves

In a voiceover, as children continued to read, I said, "I'm going to ask you to make a prediction very soon. Keep reading, but as you read, push yourself to find a place in which you can predict. Then, jot a prediction on a Post-it note." After a few minutes, I said, "If you haven't had a chance yet to predict what might happen next, do so now, jotting your thoughts on your Post-it notes." I gave the children who hadn't already done this a minute to do so, while the others continued reading. As they worked, I walked the room, gleaning a sense for the sorts of predictions many of them were making.

Then, I said, "Readers, eyes up here." I waited. "As I look around the room, most of you have been able to think ahead in the story, to suggest what *might* happen. That is totally great. Now that you're all the kind of readers who predict, can I help you lift the level of your predictions? So, to start with, reread your predictions, and think, 'How can I make this prediction even better? What do I know about wise predictions?' I looked over at the chart, 'Strategies Readers Use When We Predict,' on the easel, touching it with my hand.

continued on next page

Once you have assessed your readers along a continuum of proficiency with the skill of prediction, you'll want to think about the sorts of teaching you need to do to support children at the earlier stages, the middle stages, and the advanced stages in their prediction work. As you read the conferring and small-group work section in this session and the sessions that follow, you may want to think about how you can capture teaching ideas that seem especially applicable to your novice, intermediate, and advanced predictors in your record-keeping system so that as you circulate among your readers and conduct small groups to support them, you'll have on hand some little reminders of the sorts of things you will be apt to teach to each cluster of your readers.

Keep in mind that your conferring and small-group work must always respond to the full range of work that readers are doing. You'll still be looking at readers' logs and thinking about the amount of time students are devoting to reading, you'll still be working with some of them to increase their fluency, and you'll still be helping some of them be more resourceful word solvers. That is, just because this section of the unit focuses on prediction, this does not mean that your teaching will focus exclusively on prediction. In fact, as you support your children's predictions, you'll definitely find yourself also supporting their envisionments because actually these two reading skills (and others as well) cluster together so they are almost inseparable from each other. When a reader

---

MID-WORKSHOP TEACHING POINT

continued from previous page

Strategies Readers Use When We Predict

- Make a movie in our mind of what has yet to happen and tell it bit by bit.
- Think about what has already happened in the book and use our understanding of the characters to imagine the upcoming text.
- Draw on our personal knowledge of similar experiences to anticipate the upcoming text.

I can predict by...
- making a movie in our mind and telling it bit by bit
- imagining what the character will do next AND how the character will do this
- drawing upon what already happened and on important details from earlier in the story
- bringing in our personal knowledge

continued on next page

---

engages in nose-in-the-book reading, creating a mental movie as he or she reads, it is the most natural thing in the world for that reader to continue envisioning those passages that he or she has not yet encountered, and when doing this, that reader will be predicting. It's also natural for these readers to empathize and to draw on personal responses as they read. Then, too, as readers get into this sort of highly engaged reading, their fluency will skyrocket.

Even If You Begin with a Clear Sense of What Constitutes Strong Predictions, Children Will Surprise You: Be Ready to Jettison Your Best-Laid Plans

Although Kathleen and I and the teachers who'd just joined us in assessing children's work with *One Green Apple* had spent lots of time thinking through the instruction we planned to provide in our conferences, when we actually watched what children were doing in the name of prediction, we found that none of our wonderful plans felt immediately relevant. First, and most obviously, we noticed that a great many children interpreted the invitation to predict simply as a call to anticipate how their books might end, and usually they could have imagined the endings that they conjured up for their books simply from looking at their covers. The prompt we'd inserted into *One Green Apple* had directed children to tell us what would happen *next,* so it had not elicited this sort of prediction. We were surprised by the number of children who would pause in the midst of reading the second or third chapter in their independent reading books and then, knowing we wanted them to predict, would write something to the effect of "I think it will be okay in the end." We'd never imagined that our prediction conferences would need to help children know that prediction is not just about forecasting a happy ending. For us, this was an important heads-up. Planning is powerful because it means we are not empty-handed as we teach, but powerful conferring requires that we listen, and this means that we need to be ready to put aside our plans and let children take us to places we'd never imagined going.

Expect that Teaching Predictions Will Mean Teaching Inference

Kobe, who had finished his run of Gary Paulsen books and begun a *Hardy Boys* mystery, wrote on a Post-it note, "He'll get the girl in the end." Of course, I celebrated that Kobe had stopped to make a prediction, but meanwhile I wondered how I could explain that a reader's predictions should be informed by the details of what he or she has read. I tried making this point in conjuction with the tip that it generally helps to predict not only *what* will happen but also *how* it will happen. I nudged, "For example, *how will they* get the girl?"

Kobe looked at me like I had lost my mind and seemed somewhat aggravated. "I didn't get to that part yet," he protested.

"But how do you think they *might* save the girl?" I pressed.

"I have no clue," Kobe said. "I'm only on page 45. That's in the next chapters."

> ### MID-WORKSHOP TEACHING POINT
>
> *continued from previous page*
>
> I gave children time to work. Then, in a voiceover, I added, "It helps to tell what will happen next, and then next, and then next in a step-by-step way, like a movie." I gave the children time to put this suggestion into action. Then I said, "Imagine not just what your character will do but *how* he or she will do it." Again I gave them a minute to let this inform their work. As children worked, I said, "I notice some of you are looking back in your book, and that's usually wise because predictions need to be grounded in what already happened. Bring in details that you know from earlier in the story about the character."
>
> A few moments later, I said, "Let's share our predictions. Partner 2, show Partner 1 your first prediction, and *then* show your partner how you made this prediction a whole lot better. Explain what you've done to improve your predictions."
>
> After children shared their predictions with each other, I said, "Continue reading, and this time really pay attention to those places in the book that give you that feeling in the pit of your stomach, like those 'Duh, duh, duh, duh' moments in movies when you know big stuff is about to happen. When you get to one of those moments, jot down another prediction, using these helpful tips from the chart 'Strategies Readers Use When We Predict,' so that your prediction is the smartest it can be. Once you've made a great prediction, of course you'll read on, looking to see ways the story matches your expectations or catches you off guard."

I felt as if every circuit in my mind was blazing as Kobe talked. As I saw his struggles to predict, I realized that for many kids, not just for Kobe, it takes a leap for them to realize that when reading, the reader literally constructs meaning, authoring text that has not yet been written, supplying words and material that the author has not provided. This work of co-constructing the text is an essential part of any skilled reader's repertoire.

Kobe and other children like him helped me realize that when we ask children to predict (and indeed, to do lots of thinking that falls under the heading of higher-level comprehension), what we are really asking them to do is to author—to generate—their reading. Whether children are predicting or they are inferring character traits or they are devising interpretive theories, at a very basic level, they must replace the text's words with their own words. When a child reads that a character slammed the door behind him and hollered a string of curses and is then asked, "What sort of a person is this guy?" that child needs to supply words that are not explicitly given in the text to produce the abstract descriptor. "He's got a temper," or "He's angry." If the character goes out to milk the cows and the grass is still wet with dew, the reader infers and, by doing so, essentially writes into the text, "It is still early in the morning." Readers regularly put words into the author's mouth; readers' words and ideas enrich the text.

Strong Predictors Are Apt to:

- Draw upon not only the immediate text but also relevant details from the earlier text to speculate about the upcoming storyline.

- Be able to provide supportive evidence that suggests the reader is drawing not only on the immediate local area in which he or she has been reading, but also on a broader swatch of the text.

- Distinguish what is and is not important within the story and use this to think ahead. The reader's projected story is influenced by the storyline and by the reader's knowledge of how stories are apt to go. When readers read more demanding texts, the sub-plot and developments in the setting also influence predictions.

- Construct a prediction that reflects not only a literal but also an inferential level of comprehension. When drawing upon what the reader has already read, the reader relies upon details not concretely specified in the text.

- Construct a prediction that reflects a knowledge of how the stories that this reader tends to read are apt to be structured. If the reader of level K–Q books predicts at the point when a character has just encountered trouble, the reader expects the trouble to intensify and for it to be resolved toward the end. Readers of more difficult texts keep several plot lines in mind and anticipate they will come together at a later part. Predictions are shaped by a reader's sense of how stories go.

Prediction is a type of inference. For some readers—readers like Kobe—part of the challenge is learning that reading involves bringing ones own words, one's own meaning, to the text.

When a child's predictions are ones that anyone could have guessed after just glancing at the title and the back blurb of the book, then that child needs help drawing on the details of what the child knows from having read the book as well as on the details of what the child knows from his or her similar experiences.

When I confer with children like Kobe who have a hard time authoring predictions, I tend to say things such as:

"You know these characters. You've been in their shoes. What specifically do you think they might do next? Then what could happen after that?"

"I know you don't *know*. But readers think about how a story *might* go, like I was thinking about how that television show might go. Try saying, 'It *could* be that. . . .'"

"Can you tell me how it might go, telling it bit by bit, stretching the story out? Don't just say, 'He'll win.' What exactly might he do next? Then next? Imagine how it might unroll."

"I'm noticing that you are predicting what will happen at the very end. Can you try predicting what might happen in the next chapter? Predict not just what will happen but how it will happen."

When You Are Not Immediately Clear How to Help a Child, Draw on Your Sources of Information: The Student Can Teach You If You Listen

Pulling my chair over to Gabe's desk, I gently tapped him on the shoulder. He was completely consumed in his book (*The Chalk Box Kid*), hunched over it as usual, and I didn't want to startle him. I took a moment to notice how wonderful it was to see Gabe so obviously engaged with his book. He even had a couple of Post-its visible! I began our conference by saying, "Gabe, what have you been doing as a reader, while you read?" Gabe told me he'd been predicting. I asked if he could show me instances in which he'd done this, so he turned to a Post-it note that read, "I predict that Vince is going to make fun of Gregory for his garden."

I felt momentarily at a loss as to how to proceed because I didn't know his book, and the prediction sounded generally fine to me. This is probably a feeling many of you have experienced.

I knew it would probably help to understand what Gabe had drawn on to make that prediction, so I asked, "What information led you to make this prediction?" and after glancing at the first page added, "I bet you collected bits of information about Vince, Gregory, and his garden. Can you show me those clues?"

While Gabe flipped to an earlier Post-it note, I glanced at my written records to remind myself of the last conference I'd had with him. I saw that a few days ago, I'd nudged him to draw on his own life experiences to imagine details in a story that the author did not explicitly state. That time, he'd recalled his excitement over an approaching baseball game and used that feeling to infer how his character probably felt. By the time I had reviewed notes on that conference, Gabe was ready to show me the evidence he'd drawn on to help him generate his prediction. Pointing to a Post-it he'd stuck onto an earlier page of *The Chalk Box Kid*, he said, "Well, right here I wrote that Vince is going to bully Gregory."

That was interesting to me. One Post-it note read, "Vince is going to bully Gregory." The one I'd seen earlier read, "Vince is going to make fun of Gregory in the garden." Those two Post-it notes seemed almost identical. I wondered, even, if these were actually *predictions* so much as reflections of Gabe's theories about the characters. One character was the bully, and the other, the victim. I did not know the book well enough to be sure whether this was an inference or whether this had been flat out stated in the book, but because I know that books at this level of text difficulty often come right out and name a character's traits, I somewhat suspected the latter.

I asked Gabe why Vince didn't like Gregory and learned this was because Vince thought Gregory had been bragging that his old school was bigger than his new school. "Can you show me places in the book that support this?" I asked (relying once again on a prompt that never fails to yield), and Gabe started looking back through the book. As he searched for and produced evidence of his theories in the book that had become ever more dog-eared and grubby as he read it, I noticed that while it took him a bit longer than others, he was very able to do this work. Clearly, he had been taking in and holding onto what he read, carrying descriptors of the main character from one place in the text to another and attaching these descriptors to times when the character's actions matched the trait.

By this time, I needed to contribute something to Gabe's learning life. Time was running out. I still had no idea how to extend his prediction work. I didn't entirely grasp what his understanding of prediction really entailed.

I cast my mind over alternatives. I could teach him to carry his predictions with him as he read on, noticing whether the upcoming text confirmed or challenged his predictions. I suspected he already did a bit of that work, but it was a harmless teaching point. I prefer, though, to tailor the teaching that I do in conferences to the specifics of that particular reader, so I regard reaching for a generic one-size-fits-all teaching point as a bit of a cop-out.

I decided, therefore, to talk to Gabe about the fact that his predictions sounded more like statements about the people in his books rather than real predictions about what might happen next. I hoped that within my conference, I'd find a way to recall the earlier work we'd done in which I'd encouraged him to draw on personal experiences to help him infer what a character might be feeling. Perhaps I could show him that his personal responses could also help him develop his predictions, but I wasn't sure.

Once I had at least some vague sense of direction for the teaching portion of the conference, I was ready to go. But again, I reined myself in. I couldn't load Gabe up with instruction about what to do next if I did not first find a way to talk with power about what he had already done. Often, when I find a way to name a reader's strengths, I can segue from that discussion of strengths into a discussion of next steps.

In general, I find it is helpful if I tell children what I notice them doing, so I decided I'd tell Gabe that I noticed he had been growing ideas about people, perhaps more than predicting, as he seemed to think he was doing. I knew I could tell him that his focus on people was a strength that could be built upon, and then I could help him use his skill at empathizing with others to bolster his reading work.

So with only a vague sense of where I was going, I plunged forward. "Gabe, I am noticing that both these two Post-its—'Vince is going to bully Gregory' and 'Vince is going to make fun of Gregory'—illustrate that you are the kind of reader who really pays attention to people and to relationships between people. You have a theory that Vince is a bully, and because of your theory of Vince (and of Gregory), you predict that Vince will bully and make fun of Gregory." Then I said to him, "Reading researchers say that readers who pay attention to people *in books* are often people who pay attention to people *in life*, too. Your attentiveness to people is a real gift of yours, and it is something you should cherish."

He smiled up at me, blushing a little, but said, "Thanks!"

stretching out the word as he decided what would follow. "Vince will probably bully Gregory in the garden because that's where I think all the kids will go, and he will probably say something like, 'You think this school's not good enough for you!?'"

"Nice," I added, and then gestured for him to say more.

"So, I predict that Vince will bully Gregory in the garden and pick on him about his old school," he summed up. I noticed again how much more confident he'd become in articulating his thoughts—particularly in small groups and conferences, but I knew that his new confidence would enter more and more into whole-class discussions as well.

"Great reading work!" I congratulated. "Boy, I'm really noticing how confident you're getting about saying your ideas! I'm so glad, because your idea about what might happen next comes from all that you know about what exactly has *already* happened, which is really wise. You aren't just imagining things out of thin air. You are using the real facts of why Vince has been bullying Gregory." Getting back to my teaching point specifically, I continued, "Do you see how you brought what you already know about these characters to the text and grew ideas about things that have not even happened yet? You can do that all the time when you're making predictions." Then I added, "The other thing you can do is to read on, and see if your predictions come true. Often as we read on, we go, 'Whoops' and we change our predictions."

When Teaching Strong Readers, It Is Not Difficult to Give Them Further Horizons

I pulled my chair alongside Sam, wondering as I did so whether I would have a lot to teach him. Sam is a strong reader, and my expectation was that prediction is not the most demanding skill on earth. I wondered if I'd be better off focusing my prediction instruction on children who were less proficient. I nevertheless plunged into the conference.

Journalists have a saying that the more you know, the more you can learn. Often when interviewing people, if I notice something that the person is doing and name what I have noticed, this allows my conference to get off to a running start. What I have already seen provides me with a platform from which to learn more. So with Sam, I started right off by admiring the huge number of prediction Post-its that filled the pages of

When You Are Grasping for Ways to Help a Child, It Usually Helps to Draw on Your Knowledge of What Proficient Readers Do With the Skill

"I want to give you one tip for a way to strengthen your predictions. When I have studied really amazing predictors, I have noticed that they, like you, rely on a deep understanding of characters to think about what the people in a story are apt to do next. But they also rely on a sense of how stories usually go. So, for example, they know that in stories, what a person wants will often lead that person into difficulties, into trouble, and the trouble will get worse and worse, and then something will happen to resolve it.

"Can you, right now, think about your story and think not only about the characters but also about how stories usually go? So, you've said that Vince will bully Gregory. Think whether that trouble—the bullying—will get worse and worse. Think how it might get resolved, or what might happen, and see if you can add to your prediction. Your new prediction will almost sound like you are retelling the book, but you'll be retelling the part that has not even happened yet. You'll make that part up."

"So start, 'Vince will make fun of Gregory.' How might that happen? Then what?"

Gabe sat for a moment, turning his gaze from the pages to the Post-it notes to the air, looking perplexed, yet pensive. "Well," he began, his book and noticing that his volume of reading had been impressive. "I wonder if those two go together," I said. "I bet that predicting so much keeps you reading on the edge of your seat. It keeps you turning the pages to find out what will happen, and that may be partly why you have been reading so much!" Notice that I could have stored up this observation and idea and planned to build my whole conference to culminate in this observation, but instead I followed Annie Dillard's advice when she suggests we don't store up our best thought for later but instead write it, say it, spend it, trusting more will come.

Sam agreed that he had definitely been predicting a ton and that in fact he had far more Post-its than usual. As I listened to him and scanned his Post-its, I began to crystallize a plan for the conference. It seemed to me that Sam may have been writing almost *too many* Post-its, each capturing a fairly low-level thought. Perhaps I could help him to write less often but more selectively, and to use writing about reading to take particular bits of his thinking farther.

"Sam," I said. "Now that you are predicting a ton as you read and reading on the edge of your seat, you may find that you do not need to write all those predictions down. They may just come into your mind and get you onto the edge of your seat, and that means they are working their magic. You may decide to only write the predictions that you decide are worth pondering a bit more deeply." We talked about that idea, and he agreed.

"When you want your predictions to be a bit deeper, one way to do this is to aim to make them more specific. So when you think about what your character might do next, you can push yourself to venture a guess about some of the specifics of what he or she will do next." Then I explained, "The way to imagine what has yet to happen with some specificity is to think back on the earlier story and to ask, 'What have I read *earlier* that might affect what happens *next*?' For example, you wrote on this Post-it, 'I don't think he is going to do good.' You could be thinking, 'Hmm, how can I be more specific?' And to do more specific thinking, you'd probably need to look back on what you already know about the character."

Sam picked up his book and flipped through it and said, "Danny hardly plays." I made a "Go on, continue" gesture, and Sam added, "'Cause he's small and strikes out a lot and usually sits on the bench during games, so he'll mess up now." I nodded and named what Sam had just done so that he could do it again and again. "Wow, Sam, in just a minute of thinking, you have already thought back to information you learned earlier in the story about the character and used that information to make your prediction much more specific. And you did this in no time. Think if you really gave it a bit of time! So always remember that when you are going to make a prediction about what will happen in a story, you need to be specific. To do this, notice details. Reach back into earlier parts. (I threw my arm over my shoulder as I'd done earlier, when teaching readers synthesis.) You'll especially want to draw on what you know about your characters and the sorts of people they are. Why don't you revise that Post-it right now by adding all that you told me, and the next time you go to make a prediction, decide if that particular prediction is worth mulling over and only record it if it is. When you do record it, though, look at this revised Post-it and be mentored by your good work. Thanks, Sam, for talking to me."

EACHING SHARE

Readers Decide How to Lift the Level of Our Reading and Recruit Partners to Support Us

Ask readers to choose a repertoire of ways to share reading with their partners, reminding them of strategies they know.

"Readers I want you to get ready to meet with your partner, but first let's look back at our chart we've made containing ways to share our books. I want you to think, 'What sort of sharing would make sense for my partner and me to do?' If your partner knows your book, you won't do a 'previously in,' for example, but if the book is new to your partner, you might. If you have been working on reading smoothly and bringing out the voices of your characters, you might decide to find juicy parts and read them to each other. Glance over our chart if you need to refresh your memory of options. You'll see I have added one new bullet to it, based on today's work.

"Turn and make a plan with your partner about how you'll spend the next five minutes together. Then get started." The room erupted into talk as partnerships each chose a way to share reading.

Coach children to lift the level of their work.

I voiced over the buzzing of the room. "Can I have your eyes and your attention for just one quick moment?" Once I had the class's attention, I said, "Listening partners, you have a special job. You need to listen in a way that encourages your partner to say more. I'll be Emma's partner. Tell me how I'm doing."

Emma started talking, and I looked away in an overly dramatic fashion, yawned, rolled my eyes—all this taking place in an instant. The kids, of course, were full of critiques that I didn't hear in any detail.

"Okay, okay, I'll rewind that and try again. If I do stuff you think you could do as well, listening partners, jot what you see on a Post-it note so you can keep it close as a prompt to yourself." This time, when Emma started to talk, I leaned toward her, eyes glued on her, nodding encouragingly, saying, "Uh huh." Then I said, "So you think . . ." and repeated what she'd said and then asked an extending question. Again, I did this quickly.

COACHING TIPS

You'll notice that with this share I'm again asking children to reflect on themselves as readers, putting themselves in charge of their own reading life. Peter Drucker, author of The Effective Executive, *wrote, "Follow effective action with quiet reflection. From the quiet reflection will come even more effective action." Shares are a crucial time to ask children to reflect on themselves as readers.*

I pulled out of the role play and looked right at the class. "You can encourage your partner to talk by using gestures that say, 'Come on,' by nodding, by repeating back what your partner has said, by asking extending questions. Today I'm especially going to notice the way you all really truly talk and really truly listen. Continue talking."

After a bit, I said, "Readers, give yourselves a pat on the back. Tonight, as you read, put a Post-it note on a scene that you feel is an important one, a scene where tons of stuff is going on. We will be using that in our minilesson tomorrow, so put a star on that Post-it note so you can find it easily."

Ways You and Another Reader Can Talk About Your Books

- Share passages that especially drew you in—parts that made you feel a strong emotion or exciting parts that had you on the edge of your seat.

- Share parts in which you really pictured what is happening, perhaps parts where you felt like you were in a 3-D movie—one with surround sound.

- Show each other parts of your books where the mental movie you made as you read got blurry, places where you thought, "Huh?" and then talk about those parts, discussing what's going on in them.

- Figure out a tricky word by discussing what the word might mean and by using words you **can** read to figure out how to say this unfamiliar word.

- Tell the big things that happened to the main character so far, either by reaching back and starting at the beginning, perhaps saying "previously in . . . ," or by starting with now and tucking in past events.

- Share a passage you flagged because it is especially well written, intense, funny, and so on. Then perform the passage, talking about how best to interpret it.

- Act out a scene that feels important (preferably one with a lot of dialogue) and then talk about the new ideas you came up with about the characters or the story as a result.

- Share your predictions. Help your partner to predict what will happen in the next chapter, not just in the whole book, and to draw on specifics he or she knows from having read the book. Predict not just what will happen but how it will happen.

Detailing Predictions to Bring Out Personalities

IN THIS SESSION,

you will teach students that readers can deepen our predictions by making movies in our minds of how our stories might unfold.

Earlier in this book, you may have been antsy, wondering, "When do we get to the *skills*?" I hope by now you've begun to relax. You *have been* teaching skills—crucial reading skills such as retelling (which includes determining importance and synthesis) and envisioning (some people call it visualization) and, more recently, prediction. And you've been teaching skills not only by demonstration and explicit instruction, but also by trying to grasp what children tend to do in the name of these skills, and then providing the coaching and the scaffolded practice necessary to help them progress along a trajectory of skill development. Books on reading development don't always spell out the difference between novice and skilled

predictions, novice and skilled syntheses, and so forth. But they should.

You will have already read aloud a book such as *One Green Apple*, asking children to predict at a selected spot in that text, and then you will have studied those predictions. That's one effort to conduct informal research—but it is just a start. To design a second informal assessment tool, spy on your own reading as you read the upcoming chapter of *The Tiger Rising*, deliberately trying to make some state-of-the-art predictions. Then, gather your class and read the text aloud to them. At places where you found that you, as one skilled reader, were apt to predict, pause and say to your children, "What do you think will happen next? Jot a pre-

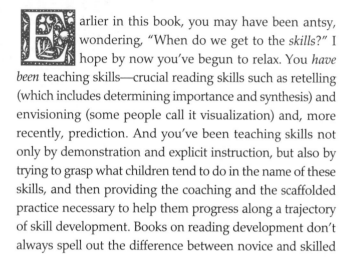

GETTING READY

- Prior to this minilesson, be sure to have finished reading in *The Tiger Rising* through Chapter 7.

- During the teaching and active involvement portion of this minilesson, you'll read aloud from the beginning of Chapter 8 of *The Tiger Rising*.

- If you're reading aloud a book other than *The Tiger Rising* for this unit, then prepare for today's session by reading up to a part that begs the reader to predict what the main character will do next.

- Place the chart "Strategies Readers Use When We Predict" in a prominent place in your meeting area so that you can reference it during the minilesson and the teaching share.

- By Session VIII, plan to have read through Chapter 12 of *The Tiger Rising*.

- You'll want to schedule extra read-aloud times outside the reading workshop so that by Session VIII you will have read through Chapter 12 of *The Tiger Rising*.

diction on your Post-it." Then gather your children's predictions and lay them out like a keyboard in front of you so you can again look between the least and most developed predictions. What do you notice? Study also the cluster of predictions you'll have gathered from one child and another. What do you notice?

The time that my colleagues and I spent trying to specify what skilled predictors do has made a world of difference

> *Being explicit about what it means to predict will remove the veil, making our hopes more transparent.*

for us. We are able to say to children, "I'm noticing that when you predict what will happen next, you often articulate *what* you think will happen, which is great, but you rarely suggest *how* it will happen. You might want to try to fill in some more details about *how* those things will play out." We can even say, "Can I show you how another reader did what I'm suggesting to you now?" And then we can show the child a few "mentor predictions." We can notice that some readers wisely let their attention to the setting inform their predicting, and others seem to attend to plot only, drawing simply on the prior sequence of events and on their knowledge of characters to anticipate the upcoming text. Being explicit about what it means to predict will remove the veil, making our hopes more transparent.

This minilesson gives you a peek at what your teaching can be like when you unveil some of the secrets to success. But a word of caution: Specifying what constitutes a skilled prediction is no easy task. For example, my colleagues and I wrestled over whether or not it's helpful to channel youngsters to provide textual support for a prediction. If a child has predicted, "He'll win the prize," do we want to encourage the child to add "because he kept practicing and practicing?" We ended up deciding that we'd usually prefer a reader to predict in a more detailed fashion or to specify more steps in the sequence, or predict not only what will happen but also why it will happen rather than digging back in the text to specify the textual basis for a prediction. That is, we'd usually prefer that the reader imagine the realm of possibilities for the future ("Perhaps the award will be A, perhaps it will be B") or specify next steps ("After he gets the award, maybe he'll react in such and such a way") or predict why ("Rob will let the tiger go . . . because he no longer needs it") rather than provide textual evidence. We made this decision because we realized that most of us draw on a whole world of factors when making a prediction, so citing one or two pieces of evidence doesn't do justice to the ways in which we tend to do this work, and most of us only produce the evidence when someone challenges our prediction.

That is, more advanced predictors seem to profit more from making predictions that construct yet-to-unfold developments in the plot, setting, and characters than from making predictions that cite evidence. Instead of including the word *because* in their predictions, we might urge these readers to instead say, "And then . . . " or "What's more. . . ." A prediction of this sort might sound like this: "I think that Rob will let the tiger go. The setting will still be a low-cost model, but the tiger—like sun in a cage—will now bring a feeling of sunshine to the place, making it less dreary. *And then* when Rob isn't holding the tiger, he'll feel weak for a bit, but Sistine will make him stronger. *What's more,* I think

Rob will get his dad to open up more. They both need to open their suitcases."

Children who are fairly advanced predictors will profit from hearing that readers imagine multiple possibilities, foreseeing various paths a character might travel or plots an author might script and foreseeing developments in the setting as well as in the plot. This sort of thinking allows for complexity and goes hand in hand with instruction children will receive later in this unit, instruction that aims to help readers develop theories about characters.

On the other hand, there *are* children who benefit from being taught to specify the grounds for a prediction. For example, children who tend to predict without regard for prior sections of the text may read in a way that does not involve taking into account and accumulating broad swatches of text. Their focus as they read may be only on the page at hand. These children will often feel as if events occur out of nowhere, without rhyme or reason. To them, *everything* that happens is a surprise, and if you ask such a child why something occurred, the child has no idea. These readers are apt to be working in texts that are within the level K–M band, or perhaps a bit beyond, and their texts tend to follow traditional story structure with a main character who encounters trouble, rises to meet the trouble, and resolves the trouble. These readers often need training in seeing the through lines that link earlier motivations and actions with later reactions and consequences. Asking these particular children to provide textual support for their predictions is a wise idea. More importantly, these children need to be encouraged to track their predictions, noting, "I was right" and "I was wrong" and speculating over the reasons.

These readers might be channeled to say (and jot) ideas such as, "I predict that Little Willy will win the race *because* he and Searchlight have been practicing so hard" or "I predict that Rob will try to befriend Sistine *because* when he thinks about her twirling, he smiles. And also *because* he carves her out of wood."

Over time, it'll be helpful to channel these readers to predict based not only on their knowledge of the prior plot but also on their knowledge of characters. That is, whereas a lower-level, or quick, on-the-run prediction, may be plot oriented and sound something like, "Because he worked for a month, he will win the prize" or "Because she took the keys, she will escape," a higher-level prediction will be more character based and may sound like, "Because he is so industrious, working his hardest for a month, he will win the prize." The prediction work you do with children is a natural segue into the character work that follows in Volume 2, *Building Theories, Gathering Evidence.*

MINILESSON

Detailing Predictions to Bring Out Personalities

CONNECTION

Remind readers that our strongest predictions are those that are grounded in our knowledge of the characters in our books.

"Yesterday, we discovered that once a reader begins to empathize really well with the main character, the reader can then make stronger predictions about what the main character will do next. We can *use* our understanding of the main characters in our books to anticipate how the story will unfold.

"We also learned that when we read, it helps to notice when tension mounts, when the accompanying music conveys that 'Duh, duh, duh, duh' feeling that tells us something big is about to happen. There are times when a story is written in such a way that it sets us up to predict the course of action our character is about to take. Yesterday we began taking cues from texts, and today we're going to take our prediction work a step further.

"Finally, we learned that predicting isn't something a person can do automatically. Predicting is a skill we develop and sharpen. And with any skill, we get better if a coach gives us tips. When I play tennis, a pro coaches me to be a better tennis player. As we play, he'll shout out, 'Follow through on your strokes. Don't punch at the ball.' Today I'll continue to be your predicting coach.

"But first, let's do a quick 'previously in . . .' to remind ourselves of the text we read aloud yesterday. Then we'll work on developing and growing our prediction muscles. Okay, previously in *The Tiger Rising*, Rob had to meet with Mr. Phelmer about his rash. The school was concerned that Rob's condition was contagious and asked him to stay home for a few days, and they sent a note to Rob's father conveying this message."

You'll see that this minilesson begins with a lot of review. You could decide to turn the job of reviewing over to the children, saying, "Often I take a few minutes to recall what I've already learned, don't you? Right now I want you and your partner to use our charts and your memory to list three things you've learned about prediction."

Many of the subordinate points that I tuck into this minilesson come from previous minilessons. Just as we want children to hold a whole text in their heads, not just the chapter they have just read, we also want them to hold all our past teaching in their heads. Tucking lessons from previous teaching into our new minilessons, as subordinate points, is one way to help them do that.

You might ask children to do a "previously in . . ." retelling on their fingers, or to a partner, before you step in to provide yours. Keeping children involved is always a priority—one that needs to be balanced by your attentiveness to the clock.

Name your teaching point. Specifically, tell children that good predictors often make movies in our minds of what has yet to occur, envisioning not only *what* will happen but also *how* it will happen.

"Today, I want to remind you that to predict well, it helps to make a movie in your mind *of what has yet to happen.* Those movies need to show not only *what* will happen next but also *how* it will happen. We can anticipate how things will happen by remembering what we already know of our characters."

Teaching and Active Involvement

Help children envision as you read aloud. Then channel them to jot a prediction of what will happen next.

"We are going to begin reading Chapter 8 of *The Tiger Rising* and, as we do, let's read in a wide-awake way, identifying with the characters so that we imagine not only *what* will happen next but also *how* it will unfold. Listen closely."

> His father read the note from the principal slowly, putting his big finger under the words as if they were bugs he was trying to keep still. When he was finally done, he laid the letter on the table and rubbed his eyes with his fingers and sighed. The rain beat a sad rhythm on the roof of the motel.

Turning back to the children I said, "Hmm, . . . I wonder how Rob's dad will respond to this note from the principal. What will he say? Do? Hmm, . . ."

Then I said, "What are *you* thinking? Stop and jot your prediction on the left side of your notebook (and I held my notebook up to point to that page)." I gave children a few seconds to get started. When I saw a few children who needed a bit of help, I got those kids started by saying, "I think Rob's Dad will. . . ."

When planning a minilesson, it helps to write your teaching point so as to work a bit on the wording. After making the teaching point as memorable as possible, you'll want to weigh the best method for teaching the content you've selected. I have sometimes taught teachers that one way to think about the different teaching methods a teacher can choose between is to consider all the ways you might possibly teach someone to put on their shoes. I point out the instructor could demonstrate, saying, "Watch me," and then proceeding to put on a shoe, step by step. Alternatively, a teacher could show an example, perhaps pointing to a series of photographs. But there is yet another way to teach people to do something, and that method is sometimes referred to as "guided practice" or "scaffolded practice." When we use this teaching method, the teacher does not do the skill first. Instead, the teacher sets the learner up to do the skill, leading the learner along step by step so that, with assistance, the learner is able to do what he or she could not have done on his or her own. Because this minilessons relies upon the teaching method of guided practice, the structure of the minilesson will be unusual. The teaching is woven into the active involvement.

Remember that your job is to hold your children's attention. One way do to this is to really be attentive, yourself, to the words as you say them. So when you say, "Let's read in a wide-awake way." You may want to go so far as to sit extra tall, to look extra wide awake.

When you are reading aloud, remember that for listeners to see what you are describing, you need to see it. So when you read a passage such as this, "His father read the note from the principal slowly, putting his big finger under the words as if they were bugs he was trying to keep still," read the words almost as if you're acting them out. Be Rob's father, taking in the contents of the letter in a slow, careful way. Make the action unfold for children. Use your voice to convey the mood of this scene. For example, I'd read this part slowly, somberly, showing how the dad, the rain, the whole scene is heavy.

Remind children to predict by imagining not only *what* but also *how* the character will act, and to do so by thinking, "What do I already know about the character that can help me predict?" Then demonstrate by starting to do this yourself, before passing the baton.

After giving children thirty seconds to do this, I voiced over their work, saying, "Notice, readers, whether you remembered to predict not only *what* a character will do, but also *how* the character will do that. How will Rob's father react? Do you think he will blow up? Yell? Or will he talk in a quiet way? You can revise your prediction if you want or try a new one."

Again I gave children half a minute to work before raising the stakes. "Readers, think about what you drew upon to make your prediction. How many of you thought, 'How would *I* react if I was the dad and I got a note telling me my son had to stay home from school?' (I made a thumbs up gesture and saw thumbs popping up and heads nodding in agreement.) 'That's smart, but it's even smarter if you also thought, 'What do I know about Rob's father that could help me figure out how *he* might respond?' How many of you thought about what you know of Rob's father and let *that* influence your prediction? If you haven't done that yet, do it now, revising your prediction or again, trying a whole new one."

Again I let children work for a minute before I stepped in to demonstrate the sort of thinking I hope the children had done. "Let me try that as well. Let's see. Hmm, . . . I know that Rob's dad doesn't dwell on emotion. After his wife's funeral, the dad said to Rob, 'There ain't no point in crying. Crying ain't going to bring her back.' He's not the sort to get emotional. But he does try hard to be a good parent, and so he probably won't just blow off school. Hmm, . . ."

Now that I'd given the children that sort of help, I again gave them a minute to work on their predictions. Some children just sat there, as if saying, "I'm done," so I whispered, "Make your prediction as wise as it can be. Let this prediction be your mentor for the work you'll do from now on as a reader."

Josh and Aly scrawled their predictions quickly. [Figs. VI-1 and VI-2]

When I teach minilessons, my goal is not simply to follow the architecture of good minilessons. I'm also hoping that my minilessons illustrate the qualities of good teaching. To me, this means that my minilessons need to be memorable. I use a variety of techniques to achieve this and in this case have chosen guided practice.

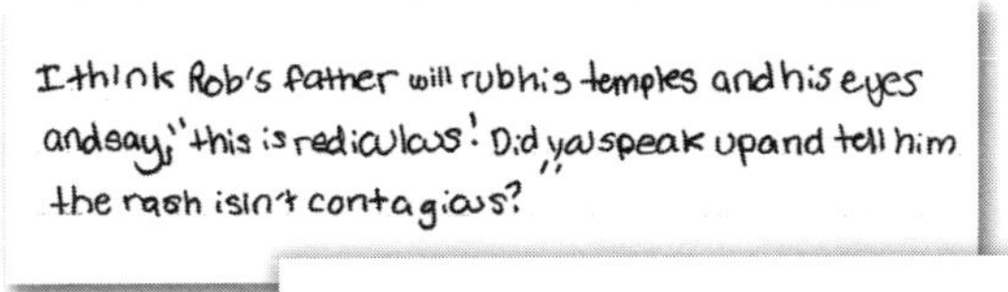

I think Rob's father will rub his temples and his eyes and say, "this is rediculous! Did you speak up and tell him the rash isin't contagious?

Figure VI-1

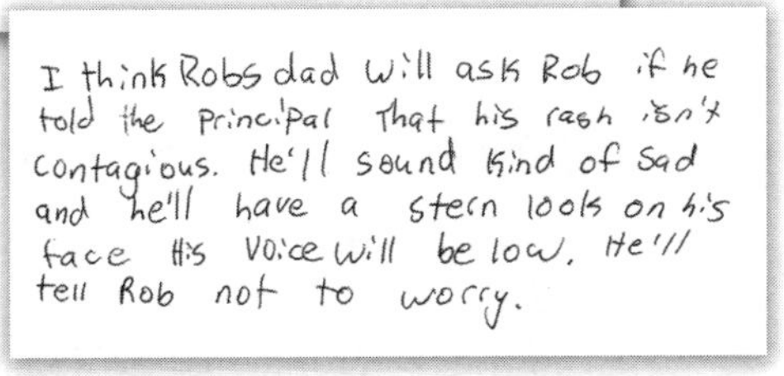

I think Robs dad will ask Rob if he told the principal that his rash isn't contagious. He'll sound kind of sad and he'll have a stern look on his face. His Voice will be low, He'll tell Rob not to worry.

Figure VI-2

The advice to predict not only what *a person does but also* how *he does it also pertains to how a person speaks. Notice the difference between Josh's and Aly's predictions—the latter conveys how Rob's father will speak to his son.*

Set children up to make a second prediction, demonstrating what they have just learned about predictions, doing this off the next portion of the read-aloud passage.

"Readers, it is exciting for me to see that you are predicting not only what the person will *do* but also *how he or she will do those actions*. And from those predictions, you are drawing on what you know about the character. Smart work. I'm going to read just a bit further in the story, and you'll have a chance to make a whole other prediction. Listen closely to this next part. It's not very long, so you'll have to use your very best envisioning and predicting skills."

I opened up my book and reread a bit, then read on.

> His father read the note from the principal slowly, putting his finger under the words as if they were bugs he was trying to keep still. When he was finally done, he laid the letter on the table and rubbed his eyes with his fingers and sighed. The rain beat a sad rhythm on the roof of the motel. "That stuff ain't nothing anybody else can catch," his father said.
>
> "I know it," Rob told him.
>
> "I already told that to the principal once before. I called up there and told him that."
>
> "Yes sir," said Rob.
>
> His father sighed. He stopped rubbing his eyes and looked up at Rob. "You want to stay home?" he asked.
>
> Rob nodded.

"Pick up your pens and predict," I said.

Again coach into children's predictions, reminding them to envision and to draw on what they know of the characters.

Before the children even had time to write much, I began coaching. Their earlier work had stayed very grounded in the events described in the text and I wanted them to extend their predictions. "I'm again going to act like a basketball coach, and call out pointers." I prompted, "What solution is the dad going to come up with? Think *what* he'll do in response and also *how* he'll do it. Remember to make a movie in your mind using what you know about the dad to help you picture what he'll say to Rob, to the principal, and how he'll say it."

You could decide to end the minilesson here, adding the link, rather than giving children a chance to cycle through this work twice. Become accustomed to seeing sections of all these minilessons that are expendable, because you generally want to limit minilessons to ten minutes, and also because you'll tailor your teaching in response to your class's attentiveness.

Read in such a way that you bring the action to life through your voice. Read the phrase "I know it," in a way that brings Rob to life, calling up his resigned, dutiful manner. Then as you read, "He stopped rubbing his eyes and looked up at Rob," show with your voice what Rob's father would look like, sound like, as he makes eye contact with his son.

A few seconds later I called out, "Remember, you need to not only imagine *what* Rob's dad does, but also *how* he does it. Then, picture what Rob will do and say in response."

Kwami and Aly jotted quickly. *[Figs. VI-3 and VI-4]*

Set readers up to share predictions with partners, pointing out to each other what they did to make their predictions good. As you listen in on conversations, guide children to grasp principles of good predictions.

"Readers, finish your predictions, and then look up at me." When I had everyone's attention, I said, "Now, look back at your predictions and select a few good ones and think, 'What makes these into good predictions?'" After giving children a moment to do this, I said, "Share your thinking with your partner."

I listened in to Lily and Jasmine. "My predictions are longer than before," Lily said. "I used to just say it in a word, what would happen."

Jasmine replied, "It is like we added details and dialogue like in a good story, like that Rob's dad folded up the note and said, 'If you stay home you're gonna have to work around here.'"

I switched to another pair of children, and this time I heard Jack say to Sarah, "I did like you and pictured the dad's face. He looks kind of sad and like he doesn't know what to do. And then, when I wrote what happens next, I stretched it out and wrote it bit by bit."

When Sarah noticed me listening in, she said, "Jack put something smart. Look at what he wrote. *[Fig. VI-5]*

Notice that I repeat the tip I've already given. Just as a sports coach will remind players again and again, "Keep your eye on the ball," I want to cement for readers the importance of trying a particular skill—in this instance, bringing what they know about characters to their predictions—over and over.

Again, this upcoming section of the minilesson is expendable, although you'll probably feel as if the children are eager by now to share what they've done. Keep in mind that if the symphony active involvement (Session V) worked well for your class, it is an alternative to partner sharing.

If time is limited and you doubt both partners will have time to share, you may want to designate when it is Partner 1 or Partner 2 who reads his or her prediction aloud. Otherwise, the dominant child will rise to the occasion.

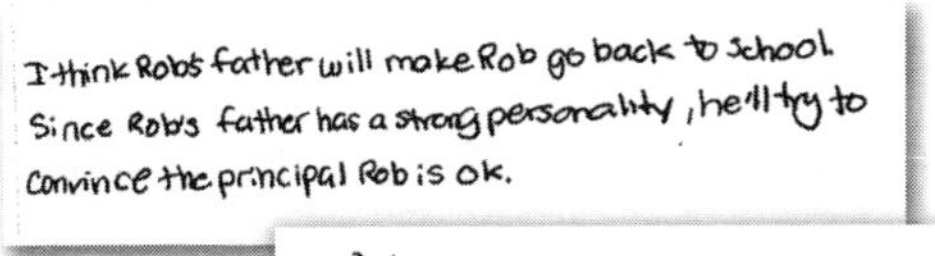

I think Robs father will make Rob go back to school Since Robs father has a strong personality, he'll try to convince the principal Rob is ok.

Figure VI-3

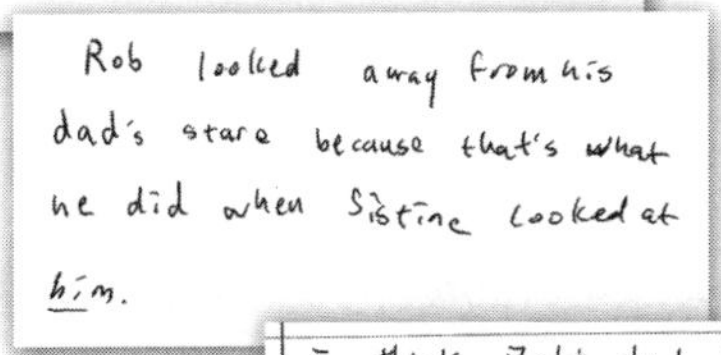

Rob looked away from his dad's stare because that's what he did when Sistine looked at him.

Figure VI-4

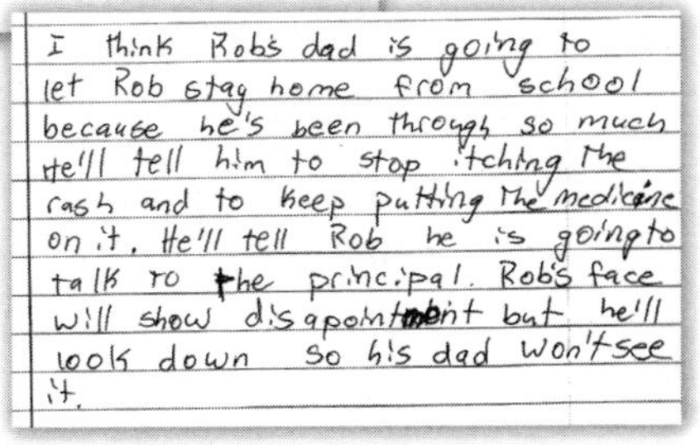

I think Robs dad is going to let Rob stay home from school because he's been through so much He'll tell him to stop itching the rash and to keep putting the medicine on it. He'll tell Rob he is going to talk to the principal. Rob's face will show disapointment but he'll look down so his dad won't see it.

Figure VI-5

Link

List the qualities of good predictions and remind readers to draw on these whenever they make a prediction. Show a chart of prediction pointers.

I convened the class. "Researchers, eyes on me. I heard you say that a good prediction lets you picture what will happen next, almost as if the story continues bit by bit. I also heard you say a good prediction sometimes includes details specific to the character, that it doesn't just say *what* the character will do but also conjectures *how* the character might go about doing it.

"Readers, today and every day as you read, remember to picture not just *what* is happening but *how* it is happening, thinking about what you know about a character to anticipate what will happen next. In life, readers don't usually record our predictions, but for the next few days, try to do that. Jot your predictions on Post-it notes or in your reader's notebook. That way we can work on making our prediction muscles as strong as they can be. I won't always be beside you, but you can be your own coach, reminding yourself of ways to lift the level of your predictions. These are strategies to make your predictions even better."

I flipped over a chart and pointed to the first bullet point.

"Off you go!"

Strategies Readers Use When We Predict

- Make a movie in our mind of what has yet to happen and tell it bit by bit.

- Think about what has already happened in the book and use our understanding of the characters to imagine the upcoming text.

- Draw on our personal knowledge of similar experiences to anticipate the upcoming text.

- Imagine not only **what** the character will do but **how** he or she will do it.

Notice that you're referring to children as researchers. Much of education revolves around taking on new identities, new roles. You may decide to lean into this, making a very big deal of your children's work as researchers.

Notice that these qualities of good predictions are actually ones you have been teaching all along, but you just gave ownership of these away, saying, "I heard you say that. . . ." Learners all the time reinvent insights and ideas. Celebrate that.

CONFERRING AND SMALL-GROUP WORK

Teaching Your Most and Least Proficient Readers

Teachers, you'll have noticed that each of the conferring and small group sections in the units of study books addresses a different theme, with one day's write-up focusing on conferences and small-group work to support envisionment, another day's, prediction. A word of caution: The conferences and small-group work will not actually fit into a nice coherent package. Just because the focus of your minilessons has turned now toward prediction, does not mean you won't still help children read with stamina and volume. You will presumably also need to confer to support children's word solving and their retelling skills. In this way, your teaching keeps alive all that the children have learned.

Having said this, it is still true that on any one day, approximately half of your conferences and small-group work will probably advance the main thrust of your unit of study. And when doing that teaching, it will help if you prepare yourself by thinking not only about what proficiency in the skill you are teaching entails, but also about how your teaching is apt to differ based on whether you are supporting your strong or your struggling readers—and predictors.

Support Your Strong Predictors: By Showing that Predictions Can Be Based on a Broad Knowledge of Literature, You Raise the Bar

When you pull a chair alongside your more advanced readers, you will find that their envisioning and predicting work tends to take in large amounts

---

> ### MID-WORKSHOP TEACHING POINT
>
> #### Readers Carry Our Predictions with Us as We Read On, and We Note Whether the Text Confirms or Challenges Those Predictions
>
> "Readers, earlier today you pushed yourself to predict in the wisest possible way. I reminded you to imagine not only what will happen but also how it might unfold, and to draw on what you know from earlier in the story. But I forgot to point out one thing. After you make a prediction, you read on, and you find out 'I was right' or 'I was wrong.' And it is interesting to take note of that. Especially when the story takes an unexpected turn, it's wise to think, 'What can I learn from what, in fact, happened?'
>
> *continued on next page*

---

of the story, not just the text on that one page or even that one chapter. Their talking and jotting is likely to reference earlier parts of the same text or even other relevant texts. You can help these youngsters by reminding them to use their knowledge of stories and the world in general to add flesh to their envisioning and to their predictions and by encouraging them to let their predictions be informed by theories of their characters. You will help them by asking, "What *type* of character do you think this is? Do you know anyone else like this?" You could then nudge them farther, saying, "Does this knowledge of other characters (or other texts) help you predict how the character will act?" You could even go a step further and help readers think about what the book is *mostly* trying to teach and to let those thoughts help them predict how the story is apt to unfurl. [Fig. VI-6]

Another powerful way of teaching these more sophisticated readers is to nudge them toward considering their books with the lens of the author's purpose. You might ask questions like, "What are you learning from the characters in this book?" or "Are you getting any sense of what the author is trying to say?" Again,

> I think Dorothy is going to finally stand up to Bears and tell him to leave her alone. She might say "why don't you go and pick on someone who is as big as you. You're a wimp."

Figure VI-6
Carolyn's predictions show she's shifting from being passion-hot to critic-cold which suggests flexibility.

you'll want to show readers that their answers to questions such as these can then function as stepping stones, helping them predict well.

Your work with readers' predicting can be influenced by your knowledge of the challenge that different bands of text difficulty tend to pose for readers. For example, when children enter the N/O/P/Q band of text difficulty, they are apt to encounter some difficulties at first because they'll find that story line, which have been so clear and monolithic until now, are often a bit more complex now. Whereas level L/M books tend to bear titles that name the story line (*Cam Jansen and the Mystery of the Stolen Diamonds*) and to tell the story of a protagonist who has very clear, explicitly stated character traits that lead him into a problem that he then resolves, N/O/P/Q books have characters that are more complex and ambivalent. Amber Brown wants both to be 13 and to be 9. She both likes and resists her mom's new boyfriend. Readers of these books will find that usually a few factors work together to cause upcoming events. You'll want to ask, "What caused this? What else caused it?" You'll also want readers to entertain more than one possibility for the story's resolution. Often characters *don't* get what they thought they wanted, but instead their deeper wants are met, perhaps in surprising ways.

Readers of level R/S/T books will profit from you keeping in mind that their books don't usually follow a single straight trajectory. There may not be one main character with one overriding motivation who encounters one obvious problem and overcomes it in a clear fashion. If you were to try to make a timeline of a book at this level, you'd find it difficult. Do you plot the changes in the world? How do you capture the side stories? What about flashbacks and flash-forwards?

MID-WORKSHOP TEACHING POINT

continued from previous page

"Let's practice by reading on for just a second in *The Tiger Rising*. Remember what you predicted Rob's dad would do? Well, let's read on, and you can get ready to think, 'I was right' or 'Hmmm. This is surprising.' And if the story surprises you, which often happens, get ready to talk with your partner about what you can learn from how it evolved. Remember your predictions about how Rob's father would respond to the principal's note saying that he was sending Rob home? Keep you predictions in mind and we'll read on."

> "You want to stay home?" he asked.
> Rob nodded.
> His father sighed again. "Maybe I'll make an appointment, get one of them doctors to write down that what you got ain't catching. All right?"
> "Yes, sir," said Rob.

continued on next page

This doesn't mean that prediction isn't as important for readers of this level of difficulty as it is for readers of texts that follow a simpler story structure, but your teaching will especially emphasize that readers draw upon what has already occurred in order to predict, and this means a seemingly inconsequential side story may return to play a surprisingly important role. It means noticing the author's craft and asking, "Why might the author have written like this, and how does this influence my sense of what is to come?"

Support Your Struggling Predictors: By Helping Children Ground Their Predictions in the Text, You Expand the Amount of Text They Deal with

Of course, there will be other children who need entirely different help. Whereas your most experienced predictors are probably apt to predict by considering ways the author will forward his or her meaning, your less-experienced predictors will be more apt to predict what will happen next. This will mean that more and less-experienced readers predict at different times. Your more experienced predictors will predict not only at the exciting moments but also at moments of significance; the less-experienced readers will be apt to predict at cliff-hanger moments. That's okay for a start. You could ask your less-experienced predictors to identify the places in the text where the author practically creates a drumroll, accompanied by the "Da Da Da dum" music. These readers should know that in moments like this, it is great for them to anticipate that something important will happen soon. That is, there are moments in a book that are like the moments in a television show in which the music cues that the action is coming to a head. In books, these parts may come right at the end of a chapter. Sometimes the author will use heavy-handed phrases such as "He knew what he had to do," or "She opened the door, and stopped dead in her tracks," or "He knew he had to make a choice." In any case, these are invitations to predict.

When these children do predict, you'll see that some instinctively predict based on what the *reader* (not the *character*) would do. If Rob is mistreated, some readers will say, "He's gonna hit back," basing that prediction on the fact that the reader would be apt to do that, but not taking into account the fact that Rob may be nothing like the reader.

Then, too, you'll see that some readers simply predict how the story will finally end, not even dreaming that they might imagine the trail the plot will take to reach that culmination. Many times, these predictions could have been made from a quick glance at the book's back cover. You'll want to teach these children that when readers predict what's going to happen in a book, rather than taking an enormous step all the way to the last page, when everything is resolved, it is helpful to take smaller steps so that we can imagine how the story is apt to unfold with as much detail as possible.

You might find that some of your readers' predictions seem to come out of nowhere. These are probably readers who tend to maintain a very local focus. If they are reading page 9, that is the only bit of text they draw upon to predict. For these readers, the powerful thing about teaching them to predict is that once they begin predicting, this skill can help them tie the entire text together, creating through lines across large swatches of text.

MID-WORKSHOP TEACHING POINT

continued from previous page

"But I won't do it for a few days. I'll give you some time off."

"That would be all right," said Rob.

"You got to fight them, you know. Them boys. I know you don't want to. But you got to fight them, else they won't ever leave you alone."

"Turn and talk. Do Rob's father's actions match your expectations of what you thought would happen? What can you learn from ways in which it is surprising?"

After partners talked for a bit, I reconvened the class. "I'm with you—I was a little surprised by this turn of events, right? He isn't as hard on Rob as usual, is he? He gives him a break."

Izzy interrupted. "But he also tells him to fight the bullies."

"What do you make of that?" I asked her and the class in general.

Izzy said, "Um, 'cause I think the father knows 'cause he's had people make fun of him, too, and he wants Rob to get tougher."

I listened, as if Izzy's ideas brought new light to the subject. "Smart work. Readers, what I want you to realize is that the big thing is not whether your predictions turn out to be right or wrong. The big thing is that when the book catches you by surprise, you can take that little feeling of surprise and think more stuff, grow more ideas. As you continue reading, try not only to do some smart predictions work but also to notice if your predictions are right or not. When the book surprises you, take some time to think, 'Hmm. What can I make of that surprise?'"

You might help these children realize that when the character comes to a place in the story where he or she needs to make a choice, choosing between one path and another (or choosing one way of reacting or another) an astute reader can usually make a pretty good guess about the choice the character will make. Those guesses do not come from nowhere. They come from thinking or looking back and seeing what the character has done and said earlier that gives some clues. For these readers, then, it is helpful to suggest they pause at turning points and think, "What do I predict the character will do, and what grounds do I have for my prediction?"

I recently met with Kobe and Malik, who were discussing the end of Chapter 6 in *The Tiger Rising*. They both agreed that Sistine and Rob would become friends and that Rob would stand up for himself even more. It had only been a week earlier when Kobe had predicted in the *Hardy Boys* book that they'd save the girl, and when he'd been unwilling to conjecture how this might happen. So I was interested in seeing whether he had grown at all in his ability to bring his own words and ideas to the text. I knew, of course, that by setting him up to talk about the text I'd read aloud and the class had discussed in detail, I was providing a powerful scaffold. "What makes you think that?" I asked them. Then I posited a scenario that was plainly wrong to push the children to explain themselves: "How do you know that Rob isn't going to go back to being quiet and allowing the other kids to bully him?"

They explained, "He's not going to go back to being shy now. He is finding a brave part of himself that he didn't know was there before. It's like, he was opening his suitcase a little bit." Malik mimed with his hands a suitcase opening a crack. "And, now that it's open, he's just going to keep opening it more and more."

"Wow," I told them. "You guys are onto something huge. I think what you are hinting at is this. In books, the author isn't just writing to tell a story. An author like Kate DiCamillo or John Reynolds Gardiner is also writing to tell a truth.

"So thinking about what the author is trying to tell you will help you think about where the story is going. Like, in *Stone Fox*, some people might say that John Reynolds Gardiner told the story of Little Willy to help us understand that we have to sacrifice and work hard in the face of obstacles to protect the most important things in our lives. So, as I read, thinking about the author's purpose helped me know that Little Willy would never give up before he had helped his grandfather, not even when the race seemed impossible or his dog died. In every story, thinking about the author's purpose can really pay off when trying to make a strong prediction."

It didn't surprise me that Malik spoke up first. "Yes," he said, "and so far I think Kate DiCamillo's purpose has to do with saying what you feel. Like, even if you're feeling something terrible, it's better to say it than to keep it inside."

I nodded. "Okay, so draw on your sense of what the author seems to be telling you to help you predict what might happen next in the story. If your theory is right that DiCamillo's message is that people shouldn't bottle up their feelings, then you need to think, 'What does this suggest about how Rob will behave next?'" As Malik started to answer, I suggested he talk about his ideas with Kobe rather than with me, and before I left, I reminded them of the bigger lessons I hoped they'd learned from the conference.

These two boys and other readers like them will benefit from encouragement to draw on earlier sections of the text. You'll find yourself asking some readers, "What do you know about this character that can help you here?" Or "Does that sound like a way this character would act?" You'll want to coach these readers to look back in order to look forward.

Help children to use phrases such as, "I think . . . will happen because. . . ." You can show them that when they predict, they should be able to go back to prior parts of the story to highlight moments where the character's actions, thinking, or feelings foreshadowed what is to come. Predictions are not random, but are instead rooted in a deep comprehension of the text. You'll probably ask these readers to jot what they predict the character will do (or what will happen to him or her) and to add the word *because* and specify the textual grounds for this prediction.

You may want to convene a small group to help children learn how to cite evidence for their predictions. You might say to your group, "Remember earlier I read a part of *The Tiger Rising* where . . . and we predicted that. . . . Remember we came up with that idea purely by reminding ourselves to think, 'What do I know about the character?' Well, I am going to reread that part again, and this time let's work together on a prediction that will include not only *what* we think will happen but also *the evidence* for that. We can say, 'I predict . . . ,' and then we can say, '*because*. . . .' So, for example, 'I predict Rob is going to spend a lot of time in the woods with the tiger *because* he felt lucky he found it, *because* he thought about the tiger all the time, he drew a picture of it, and he felt the picture in his pocket when he was in the principal's office.'" Then I named what I'd done, saying, "Did you see how I grounded my prediction of what Rob will do now that he doesn't have to go to school in what I already know? Let's try it together."

After practicing this using a shared section of the read-aloud book, you could ask children to do similar work with their independent reading books. You might give all the children, all at one time, a lean coaching prompt such as, "What do you think will happen next? Stop and jot." Or you could say, "Point to a part of the story that makes you think that." Then you'd want to send out another prompt: "Now, point to another part of your story that makes you think your prediction is grounded in the text." These methods, of course, can be used one-on-one in conferences as well as in small-group strategy lessons.

And because your real goal for these readers is to encourage them to synthesize the text, to see cause and effect relationships, to accumulate earlier sections of the text as they encounter new text, it will be important for these readers to be especially careful to carry their predictions with them as they read on, later pausing to think (and jot), "I was right because . . ." or "I was wrong because. . . ."

TEACHING SHARE

Readers Think About the Qualities of Effective Predictions

Give an example of some good prediction work and ask children to select and discuss an instance in which their own prediction work is good.

"Readers, in a minute you'll have a chance to meet with not just your partner but with a small group. First, look back over your predictions and identify the prediction that you think is your best one. Remember, it might be an instance where you wrote not only *what* will happen but also *how* it might unfold. Then again, it might be an instance where you drew on your understanding of the characters. Possibly your best prediction is actually several Post-its that fit together into one prediction"

After a moment, I asked children to meet with others at their tables, that is, their partners and both members of another partnership, and to look across each others' predictions, "Look for one prediction that seems to the group to be especially effective," I asked. After children selected one of their foursome's predictions that felt like it illustrated all they'd learn about predicting well, I suggested they talk about what they felt worked in the selected prediction. One group chose Brendon's as their mentor Post-it; a second choice was Sam's. *[Figs. VI-7 and VI-8]*

Notice that today I've set up a table share, not just a partner share. If you do this and find it brings new energy to your classroom, as it may, then you can return to this often. Today's entire share session, actually, is a replicable one. You could alter it in ways that allow you to use adaptations of this often. You are asking readers to identify their best work and to name why the work is good. This is a powerful way to nudge youngsters to clarify their images of good work.

> I think that Rockys notebook is going to be a monument. She'll put Sketches and writing in it about the town, the grain elevators, the popsicle stick graveyard. Maybe Rocky and Mick will teach peo in the town what a monument wi be. They'll make the town f better about themself

Figure VI-7
Brendon's entry about Gary Paulsen's *The Monument.*

> . This lets me know that Bastian isn't going to leave. I think his dad is going to change his mind and stay here. I think in some way this will really affect the story because Bastian seems like an important figure in the class.

Figure VI-8
Sam's prediction shows tentative, flexible thinking and an attention to story structure. I picture him sketching his prediction with pencil and a light hand. Although this is admirable, I'd also like to see more grounding in precise details from earlier in the text.

Coach children to not only talk about the quality of their predictions but also to use those predictions as jumping-off places for talking about texts.

I then nudged the children to talk about the content that surrounded the prediction they'd shared. I listened in to Tyrell's conversation with Max, Lily, and Jasmine. Tyrell was reading *Freckle Juice* by Judy Blume. He read his Post-it aloud [Fig VI-9]

Then Tyrell talked off his jottings. He said, "I predicted that Andrew was going to get in big trouble by Miss Kelly. He got caught with a note from Sharon. Miss Kelly took the note and told Andrew to see her after school. I predicted that Andrew was going to get a note home telling his Mom what he had done. I was surprised that Miss Kelly gave him back the note and only said he had to pay attention in school," said Tyrell. Tyrell knew he was supposed to talk to his classmates, but couldn't help shooting a glance in my direction to make sure I heard his ideas.

Max got to the crux of the matter, asking, "What was on the note?"

Figure VI-9

Usually as I listen, I jot down what the child says so that I can remember his or her words later. I often find myself wanting to rewind a conference. It also never hurts to have children see you write what they say. Children love to know that their words are heard. Transcribing also helps me to assess the types of thinking kids are doing.

"It was a recipe to give him freckles. He really thinks that if he had freckles, he won't have to wash his neck. Andrew is weird." Tyrell chuckled as he explained the story to his classmates.

I coached, "When someone acts out of character like Miss Kelly did, try to remember that those are times not only to predict but also to think about the character, asking, 'Why might the character have acted in this puzzling way?' Why do you think Miss Kelly did that? What do you now know about Miss Kelly from this surprise?"

There was a long pause as Tyrell thought. He looked back to the book while he tapped both feet on the ground. "Maybe she felt bad for Andrew because he was already embarrassed in front of the class when he fell out of his chair and when he had to give the note to her. And plus he's usually not in trouble. Or maybe she is being nice to him because she can tell he really wants that recipe. She could've ripped it up but she didn't."

I interrupted, "I like the way that you're thinking about details you learned earlier in the story to figure out why Miss Kelly did what she did. Keep thinking. Try asking, 'What does this tell me about the character?'"

Tyrell said, "She is really nice and not a mean teacher."

Jasmine piped in, "Or maybe she cares a lot about Andrew and she's understanding."

"And she forgives people when they do something kind of bad," added Tyrell, talking excitedly over Jasmine.

At this point I interrupted the whole class. "Readers, I hope you see that a prediction can lead you to talk at length. It can also lead you to *think* at length—and that's what good readers do."

In this instance, I noticed later when I reread Tyrell's commenting that his prediction shone a spotlight on an inconsequential point of the text, bypassing the more important drama around the freckle recipe. Perhaps Tyrell connected personally to Andrew's troubles with his teacher.

Teaching your children to ask and to entertain provocative, significant questions of a text is worthwhile work. In real life, of course, readers need to generate their own questions because there are no questions at the ends of chapters. Skilled readers generate and muse over questions to ratchet up our thinking work.

Notice how I nudge Tyrell to pursue a line of questions and to follow a line of thinking. I want to push him to hold on to a particular idea, to say more, and to think more deeply. This is critically important thinking.

IN THIS SESSION,
you will teach students that
when readers connect to our
characters with open hearts,
we envision, predict, and
think about our characters
simultaneously.

Mining Details About Characters

I was in Boston a few years ago for a policy meeting of leaders from many major cities. The person who convened the meeting started it by saying, "Let's go around the table and hear what one representative from each city believes is the biggest challenge in your city, related to teaching reading."

The representative for the first city said, "Comprehension, starting grade 3."

All eyes shifted to the representative from the next city. She thought for a moment, then said, "Comprehension, starting grade 3." As we proceeded around that table, one by one, each of the others responded, "Ditto," "Ditto."

Listening to this, I was reminded of how many times a child has come to me and announced, "I finished! I read the whole book!" and then, when I've said, "I don't know that book. Tell me about it," the child has given me a blank stare, and started stuttering . . . "Um, uh, um," before hurrying to add, "I read it, honest. I just don't remember it."

When children read as if they are made of Teflon, letting the text roll off of them, I want to say to them, "If you've gone through every page in the book and then, after you close the last page, you remember nothing, you haven't really read the book." Part of the trouble might lie in the skim-and-scan way that some kids read—searching for the general story—the basic plot or gist—and tossing the book aside once they do. "There is so much more to a story than merely what *happens*," we might tell our children. "Search. It's all in the details."

"We think in generalities but we live in detail," said Alfred North Whitehead. To this I'd add that we remember in detail, we recognize in detail. Think back to your first conscious memory—a snatch of color, the specific feel of a milk bottle's comforting warmth in a curved palm, the odd shape of the mole on a caregiver's brow, falling off a tricycle—our very first perceptions of the world did not include its vastness or its generalities. Our first perceptions were the smallest of details. It was around these details that larger stories

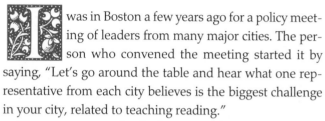

GETTING READY

- In today's session plan to read aloud Debbie Allen's gorgeous picture book *Dancing in the Wings* or another relatively simple yet emotionally powerful text centered around a main character with whom children will easily connect.

- By the next session, Session VIII, you will need to have read through Chapter 12 of *The Tiger Rising*. If you've selected an alternate read-aloud for this unit, then read up to a part in the text where the characters are interacting in a way that reveals the relationship they have with each other.

- You'll be adding to the chart "Strategies Readers Use to Grow Ideas About Characters" in the teaching share.

formed and bigger events occurred. Once these details, in themselves, acquired significance, they became the familiar reference points around which life unfurled and began making sense of itself.

The most powerful narratives mimic this sequence. Stories begin in detail. Around these few details, almost rising from *within* them, a plot begins to form. Gradually, it thickens and acquires layers and dimensions through yet

> *Stories begin in detail. Around these few details, almost rising from within them, a plot begins to form.*

more nuance, more detail—fingers that fumble across rosary beads . . . scores of kites across the Kabul sky . . . the slant of a villain's eyes. . . . Years ago, I remember once trying to put my sons to bed with a hastily concocted 'bedtime story' when I didn't have a book at hand to read aloud from. I remember constant interruptions. "Was the bunny white or gray? Did it have red eyes like the neighbor's pet rabbit? Was that grassy patch in the middle of the forest or on the edge of it?" At first I'd suspected the endless questions were a ploy to secure more awake time, but I soon realized that these details were as integral to the boys' understanding of the "story" as the larger plotline—perhaps even more so. Without them, envisionment fell flat and so did any chance at empathy; who could identify with a faceless, nameless rabbit? I had to begin the story anew, this time fleshing the

characters out until they felt real and alive, until they began to matter.

Yet the "details" in a text have conventionally had a tricky reputation with reading comprehension teachers. When students are prepared for high-stakes tests, they are advised to think, "What is the main idea of the story?" and "What is this story mainly about?" There is no doubt that reading to ascertain the gist of a story is an important skill to master. But when helping kids read texts as if they are gold, we help them take texts in and let it *matter*. I want to suggest that gold is in the details.

So much is conveyed in Tolstoy's *Resurrection* when a society woman, conscious that she is aging and desperate to appear young, keeps turning from her festive lunch to eye the window through which a beam of unflattering sunlight has begun to shine. So much is conveyed, similarly, when a man's coat seam splits under the arm when he raises it to hit his sobbing son at his wife's funeral. These details are not accidental—their insertion in the folds of a story allows the readers to see more and feel more of the story. This, then, is the note at which you'll finish this bend—an invitation for your readers to see more and feel more, panning for gold in the telling gestures and slight details that make their character alive and unique, familiar yet complex.

Prepare for today, then, by finding a picture book that you are absolutely sure your kids will love, a book that reminds you of all that reading can be. Read the start of that book within today's minilesson, and finish it during read-aloud. Before you teach, reread the book to yourself; let it work its magic on you. There are lots of ways to read a book—for now, do the sort of reading you have been helping children to do. You have been helping your children make mental movies as they read. You have helped them not only follow the characters but also read in advance, predicting what might occur just down the road of the story. Do this work now as you read the book you select. Then practice talking and thinking about the specific details that help make this envisioning and predicting work possible.

When I did this, I chose to read Debbie Allen's *Dancing in the Wings* because this picture book has been utterly beloved in literally thousands of the classrooms in which my colleagues and I have worked most closely. After reading the book, I tried to capture what the experience of reading is like for me. "Reading," I thought, "is really living a second life—many other lives!—in high-contrast, Technicolor fashion through the lives of characters in our books." I remembered that Anna Quindlen, when talking about falling in love with reading as a child, has said that to her, all the characters in her favorite books "were more real than the real people I knew. My home was in that pleasant place outside Philadelphia, but I really lived somewhere else. I lived within the covers of books and those books were more real to me than any other thing in my life." I'm betting that Quindlen savored the details, that she embellished her imagination with them until she entered the world of her story effortlessly. We can aim for our children to do the same.

MINILESSON

Mining Details About Characters

CONNECTION

Tell the story of someone who was so intent on rushing between one place and another that he never really saw the terrain he passed through.

"Readers, yesterday I met someone who told me that he'd driven across the United States—from New York in the east all the way to Los Angeles in the west—to spend Thanksgiving with his family. 'What a great drive that must have been!' I said. Of course I was imagining driving through open highways and swaying golden cornfields, crossing rivers and desert roads. 'You must have seen some beautiful country,' I said.

"'Not really,' he told me. 'All I saw was the rear of a brown SUV—the one we were following.' I must have stared in stunned silence because he explained, 'We had to get there for Thanksgiving so we hit the road and just drove, following friends who knew the way. I guess we didn't have that much time to look.'

"Readers, I have to say I was appalled at the thought of driving through some of the most beautiful areas in this country without looking left or right out of the windows to appreciate the colors and the sights and the changing geography. I thought, 'I hope I'm never in such a hurry that I forget to look around me, that I forget to *live*.'

"I know that in our reading workshop, we've talked about reading faster, longer, stronger. I hope you know that reading your books from start to end the way that driver zipped from New York to California may well be fast and long—but it certainly won't be *strong*. In the past few days, we've been learning the work of stepping into our character's shoes and envisioning the world of the story, predicting not just *what* will happen next but also *how* this will happen. This is the stuff that *strong* reading is made off—you can't do this work if you zip through texts with blinders on.

COACHING TIPS

When you tell stories in your minilessons that end up being symbolic, meaning more than at first meets the ear, you are bringing kids into the world of metaphor, of language that is layered with meaning. Without talking about it, you are immersing children in lessons about symbolism and figurative language. Glance at the assessment section that follows this session in which I describe the work that readers need to do when reading texts in the U/V/W band of text difficulty, and then consider, for a moment, ways in which minilessons may induct them into that sort of mind work. After all, you are showing kids that stories can mean more than they at first seem to mean, that comprehension can involve building bridges between two seemingly disconnected sections of a text, that readers fill in the gaps of a text . . . and all this is work that readers need to do to read complex fiction.

"Here's what I thought about that driver: Sure, he got to California, the end he set out for, but . . . if he didn't have that brown SUV ahead of him, I bet he wouldn't have known one state that he drove through from another. If he never stopped once at a quaint-looking roadside diner to have a cup of coffee and chat with the local people, if he never once looked out to track the changing tree line or to note the earth and the rocks changed as he got further west . . . why, then, he probably couldn't even recognize the areas he'd driven through if he saw them again. Nothing along the way meant anything to him; he found significance in nothing. I've met people who've been changed forever by road trips such as this and here was this guy who might as well have never taken the trip *at all*.

"I mean, if I were driving west from New York all the way to California, I'd keep my eyes open for important details such as the Gateway Arch in Missouri, the tallest monument in the US. I might have planned my route to cross through a real ghost town, a detail that many travelers find fascinating about Kansas. And I'd certainly expect to note Pike's Peak in the Rockies. I'd be able to predict, just by looking at the change in the color of the rocks and the earth, just by the changing trees and shrubs, where we were in terms of latitude and longitude.

State your teaching point. Specifically tell children that in order to envision and predict with strength, readers pay attention to details.

"Readers, my point is that all this predicting and this envisioning requires a traveler to take in *details*. If a traveler—or a *reader*—skips details, reading faster just to find out what happens next and next and in the end, I'm betting a month later, they'd probably not even remember they'd taken the journey *at all*.

Teaching

Pick up a picture book, one that you've chosen especially to read aloud in today's minilesson. Demonstrate how you might skim the book for its basic plotline, with minimal attention to detail.

"Let's look first at the cover of the book *Dancing in the Wings* by Debbie Allen. I'm going to show you how my friend of the boring SUV-tailing road trip might have read this absolutely beautiful book." So saying, I flipped the book over and proceeded to skim and scan, flipping pages quickly, all the while muttering, "Dancer girl . . . wants

Notice the chatty, conversational quality to this minilesson—it almost feels like gossip. "Here's what I thought about that driver: Sure he got to California . . . but I bet . . ." And yet, notice that this teaching is studded with details. I've sometimes asked teachers to watch as I give a minilesson and to notice which aspects of the minilesson seem to draw listeners in. You won't be surprised that it's the details that do this. Had that driver simply said, "I followed another car" the story would be far less powerful than it is now: "I followed a brown SUV."

Note that I'm taking maximum mileage from this metaphoric reference to a road trip, suggesting that a failure to take in details makes a road or a book indistinguishable from any other.

to dance . . . brother is a pest . . . there's a talent show . . . she enters . . . two girls laugh at her . . ." I give up flipping and skimming and look up in mock horror. "I hope no one here thinks that what I'm doing is reading! It most certainly isn't. Skimming or scanning is not the same as real reading.

"Readers, even though I was using the illustrations to figure out the story, I certainly didn't have a mental movie going on. And though I can kind of predict the end, I have no idea *how* it will happen—just a vague notion that all will turn out well for this dancer girl—see I haven't even picked up her name. It's clear: no attention to detail— no mental movie or predicting.

"Here's how I might read the book, like a true *reader*. I showed the class the front cover of the book and then turned it around and studied it myself for a moment. I said, "Wow, she's so beautiful in her fancy tutu and she looks so graceful. Look how she is able to stand on her toes and the way she extends her leg. She must be an amaz- ing dancer. Don't you think?" Aside I added, "See? I'm already using the cover illus- tration to predict things about this character." There were some quiet nods and murmurs of assent as I thought aloud.

"Look at that—we haven't even opened the book yet and already we're starting to wonder about and care about this lovely, tall girl! There are so many different reasons to care about a character. Some people like reading about characters they identify with, that they relate to, because this helps them feel as if the line between reading and experiencing is a thin one. Others find it more exciting to read about characters that are very different from them. I wonder how we'll connect to this character." I pointed to the cover. "It will probably be a little different for each of us, because each of us will connect to her in our own way, coming from who we are as people and as readers.

"So, I've been dying to find out more about this dancer on the cover. I'm going to start reading, and I want you to listen to the story, of course, but also sort of watch my thoughts as I pay attention to details, working to envision and predict all in a whoosh."

> Ever since I was born and could see,
> Everywhere I looked, I saw dance.
> In the clouds as the wind blew them across the sky,
> In the ripples on a pond,
> Even in the sea of ants marching up and down their hills.
> Dance was all around me. Dance was me.

I've gone so far as to suggest that scanning or skimming, in fact, are a process entirely different from real reading. In actual fact, previewing a book to grasp its basic plotline hardly does justice to its content—so I have few qualms about making this distinc- tion.

The beginning phase of this teaching section is much more explicative than demonstrative. However, I want children to really understand that caring about characters is what readers, all readers, do. One could even say that reading is caring. Reading is the miracle of being moved by what at first glance are merely marks on a page. This teaching section bears testimony to that. I want to show children that it's not just their teacher who thinks this way. People from all walks of life—anyone who carves out a place for reading—allow themselves to be moved by the charac- ters in books.

"Wow. That sounds like poetry. I can almost see the clouds, water and ants dancing! This character seems to breathe dance. I wonder if this means she's going to become a dancer herself . . ."

My mom calls me Sassy, 'cause I like to put my hands on my hips and 'cause I always have something to say. Well, if you had feet as big as mine, you'd understand why.

"Uh-oh! Maybe I was wrong. Big feet might make her a clumsy dancer. Now I know two things about her—she's sassy, in name and as a person, and she's conscious about having big feet."

You should join the swimming team, since you got those long toes and don't need any fins," my older brother, Hughie, teased.

I shot right back, "At least I don't have that big forehead lookin' like a street lamp."

"She sure sounds sassy, just like her name. She can really give it back."

Mama said, "Stop all that bad talk! You act so ugly sometimes. Hughie, your big head is a sign of intelligence. And Sassy, your big feet will make your legs look longer and prettier in your ballet shoes."

"I'm predicting that her big feet—and their role in her dancing the ballet—are an important feature in this story."

Make the Connection with Your Class: Tell Them You Hope that When They Read, They Care About Characters

"As we read on, we'll notice other details about Sassy, details that will enable us to picture the way Sassy talks, the way she holds herself, her movements, the expressions on her face. These details will help make our mental movie clearer and they'll help us predict what Sassy might do when confronted with a certain situation. Sassy should begin to feel more and more "real" to us, so we find ourselves seeing through her eyes and we can hear her voice without even trying or thinking about it. Anna Quindlen, a well-known author, wrote that characters in books always seem even

Note that I'm not stopping to ponder each detail that I read—that would merely distract from the story. Your read-aloud will do this teaching effectively if you allow your voice to enunciate details clearly and with engagement and expression as you read. You will want to summon all your storytelling abilities and talents. Use particular emphasis when referring to the main character; show how much you care for and sympathize with her. Try to talk and even hold yourself like the character would.

more real to her than the people in her life. When you start to get that feeling about a character, that's when you know that you are listening to that character the same way you would with a friend. You are picturing the events, trying to predict what might happen next, and thinking about the character's feelings naturally, all at once."

ACTIVE INVOLVEMENT

Read aloud a brief text, channel readers to talk with each other about their responses to the text, and then help them see that for engaged readers the skills you've been teaching become second nature.

"As I read on, I want you to continue to listen in such a way that you are getting more and more connected to Sassy with every sentence. Listen to all the little details about Sassy's character that the book provides—and you'll notice that your envisioning, predicting, and thinking about her happen all at once, in a whoosh."

You can continue your out-loud responses to what you're reading, nudging children to do the same internal thinking that you are doing out loud.

> My legs were longer, all right. So long, that when I went to *tendu*, point my toe, at the bar, I tripped Miss Katherine, our teacher, who was coming down the line, looking the other way. SPLAT! She landed under the piano,

"Oh, no!"

> her legs up in the air. *Ooo!* It was so funny. Even she had to laugh.

"Phew!"

> "Sassy!" she called out. "I'm going to tie orange bows on those big feet."
>
> "Sorry, Miss Katherine," I answered. "But if you don't wear your glasses, you still won't see them."
>
> One thing for sure—because of my long legs and big feet, I could jump higher and spin faster than everyone else.

"I *knew* she was good! I can picture her higher and faster than everyone else in that dance class. This girl stands out."

> I was taller than the rest of the kids at school, even the boys. At our recitals all the other girls got to dance solos and duets, and wear pretty

tutus. I was too big for the boys to pick up, and too tall to be in line with the other girls. So I watched from backstage, dancing in the wings, (I flipped quickly to the cover of the book and nodded showing that I now got the meaning of the title) hoping that if I just kept dancing and trying, it would be my turn to dance in the spotlight.

One day at the end of ballet class Miss Katherine announced, "Mr. Debato from the Russian school is coming next week to look for talented young people for the summer dance festival in Washington, D.C."

The whole room turned into a whirlpool of excitement as the sign-up sheet was posted. Everyone wanted to try, especially me.

"I bet I know what's going to happen."

But as I wrote my name down, I heard two girls, Molly and Mona, giggle. Mona said, "Oh please, she'll never make it. They said talent, not a tyran-nosaurus."

My heart seemed to stand still. For once I had nothing to say. I couldn't hide the tears I felt welling up in my eyes, so I just grabbed my dance bag and ran to the parking lot.

I pressed my hand to my heart and looked up at the class, showing that I was think-ing about what we had just read. I turned to the children and said, "Open your note-books and, in a whoosh, write all that you are thinking right now.
[Figs. VII-1 and VII-2]

"Looking over your shoulders, I see some of you writing things like, 'I was worried Sassy was going to get in trouble and get yelled at when she tripped, but when Miss Katherine made a joke of it I was relieved,' or, 'I can't believe how mean those girls were to Sassy. I would've cried too!' Those responses show that you care about this character, that she's become real to you. She's not just words on the page."

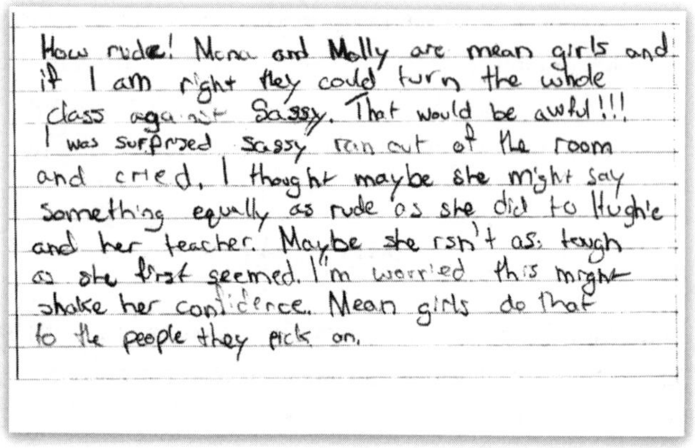

Figure VII-1
It's terrific to see that Jean's predicting grows from the theory that Sassy is tough—and yet the theory's open to revision.

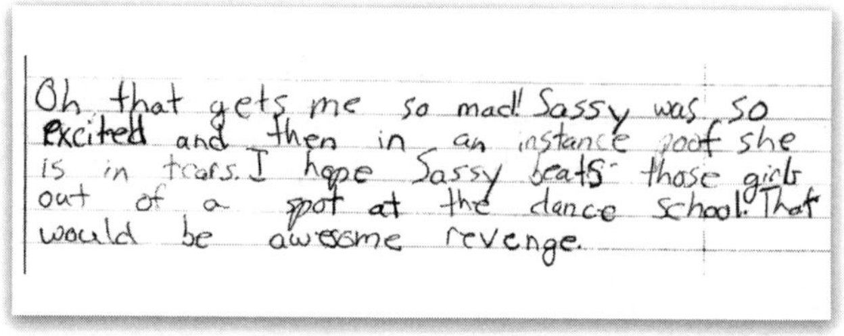

Figure VII-2
Daniel is invested enough in Sassy that he is furious over the catty comments other girls make about her. His interest is revenge—eventually he'll fine-tune his skills enough to differentiate the character's response from his own.

Although writing can take a bit longer than talking, I wanted the children to push themselves to say more and writing can make visible who is and isn't doing that. It is also a way for me to research who is and isn't getting the work we've been talking about. This will help me in my conferring and small-group instruction and in determining future minilessons.

As my colleague, Randy Bomer, once put it, "Response is not an extra credit option for the gifted readers who finish early. Response is what reading is all about." Our goal as teachers is to not only give children the tools to be better readers—and learn-ers—but to inspire them so they want to be better in the first place.

LINK

Remind readers to read with an attentiveness to detail, allowing the little things about the way a character dresses, talks, acts or moves to help us know the character well enough that we can predict what this character might do in a situation.

"Readers, what I'm hoping you realize is that when you read strong and long, getting lost in a book, you also feel for characters like you feel for people in your life who matter to you. Just like you know the tiny details about your best friend—how she holds her pencil, the unique slant of her handwriting, the lunch she always brings, her favorite author, favorite T-shirt, favorite TV show—you need to come to know the tiny details that a book provides you about the characters. You need to know these in order to climb into this character's shoes and to imagine or predict how this character might act.

"As readers, you know to envision—making a movie in your mind as you read—to use all you know about a character to predict, to revise those predictions as you read on . . . but really, above all, I don't need to tell you that as you read, there will be times when the text propels you to envision and to predict and to put your response on to the paper. Some of you will write on Post-its, some may have graduated to writing on pages of your notebook. Either way, I'm trying to say that you read with your heart on your sleeve, caring about characters just as you care about people in your life. When you are in a relationship with a character, you read with not just your mind but also with your heart—and those important things we've been practicing—envisionment and prediction—happen all in a whoosh. [Figs. VII–3 and VII–4]

"Today, and always, try to open yourself to your text. And when you gather with your partner, you'll have times to talk about—and to read aloud—places in your book where tiny details help you envision your character better or predict how this character might act." [Figs. VII–5 and VII–6]

Shirley Brice Heath has said that one of the most important gifts we can give children is allowing them to form bonded relationships with richly literate adults. To that end, we need to wear our love of reading and writing on our sleeves. Minilessons provide opportunities not only for teaching but also for preaching.

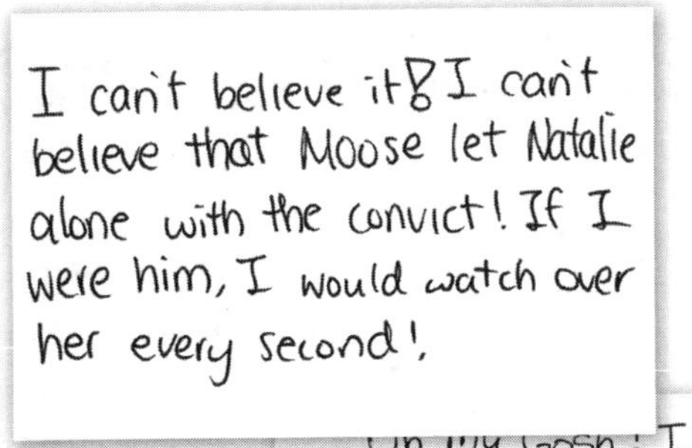

I can't believe it! I can't believe that Moose let Natalie alone with the convict! If I were him, I would watch over her every second!

Figure VII-3

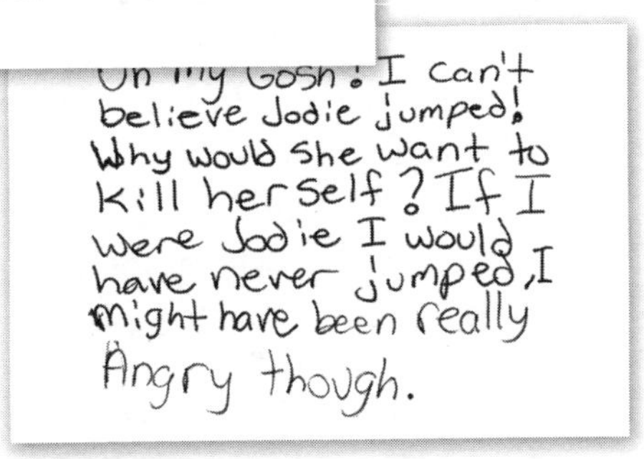

Oh my Gosh! I can't believe Jodie jumped! Why would she want to Kill herself? If I were Jodie I would have never jumped, I might have been really Angry though.

Figure VII-4

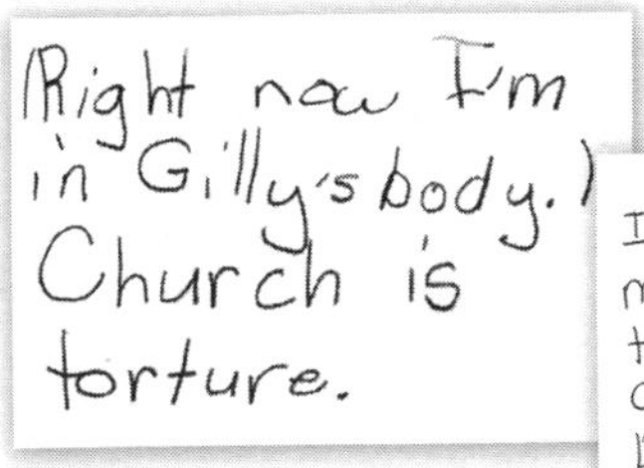

Right now I'm in Gilly's body. Church is torture.

Figure VII-5

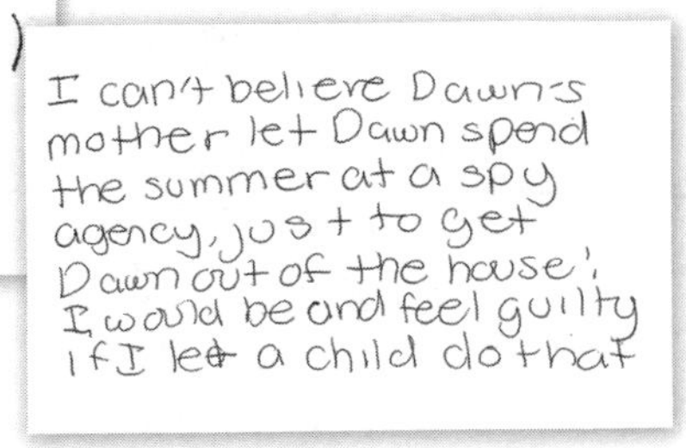

I can't believe Dawn's mother let Dawn spend the summer at a spy agency, just to get Dawn out of the house! I would be and feel guilty if I let a child do that

Figure VII-6

CONFERRING AND SMALL-GROUP WORK

Use Compliment Conferences and the Power of Literature

It would be easy today to continue the conferring and small-group work that you've been doing over the past two weeks. Each days' work with children will set you up for work you can do on other days, because once you've broken a conferring trail and once you have examples of students who have gone from one way of thinking to a better way, all of that equips your next conferences.

So absolutely, sneak in a few last bits of advice, a few final reminders about ways in which readers can take their work with prediction and envisionment one step further.

But mostly, you will probably want today to be a miniature celebration of what children have begun to do because there is no better way to be sure that this work makes a lasting difference in the lives of children than for you to move among your kids, joining them in seeing their growth and in naming what it is they have learned to do.

You may decide to devote today entirely to compliment conferences. You'll remember that compliments are a part of every conference (save for the times when you want to call a child on doing less than his or her best work), so if you spend today devoting your attention simply to compliment conferences, you'll find this one day can strengthen every conference you do forever more in your life.

MID-WORKSHOP TEACHING POINT

Readers Draw on Our Unique Strengths as People and as Readers When We Envision and Predict

"Readers, may I interrupt for just a second? I am blown away by the work you are doing today. You all are making movies in your mind as you read, and you are predicting so much that you are sitting on the edges of your chairs as you read, reading on and on to see if your predictions come true. After today, we're going to turn to focus on other ways of thinking about books. We'll be thinking about growing theories about characters. So when we shift to that work, it will be up to you to remember that the learning we have been doing together wasn't just for the last two weeks' reading workshop. It was for the whole of your life. I am hoping that forevermore, you read differently because of the learning we have done so far this year and in this unit.

"And specifically, what I am thinking about today is that when I stop coaching you in how to envision and how to predict, what ends up happening is something really beautiful. And it is this. Each one of you ends up bringing who you are as a person to your envisionments, your predictions.""For example, some of you have the minds of mathematicians, of scientists. You see patterns everywhere, and you practically walk through life doing math problems. Well, what I am noticing is that those of you who are more mathematical, more scientific, are bringing that stance to the thinking you do as you read. You have calculated how the characters tend to act, you have seen patterns, and you practically rely on a formula to tell you that the likelihood is high that they'll act in such and such ways in the future.

continued on next page

Let me coach you a bit on compliments—and this coaching will help you whether you are conducting conferences, which are nothing but compliments, or whether your compliments are a portion of larger conferences.

Some Suggestions for Using Compliments

When you draw a chair alongside a child, listen to what she says and study what she shows you, and do so thinking, "What can I compliment?" Your instinct will be to notice whether the child has done as she's been told. Has she done the very things you have asked her to do? If you've taught the class to picture (or to predict) not just what a person does, but also how that person does this thing, your temptation will be to see if the child has done this, and, if he or she has, to say, "I want to compliment you on the fact that you pictured (or predicted) how the character does things."

This is a lot better than not noticing that the reader has made an effort to incorporate your instruction into her life, but that youngster is not going to go home and tell her mother that she received an amazing compliment today—she was told she did as the teacher told her to do. Giving her a gold star for doing as told is not going to make a reader's day or change the course of her learning.

I once had a quote pinned to my bulletin board which said, "I can live three months on a good compliment." In my own life, I've actually carried really good compliments with me for far more than three months! So when you compliment a reader, your goal is to do so in a way that leaves a lasting impression. To do this, it helps if you try to see exactly what it is that the person has done that is special. Sure, you may want to tuck in mention that the reader has pictured not only what the character has done but also how the character did that thing . . . but what was idiosyncratically special about the particular way the reader did this? Did the reader practically stand up and act out the book as she told you what would happen next? Did she start to say what she predicted and then pause, thinking really long and hard, using that silence to try on and discard a few possibilities before arriving at what she thought was the most true, more perfect, prediction? Did she involve a partner so the two of them thought together about what was apt to happen next in the book?

If you want to make your compliment into a lasting one, it will help if you sometimes talk not only about the child's reading but also about the child as a person. Every reading skill is actually a way of thinking, not just a way of reading, so it is easy to compliment a child's work with a reading skill by noting times when the child has done similar work not just in books, but in her life. If a child comes up with a whole raft of different possible predictions, saying, "It could go this way . . . or that way . . . or that other way," you can tell her that you notice this, and point out that this kind of thinking is characteristic of her not just when she reads but throughout her life. "Lots of people just come up with one idea and then think, 'that's it,' but you . . . you are incredibly fluent at generating possi-

> ## MID-WORKSHOP TEACHING POINT
>
> *continued from previous page*
>
> "Others of you are the most avid readers of mysteries. Because you read so many mysteries, you are really talented at seeing the little clues that mystery authors give along the way. You are accustomed, when reading mysteries, to using these small pieces of the puzzle to help you figure out 'who dun it.' But what I am noticing that is so cool is that you bring your talents as mystery readers to books that aren't even mysteries, and you read all books looking for clues as to what will happen next.
>
> "So all of you, take a second to share you predictions with others at your table, and notice how your predictions are like fingerprints. They are uniquely yours."

ble ideas. You know how we talk about how important it is to be fluent as a reader, to read quickly and smoothly and in a way that flows? Well, you are fluent as a generator of ideas. Even when we were thinking about how we could decorate our reading notebooks, in the space of three minutes, you came up with all these lovely possible alternatives. 'We could do this,' you said, 'or, on the other hand, we could do that. . . .' That's a real gift."

When you are complimenting children, aiming to make these compliments memorable, one way to do so is to borrow the power of wonderful literature. Because you read aloud *Dancing in the Wings* today, you may want to carry that beautiful book with you when you confer with your readers. You might find opportunities to recruit those feisty, strong characters as a way to highlight the work your readers are doing.

For example, when I spent a bit of time with Kobe on this last day of this bend, this part, in the unit, I definitely wanted to support the hard work he'd done to lift the level of his predictions and his envisionments. So I said to him, "Kobe, you are like Sassy. You are so determined. I

remember that first day when you and your table looked over your envisionment Post-its and you told me the group had decided that yours just repeated the stuff that was in the book—other kids might have gotten all discouraged and said to themselves, 'I'm not going do this kind of thinking, it is not my style.' Others might have folded their arms in a huff and said, 'I'm not the type to envision.' But you—you have been so determined and bit by bit you have worked harder and harder. Look at the difference in your envisioning. At the beginning, you just wrote, 'He is a good basketball player.' Now look at your envisionments!" We looked together at the progression in his work.

Then, continuing, I said to Kobe, "To me, you are a lot like Sassy, in *Dancing in the Wings*. Remember how after Mona and Molly told her she had no talent, that there was no way she'd get picked to go to the dance festival, she didn't let them discourage her. No way. Remember how that very night she dreamed that she was dancing on the Milky Way and she went right on to those tryouts and didn't let Mona and Mollie's snicker-

ing get to her. You are just the same Sassy because the two of you never give up."

Meanwhile, when I got a chance to look over Jasmine's Post-its, I said, "Oh my gosh, Jasmine! There is something about your predictions that are so unbelievably fresh and powerful." She and I read some of her Post-its together. [Figs. VII-7, VII-8, VII-9, VII-10, VII-11, and VII-12]

It took me a while to find the words to capture what I think are the unique qualities of Jasmine's work. "Hmm . . . I'm trying to think how to put into words the special talent you have," I said, letting her see me reach for the honest and true words. "I think that when you predict, you aren't just thinking in a detached way about what will happen next in the story. You are actually almost talking to your characters like a parent might talk to a kid. You are saying to your characters, 'It's gonna get better. Hold on. Don't give up.'"

Then I looked Jasmine right in the eyes and said to her, "Your predictions and your relationship to characters remind me of Uncle Redd's

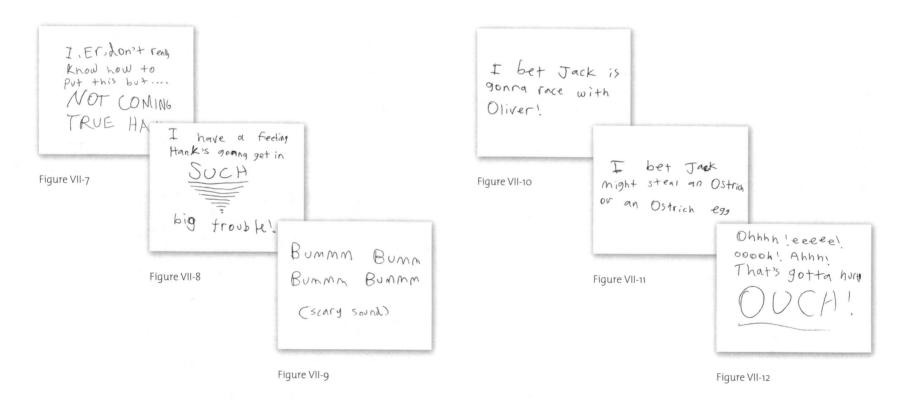

Figure VII-7

Figure VII-8

Figure VII-9

Figure VII-10

Figure VII-11

Figure VII-12

relationship to Sassy. Remember when Sassy tells Uncle Redd she is just too tall, he tells her, 'You gotta look at that as a gift.' Then he cheers her on like you cheer your characters on. He says, 'It'll get better,' like you say to your characters. And just like you, Uncle Redd helps Sassy imagine *how* things will probably turn out. Remember he says, 'Listen, gal, all you gotta do to make your mark on the world is walk into a room.' That meant the world to Sassy and it turns out to be the prediction that holds the whole story together."

I end my compliment conference by saying to her, "For the rest of your life, Jasmine, always hold tight to this talent you have. Always forge that special bond with your characters, and think ahead for them so you can say to them, 'Hold on, it'll get better,' or 'Watch out girl, you could get in trouble. Be careful.'"

I also had a chance to review the work Sam had done since our conference. At the start of the unit, his Post-its had tended to look like this: (*Figs. VII-13 and VII-14*)

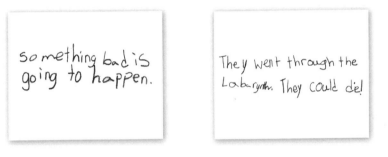

something bad is
going to happen.

Figure VII-13

They went through the
Labaryth. They could die!

Figure VII-14

Now Sam's Post-its were more apt to look like this: (*Fig. VII-15*)

"Sam," I said. "I am just bowled over by what you have done. Was it just two days ago when you and I talked when we agreed that you had tons and tons of prediction Post-its, and I challenged you to perhaps make a few less, but to use writing and thinking specifically about the book to try to make the predictions that you did do, those that matter to you, more specific? I was not at all sure you'd be game for that. There are lots of strong reader who'd just say to themselves, 'Other teachers have said my work is fine and I read hard books so get off my back.' But you are a lot like Sassy. She didn't just want to be on okay dancer. She wants to dance like she's dancing on the Milky Way. So when she was doing perfectly adequate work that wasn't superb, and Mr. Debato went so far as to practically yell at her saying, 'Young lady, you must learn to dance to the music. Up on the count of one, down on the count of three! Three! Not five! You have the rhythm of a troglodyte. Again!' she was crushed, sure, but did she let that stop her? No way. She took all his coaching in and worked to make her good dancing into great dancing. That's what real pros do, and that's what you do. I am so proud of not just your work, but your willingness to work."

You'll probably feel that your kids' energy is sky-high. Learn from this. Learn to make better use of compliments throughout all your teaching. And learn, too, that human beings have a need to be seen. Perhaps, during a bit of free time, you could visit the classroom of a colleague or two, and try using compliments as a way to help each other, not just to help your students. After all, the one thing that you need more than anything as a teacher is professional company. You need colleagues who are on this learning journey with you. And there is no better way to create a collegial workplace than to be generous with each other.

I think that Bastian
isn't going to leave. I
think his dad is ~~going~~
going to change his mind
and stay here. I think
in some way this will
really affect the story
Maybe it will make him
Feel less sad and he'll
be less of a Jerk.
Bastian seems like a figure
in this class.

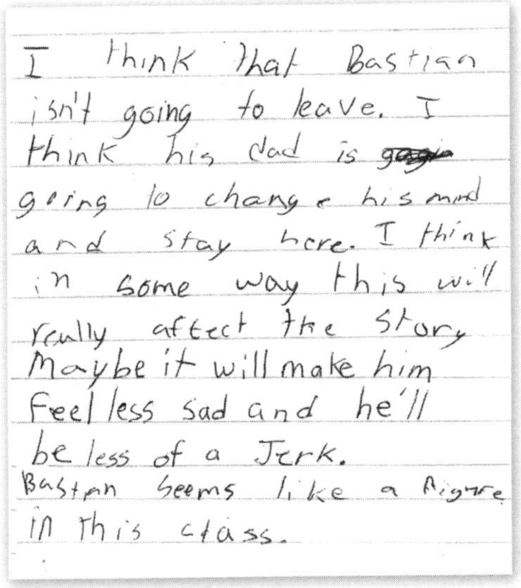

Figure VII-15

TEACHING SHARE

Readers Grow Ideas By Identifying with Characters

Recall a previous read-aloud, one that children listened to with their hearts on their sleeves. Suggest that this care is essential to readers.

"Readers, earlier today I was thinking about something that happened to my friend that left her feeling upset, and I noticed how strongly I was picturing the scene, feeling my friend's emotions and even predicting what might happen. I realized that the most careful readers and listeners are also the most *caring* readers and listeners. It's as if we wear our hearts on our sleeves. It's like we're experiencing the same moments the characters are. And when we do that, we can grow new ideas about the story, the characters, and the world.

"Right now I want us all to think back to the last chapter of *Stone Fox*. Remember how still we were, barely breathing as I read aloud how little Willy walked the last ten feet and crossed the finish line cradling Searchlight in his arms. In that moment we all were readers who were giving ourselves over to the story, vowing not to be stone. We were experiencing that moment with little Willy. We understood what he felt because we read the eighty-three pages of this book in such a way that we came to care about little Willy and Searchlight. In life, just like in books, we meet people with whom we develop deep bonds. We care for them, we identify with them, and we are forever changed by having known them in our lives.

Channel students to talk with partners about characters who have mattered.

"So, today as you talk with your partner, let's all be the most careful listeners and wear our hearts on our sleeves. Let's bring the characters that we feel so connected to into our conversations. And as we talk about them, let's think, 'Why does this character resonate with us? What is it about this character that we identify with?' When we ask these questions, we'll grow new ideas. I'll give you a minute to prepare, and then you will talk with your partner."

I listened in on Emma's conversation with her partner, Izzy. Emma had finished Katherine Patterson's *The Great Gilly Hopkins* and also *Cassie Binegar* and was now reading a somewhat similar book, *Journey* by Patricia MacLachlan. Emma began with a big question. "I wonder if Liddie really ever loved Cat and Journey. She's not a very good

COACHING TIPS

I know that this beginning has a high beauty quotient and may be a bit low on practical nuts-and-bolts information, but I'm also aware that when I preach a little sermon like this, some kids won't actually take in all of what I am saying. That's okay by me. I hope by this point in the year they still glean that I'm trying to talk about really important issues.

You may wonder about my use of "big words" such as resonate. I make a point of weaving what I suspect will be unfamiliar vocabulary into my teaching. I do not usually stop to provide a definition, but I do try to surround the difficult term with an explanation of its meaning. That is, I try to enable children to use contextual knowledge to grasp the meaning of the term. This is how most human beings learn the thousands and thousands of new words we learn each year. I recognize that you will alter these minilessons so they work for your kids, and this may include altering the level of vocabulary.

mother to leave them with their grandparents. She didn't even say good-bye to them." The question interested me because Emma was thinking not just about the characters who are present in *Journey*, but also about an absent character—the mother who is long gone from the lives of her children. I would have inserted a lean compliment, but the conversation had already moved on.

Izzy said, "I think it is not right when parents just leave their kids. The kids can be injured for life. I know I would be if my mom left me, wouldn't you? Why didn't she say bye to her own kids? Did she have good reasons?"

I inserted, "I love that you are asking questions about characters in a book that you'd ask of people in real life."

"It didn't really say why she didn't say 'bye,' but it said she was screwed up, and she always wanted to get out of the town, and I think that's why she named her kid Journey."

"What do you mean?" asked Izzy.

"Because *she* wanted to go on journeys, explore the world and all, so she named her kid Journey." Then Emma added, "And Cat. I don't know why that name—she had a cat."

"Does the name make Journey think about his mother going away?"

"Well, no, not exactly. It's like Journey doesn't really get what's going on."

I joined their conversation for a moment and asked, "Do you know anyone like Journey?"

Emma nodded quickly, as if she had already considered this question. "My little sister is like Journey and I'm like Cat. When my parents got separated, my sister just thought it would be fun to have two houses and rooms and more stuff, 'cause she's littler and more naive and doesn't really deal. I knew it wouldn't be fun, 'cause I'm more mature, same as Cat."

At this point I interrupted the whole class and said, "Readers, partners, may I have your attention? You're really pushing each other to dig deep into your character's lives and minds. And I want to tell you something else too. One way to grow new ideas is to think about why we identify with a character. One way partners can help is to ask, "Do you know anyone like this character? Or which characters are you most like? When you and your partner push each other, by asking these types of questions, you'll be able to go beyond observations and into the hearts and minds of your characters."

Strategies Readers Use To Grow Ideas About Characters

- We make a movie in our mind, drawing on the text to envision (or become) the character.

- We use our own experiences to help us walk in the character's shoes, inferring what the character is thinking, feeling, experiencing.

- We revise our mental movies as we read on, getting new details from the text.

- We notice when we feel connected to a character and use that feeling to deepen our understanding of the character.

Analyzing Text Difficulty to Inform (and Transform) Instruction

When I was a doctoral student, studying methods of research, one of my professors told me that a good rule of thumb to keep in mind is that one should always spend at least as much time analyzing data as one spends collecting data. I am convinced that this single bit of advice could turn school systems upside down. Think of the time you and others spend collecting running records that show kids' abilities to read texts at different levels of difficulty. We corral the assessment texts, duplicate and distribute them; we hunker down with one child after another, noting their readings and miscues. Think of the time spent entering this data onto individual and class records. By now, you and others will have invested at least a hundred hours collecting data on your kids' abilities to read texts at particular levels of difficulty!

Now imagine how you'd go about spending an equal amount of time analyzing this data. Could we physically accomplish this? This assessment section will help you harvest insights from all the work you have done to assess your children.

Take a Bird's-Eye View of the Text Levels in Your Class

To make the most of the data you have collected, step back from it a moment and look across all the information you have in order to inform your teaching.

Rethink Your Planned Units of Study in Light of Your Text Levels

Use the data that you've gleaned from your class as a whole to think about and revise your plans for the year. The following are a few examples of how you might tailor your teaching based on the text levels in your class.

If Most of Your Children Are Reading at Levels J-N

For example, if you know now, in October, that most of your children are reading texts that are levels J-N, then you'll know some specific challenges they'll face. For example, as readers progress from reading texts such as *Frog and Toad* toward texts such as *Amber Brown is not a Crayon,* their fluency needs to strengthen dramatically; within those five levels of text difficulty, children need to move from reading 85 words per minute to reading closer to 130 words per minute. This is a challenge particular to this band of text levels. As children progress up the *next* four levels of text difficulty, the expected reading rate only rises thirty words per minute, and, after that, the reading rate rises even more slowly. Not surprisingly, readers at this band of text level tend to benefit from a bit of fluency support. This might involve support in:

- Reading the punctuation involved in dialogue
- Understanding "untagged" dialogue
- Leveraging known syllables, prefixes, and suffixes to word solve
- Synthesizing across the arc of a story

A teacher whose class is primarily reading at this level will want to consider her planned sequence of units of study. Units on reading series books, mysteries (see *Constructing Curriculum*), humor (see *Constructing Curriculum*), and biography will be more supportive for such a class than units on reading historical fiction and fantasy. Units of study focused on reading with fluency and on predicting and growing theories about characters will all be very helpful.

This teacher may decide to postpone the use of a reading notebook to protect as much time as possible for actual reading. She may try to move heaven and earth to make it more likely that her children can be in same-book partnerships so that her book introductions and her coaching can support two children at once, and so partners can be more supportive of each other.

If Most of Your Students Are Reading at Levels R and Above

Meanwhile, a teacher whose readers are almost all reading levels R and above may want to support her readers in:

- Growing especially nuanced ideas about characters
- Using reading notebooks rather than Post-its as a response tool
- Bringing more critical reading, interpretation, and intertextuality work to bear

This teacher will draw on her knowledge of texts at higher bands of text difficulty to tailor her content toward her readers and will consider teaching some more advanced units of study, either from the *Constructing Curriculum* book or those she invents on her own or with colleagues.

Rethink Your Assessment Schedule in Light of the Text Levels in Your Class

As you look over the landscape of the levels of text difficulty that your readers can handle, you'll want to think about your schedule for reassessing readers. Children who are reading lower levels of text difficulty tend to progress through these levels much more quickly (this is true even without considering that these readers have some catching up to do). A second grader who is reading at grade level will enter second grade reading level J and leave reading level M, progressing four levels in that one year. Meanwhile, a reader who is reading at grade level will enter sixth grade reading level U and leave reading level W, progressing two levels during that year. The moral of this is that when you look over the levels at which your class is reading, you can, at that time, devise a schedule for reassessing readers. You'll need to assess more frequently for readers who are reading at the lower levels of text difficulty than for the others. You might, of course, reassess well before the scheduled assessment, but it is still wise to schedule assessments so that you don't end up sleeping on the job.

Support Readers Who Merit Extra Attention

Once you and your colleagues have accumulated data on all the children, it will be impossible to ignore the fact that some children need extra help urgently—immediately. There are three things to do for these children straight away.

Get them books they can read. First, what we know is that too many children who struggle never get a chance to read books they can read with proficiency. It is urgent that each of these children pull out all the books he or she has been "reading" and read a fragment of each aloud to us. If the child cannot read any one of the books with proficiency, then that book needs to be replaced with one that the child can read. Otherwise, as Allington says, "These children come to school for the promise of an education and instead they are given sawdust" (Teachers College 2008). These children need to read books they can read *all day, every day, in every subject.*

Find and honor their talents. Second, these readers need to find ways in school to excel. Is one an artist? Can she be recruited to lead the team that is making a mural? Is another a DJ? Perhaps each day can begin with a song, played by that youngster. Does one child speak a language other than English? Let's begin a study of that language, led by that child.

Conduct deep, careful assessments. And finally, these children demand more complete assessments. For example, if a child reads very slowly, it is worthwhile to assess her knowledge of high-frequency words. Could that be getting in the way? What about the child's abilities to use letters and clusters of letters to spell? What about the child's listening comprehension. Is it significantly higher than the child's ability to decode? We need to learn what she can do and what she does do and why.

You will need to invent more ways of responding to individual children who need extra help, and also to groups of children who need extra help. You will probably find that there are some levels at which many of your readers' growth seems to stall. We've seen this happening, for example, between levels M and N, and between T and U. A school I know recently convened a parent-child "Turn Around" meeting for a group of fourth-grade students who seemed stuck at level

M texts, those like the *Magic Treehouse* series. This meeting was scheduled just before December break to not let these readers lapse any more over that vacation. The teachers said to students who'd been invited, "We set up this meeting because we have been seeing signs that you are ready to zoom forward as readers, and if you and your caregivers are up for joining Project Turn Around, we're game for working with you for the next four weeks. We have the expectation that during this time you can—if you are willing to work at it—make giant strides forward as readers." Children who participated went home that day with stacks of books both at level M and at N, after receiving text introductions and some read-aloud support.

Of course, the powerful thing about Project Turn Around is that we, as teachers, need ways to knock ourselves out of our complacency and to remind ourselves that if children are not reading at the text levels we expect for them, this is not just a descriptor of our kids. It is also a descriptor of our teaching. Our job is to maximize each child's progress, and the first step in doing that is believing that we can.

Cross-Check Your Running Record Data with Standardized Test Data

Again, as you look over the landscape of your readers' text levels, you'll want to notice correlations that do and do not exist between those text levels and the scores these youngsters have achieved on standardized tests. You should see a great deal of correlation. If a reader is reading texts that are generally what you'd consider on grade level and yet scored a level 1, far below standards, or even a low level 2, on the standardized test, then this should function as a flashing yellow light for you. Proceed with caution. Could it be that your running records weren't truly accurate? Did you turn a blind eye to comprehension problems or overlook fluency and reading rate, thinking you were doing the child a favor? If your standardized test scores paint a different picture of a particular child as a reader than the one you have, you'll want to use this as a way to cross-check your own conclusions.

You may want to look at the benchmark text difficulty levels that the Teachers College Reading and Writing Project has recommended for each grade level (or another set of benchmark levels for grade levels, for that matter) and decide whether or not they are right for your grade or school. If they are not, alter them; set your own benchmarks to match your own circumstances. One way to do this is to find the set of children at a grade who achieved a particular score level on the standardized text, and then see which level of text difficulty most were reading at that time. For example, you could find the band of children in fourth grade with a score level of 3+. If most of those children were reading at least level R books at the time of the test, then you may want to establish R as your school's benchmark level for fourth grade.

You can use the benchmark levels we've provided in other ways as well. According to our chart, most of the time children who are reading level R in March of third grade score at about level 3 on the standardized test. If, in your classroom, only half of the children reading level R brought home that 3 on the standardized test, then something may be wrong. You'll want to look again at your methods of conducting running records and matching children to books, because chances are good that your levels have become inflated.

If you have access to last year's testing and text level data across your school, look especially for places where students' growth in reading accelerates and places where it stalls. In many of the schools we know best, children make significant progress in the fall of every year, and then their progress stops. Now that we have seen this trend, we've alerted the schools where this occurs, and teachers there are poised to break out of this trend during the coming year. If you look across years and across the school, you may find that children's text difficulty level sinks two to three levels every summer—a trend that has been widely recognized among high-poverty schools. If this is the case in your school, provisioning children with backpacks full of high-interest books for summer reading might be one of the most important developments your school could make.

A few words of caution: This correlation between text levels and reading test scores is even less dependable when you are looking at the top and the bottom of the score zones. For example, sometimes to get a top score, a test-taker must answer 100% of the test questions correctly. Even one wrong moves them down a zone. In cases like that, chance and other extraneous factors can weigh heavily and certainly shouldn't outweigh, or even cast too much doubt on, information about the reader you glean from other sources. Then, too, there will never be a perfect congruence between the levels of text difficulty that a child can handle and her scores on standardized tests. Achievement on the tests reflects a set of skills that might include, for example, an ability to write about reading, to understand test lingo, to read diverse genres including fables and poetry, to work quickly and under pressure—all of which are different skills than those needed to read at certain text levels.

To be able to use your running record and text level data to correlate with tests and to examine across your school, you'll need to keep it true to what you've found. It will sometimes happen that you come to the conclusion through running records that a child's just-right text difficulty level is, say, M, and yet because you know this particular child and his abilities, you want to push him with a course of level N books. Do this. You should make whatever instructional decisions you deem wisest based on your assessments! At the same time, you will want to maintain precisely true assessment data. That is, you can vary the instructional implications of your assessment data without "cooking the books." Record this student's level as M and note that you've given him N texts for the reasons you name. That practice will keep your data intact for correlations and for system-wide use.

Consider Communicating Your Data with Parents and Other Caregivers

As I mentioned earlier, you'll want to think about whether you will communicate to parents the level of text difficulty that a child can handle and whether you will also convey the benchmark levels for this grade level and time of year.

Increasingly, the decision of whether or not it is helpful to convey such information to parents has been taken out of teachers' hands. In many cities and towns, teachers are required to send information home regularly to parents, keeping them informed about children's reading progress. In New York City, to meet that requirement, every teacher has a choice: He can administer a standardized McGraw-Hill test repeatedly throughout the year, sending quarterly reports of the child's scores, or instead, the teacher can use the Teachers College Reading and Writing Project's assessments, found on our website and described throughout this series, to keep parents informed of the child's progress along a gradient of text difficulties.

On the CD-ROM, you will find examples of the letters that I've written to help teachers communicate these assessments to parents in ways that we've found are helpful. You'll notice that the letters convey that these assessments are based on one-time samplings and are fallible and open to revision, and above all, the letters convey that children can progress as readers if they are given access to lots of books that are just right for them and opportunities to talk about the books they are reading. The letters include book lists that are tailored to the child, of course, and other suggestions for parental support. The letters are also worded in ways that remind parents that children grow in fits and starts and that encourage parents to take this information with a grain of salt, because certainly the child's entire story as a reader is far more complex than the information that can be encapsulated into a level of text difficulty that the child can read.

Information from other assessments—high-frequency words, sound-to-letter correspondence, concepts of print, spelling inventories, and the like —is also sent home to parents and tracked, with a similar attention to the question of "How good is good enough?" That is, if a child's knowledge of sight words is a cause for concern, this information is also included in the letters home. Again, these developmental expectation charts are included on the CD-ROM.

Then too, as I've written earlier, you and your principal will want to look back over cumulative data, collected across the years, to note when growth in reading tends to happen (and not to happen). I recently told a large group of principals that their data suggests that the vast majority of growth that their kids' make in reading levels is between September and November—and that the learning curve flattens after that. Could this be because their schools are so consumed with test preparation during the second semester that kids' opportunities to read just-right texts nose dives, as does their growth in reading? If the children in one classroom in the school regularly climb levels of text difficulty over the summer, and the children in other rooms follow the predictable course for high-poverty kids and decline by two levels every summer, you'll want to learn what the kids in the one classroom are doing differently.

Take a Bird's-Eye View of the Challenges Posed by the Text Levels Your Students Need to Read

Once you have calculated the level of text difficulty that each of your students can handle, you can not only steer *the child* toward books that are apt to be supportive, but you can steer *your teaching* toward skills that are apt to be required by those books. What a bonanza this is! This means that when you pull a chair alongside a youngster to talk about the text he or she is reading, even if you do not know the specific text the youngster has in hand, you can draw on your knowledge of books that are within that text's general place along the gradient of text difficulty to ascertain the sort of work the reader is apt to be doing.

Why Rely on Bands, Not Single Text Levels?

There is some debate over whether each and every precise text level will be informative to you, or whether it's the band of text levels that can inform your teaching. My colleagues and I believe it's the latter, although we've considered both positions carefully. We ordered 100 books for each level, J–Z, and looked across all those books to clarify for ourselves whether one can really say there are specific features for each and every level of text. We came from this work believing that although there is validity to saying that books can be categorized according to ascending levels of difficulty, there is less merit to attempting to say that all books at a particular level are at that level for the same reasons. That is, there are lots of ways for a book to be hard: One book may include foreign language words, another, a sea of characters, and in yet another, the passage of time may be especially complex. There is no one way for a book to be hard—or easy! (Although it's true that the books in levels A-K are vastly more amenable to being differentiated by precise level.) One need only look at a collection of books at any level above K, and you'll quickly see that books ascribed to that level are not easily described by a precise list of traits.

Having said that, my colleagues and I have found that it is not only possible but extraordinarily helpful to describe some of the main ways in which books within a *band* of text difficulty, a clump of several text levels, tend to pose new challenges for their readers. To cluster text levels into these bands, we studied data from several hundred schools and found, as mentioned earlier, that kids tend to move fairly easily between some levels and to get stuck at the transition to other levels, suggesting those places where kids are prone to get stuck might involve larger step-ups. For this reason, and others, we have come to think of upper-grade text levels as falling within these bands:

- K/L/M
- N/O/P/Q
- R/S/T
- U/V
- W/X/Y/Z (Our work is very much in progress at these levels, and they are complicated to talk about because many texts have been categorized as Z not because of text complexity but because of adult content.)

What Kinds of Reading Work Are Called For at Each Band?

For each band of text difficulty, it is helpful to ask, "What is the new work that readers who are working with books in this band of text difficulty will be apt to do?" If we, as teachers, have a sense for what the new work is that readers will be apt to need to do, then we can draw on this knowledge when we want to help a reader move into one of these bands. For example, we can provide book introductions and strategy lessons that help equip readers to do this new work, and we can keep an eye on readers' progress by paying attention especially to their abilities to do the new work required in the band of texts in which they are working. We can also think about whether our minilessons and small-group work are supporting the kinds of skills that readers in our classes are being required to use.

It is possible to catalog a huge list of all the work that readers are apt to do when working in a band of text difficulty, but I think it is important to restrain ourselves from doing this. First, the longer and more detailed the list, the less broadly applicable it will be. But more importantly, the reason to talk and think about bands of text difficulty is that this knowledge can inform our teaching. The reason that it helps to describe the new work readers are apt to need to do within a band of text difficulty is that then, when we draw a chair alongside a reader and ask, "How's it going?" we'll have some hunches about the challenges the reader is likely to be facing. The whole goal of this work, then, is for it to be portable. The point is for a teacher to be able to look at a book that a child is reading, a book the teacher may or may not know, and for the teacher to be able to draw on her internalized knowledge about a gradient of text difficulty to predict the sorts of challenges that book is likely to be posing. My colleagues and I, then, have worked hard to develop the shortest possible list of characteristics for any one band of text difficulty and to be sure we talked about the work readers are required to do in language that does not require a PhD in reading instruction to understand.

What Kind of Work Is Called For in the Band of K/L/M (*Nate the Great to *The Paint Brush Kid)?

Structure

When readers move into books that are within this band of text difficulty, they are apt to find that instead of reading episodic chapter books such as one finds in the earliest chapter books, where each chapter is essentially a self-contained story involving the same characters, they are now reading books in which a single story line spans the entire book. This means that readers are required to carry a lot of content across a broader swatch of text, so synthesis and determining importance are important skills. Readers profit from understanding how stories tend to go because when reading fiction at these levels, most of it fits in a straightforward fashion into the traditional story structure of a character who has traits and motivations, and who runs into problems and ends up somehow resolving those problems.

The good news is that books at this level tend to provide youngsters with a lot of support. Both the books and the chapters are short. The title of the book (and sometimes of the chapters) and the blurb on the back cover help readers grasp the main through line in the story (as is the case for the book *Horrible Harry and the Ant Invasion.)

Characters

There is a lot of dialogue in these books, often between several main characters. It is not always tagged and is sometimes interrupted, as in this example: "I'm going," Mark said, getting up to walk out. "I won't ever come back."

The characters in these books have a few dominant characteristics, and these are explicitly labeled, repeatedly. Horrible Harry is. . . horrible!

The characters tend to be relatively static. They change their feelings over the course of the story, but their traits are fairly consistent throughout the book, and often these are related to the main problem. In *Horrible Harry and the Ant Invasion*, Harry likes creepy things, so when the teacher asks, "Would you like to be the ant monitor?" things coalesce around this character trait.

In these stories, the character often wants something concrete—to take care of creepy creatures, to win the prize, to get the shoes that popular kids wear.

In the books at the high end of the band, it fairly often happens that the character ends up getting not the concrete thing he or she wanted but rather the deeper motivation that made the character want that concrete object in the first place. The boy does not get the shoes that the popular kids all wear, but he does get a friend and a chance to feel popular.

Vocabulary and Syntax

Readers of books in the K/L/M band of difficulty will find themselves required to tackle an increasing number of two- and three-syllable words. Readers of books in this band of text difficulty will find that more and more words in their books are not words they use conversationally—and many of these will be subject specific. A story about soccer will include *opponent, cleat,* and *positions,* for example.

What Kind of Work Is Called for in the Band of N/O/P/Q (*The Chocolate Touch and A to Z Mysteries to *Fudge-a-mania)?

Structure

Before now, the narratives that children tended to read fell neatly into a traditional story structure in which a single main character has a big motivation. He or she wants something and gets stymied, but like *The Little Engine That Could*, the character tries, tries, tries, and eventually makes it over the top of the story mountain.

Once readers are working with texts in the N–Q band of text difficulty, however, the texts will be more structurally complex. The narrative frame is still present, but the character encounters not just one concrete problem but a blend of pressures, or a multidimensional problem. In *Amber Brown is not a Crayon,* the big problem is that Amber's best friend Justin is moving away, but because Justin puts the best face on this, Amber feels that he doesn't share her agony over the impending separation, and consequently they get into relationship problems. Then, too, there are smaller problems that come along the path. Will they be able to convince the family that is considering buying Justin's home that it's not at all the house they want? When reading texts in this band of text difficulty, a fair amount of abstraction is required for readers to extract the one overarching story line that provides the bearing walls for stories.

This means, of course, that the work readers were doing earlier in synthesis and determining importance is all the more necessary now, and the question "What seems to be the central problem in this story?" is both important and challenging. Readers should expect that thought is required to respond to that question, and often the answer has several parts to it. Problems will start to be a bit multidimensional, and between the character's motivation and the story's resolution, there will be a few subplots.

When working with readers in this band of text difficulty, then, it is helpful to show them that readers work to keep focused on the central story line. It helps if readers understand that the question "What *now* does this text seem to be mostly about?" will produce an answer that evolves a bit over time. As they read more deeply into a book, and as more information is provided to them, readers should expect they'll refine their sense of the overarching problem (the one that holds the whole story together). A reader might read about a point of contention between two important characters and think this will be central to the story and then be shown that actually that one conflict was only a small part of the main story line. The important thing is that the reader be willing to let go of his or her first expectation to fashion one that is more grounded in the text as it actually unrolls.

Characters

One way to help readers who are working in this band of text difficulty synthesize the text is to help them think about *why* characters do what they do, ascribing more than one cause to an effect, using phrases such as "Another reason is . . ." or "Another part of this is . . ." and Another part is. . . ." To talk about cause and effect, readers need to link earlier parts of a book to later parts, uncovering the through lines.

It's not only the story line in these books that is more complicated. The main character will tend to be complicated as well. The character is often conflicted. Amber wants to be a little kid and wants to be a teenager at the same time. She is part thirteen and part nine. She both likes her mother's new boyfriend, and she resents the way he has replaced her father. She both adores her pal Justin and is furious at him for moving away. Feelings tend to be ambivalent and often at least some of the trouble in the story is internal, related to these ambivalent feelings. Usually, however, readers do not need to deduce these characteristics. The characters are complex, but readers are told about this complexity. It will not usually be subtle. Someone—the character or the narrator—will come right out and tell the reader the traits of the main characters. Readers need only pay attention to these descriptors and then carry them so that when the character later acts accordingly, the reader is able to think, "Yep, there she goes, acting. . . ."

Vocabulary and Syntax

Earlier, I suggested that readers who are working in the K/L/M band of text difficulty need to be prepared to work with tricky words, because they will begin encountering many more multisyllabic words, and this trend will continue. There are two things to note as readers move into level N/O/P/Q books.

First, readers will encounter many words that live in the world of written language and are rarely part of a child's spoken language. A teacher may not, at first, think of *unique* as a tricky word—after all, it is not a term such as *ambivalent* or *morose*—but it is helpful for teachers to realize that reading is now taking children into a world of academic language, and there are far more unfamiliar or vaguely familiar words in that world than a teacher might realize.

But my main point is that at this band of text difficulty, readers encounter not just tricky *words*, but tricky *phrases* and tricky *passages*. Usually these are tricky because they include a play on language, perhaps a pun or a metaphor or another figure of speech. The title of the book *Amber Brown is not a Crayon* is a perfect example. The reader who knows there is a character named Amber, surname Brown, and who has never had one of those boxes of 300 crayons, including one bearing the title Amber Brown, might well miss the entire point of that book's title. Another example is in **Forever Amber Brown*. Readers know that the mother's boyfriend and Amber both like to bowl. At one point, Amber is discussing whether her parents might get reunited, and she says that the chances are about as great as that of her scoring 300 in bowling. There are a few challenges in these tricky parts of books. One is that often some world knowledge is required to grasp the point:

Readers need to know that Amber Brown *is* the name of a crayon and that 300 is a perfect score in bowling. The other problem, though, is that passages such as these could lead readers astray. A reader might misread Amber's comment about her parents getting back together and somehow get the idea that the characters are now going bowling. As the language in texts becomes more complex, it is almost inevitable that readers will misinterpret in ways that could lead them astray; the important thing is that readers need to be able to self-correct erroneous interpretations if, as they read on, they are not borne out.

What Kind of Work Is Called for in the Band of R/S/T (*Because of Winn Dixie *to* *The Tiger Rising *and* *Bridge to Terabithia*)?

Structure

In general, there is a trend toward stories becoming layered with meaning. It is as if the characters and the events, too, are like icebergs—with the part that shows, that is labeled and discussed, being only part of what's really going on. The problem may seem to be the relationship between these two characters, but really, deep down, the problem is a bigger sense of loneliness or homelessness. The problems are big enough and layered enough that they are not all solved. In fact the story line is less about a character who encounters a problem and rises to the challenge, solving the problem, and more about characters who encounter problems and work to respond to those problems, changing and learning in the process.

It is especially notable that in this band of text difficulty, readers need to follow not only the evolving plot line but also the evolving setting. The setting becomes a force in the story, influencing characters and the plot, just as, say, an antagonist might. In historical fiction, for example, readers need to construct a timeline of the historical events as well as of the protagonist's events, and more than that, to see the two timelines intersect. But in most well-written novels within this bend, the setting evolves across the story and plays a role in the story. There is an evolution to Terabithia and to Winn Dixie, for example. Settings change because characters relate to them differently across the story. Readers are expected to cumulate a growing understanding of the setting, just as we cumulate a growing understanding of main characters.

As more elements emerge as important in these more complex texts, it becomes important for readers to hold more parts of the book in mind. In particular, there are subplots and minor characters in books in this band of text difficulty that might seem to be inconsequential, but in the end, fit into a synthesized whole. Readers, then, are expected to keep some of these in mind as they read, predicting, for example, that the sister who was mentioned in passing at the start of the book may return to play a role at the end of the book.

Character

In the preceding band of text difficulty, the main character was often ambivalent, and the problem often had several parts (as in Amber being upset with Justin for moving away and also for not being crushed that he was moving away). The trend toward complexity increases in this band of text difficulty, and increasingly the characters are characterized by complex internal, emotional lives. Jesse, in *Bridge to Terabithia*, is full of anxiety, self-esteem issues, and self doubt. Rob, in *The Tiger Rising*, is equally conflicted. One difference is that whereas in the level N/O/P/Q texts, the characters or the narrator often comes straight out and labels the character's emotional life, now readers are left to infer what the character is feeling. In fact, often readers realize things about the character that the character does not know himself or herself.

Vocabulary and Syntax

Whereas the previous level contained tricky sentences—usually figurative language—books in this band of text difficulty often contain tricky chapters. A teacher might say to these readers, "Before, if you came to a tricky chapter and were totally confused, you might think the book was too hard for you. Now, at this level, you need to expect that sometimes books are hard on purpose, and you are not supposed to entirely get what is going on. You can say, 'Huh?' and read on, expecting things will become clearer in the end."

What Kind of Work Is Called for in the Band of U/V/W (from *Loser *to* *Walk Two Moons*)?

Structure

Books in this band of text difficulty exacerbate most of the challenges described in band R/S/T. A few elements of story are apt to become especially complex at this level, and one is the passage of time. These stories still tend usually to unfold somewhat chronologically, often in a relatively straightforward structure, yet there is often some big event that occurred before the novel begins, and we have to read on to learn about that event and to find the meaning of it. Backstory, then, becomes increasingly prevalent, and a reader can be two thirds of the way through a book and still be learning more about the backstory. Usually the backstory is not a flashback, in which the character actually relives the event, full of action, but instead involves a character telling or discovering some background information.

Sometimes these texts have multiple plotlines. Readers will be apt to discover this first when they are reading along and find that as a new chapter begins, there is a new narrator, or a character has been left behind. Usually when this happens readers are not utterly mystified. It's usually easy to see the connection between the different fragments of the story. In *The Thief Lord*, by Cornelia Funke, for example, one chapter tells the story of two boys who are runaways in Venice. In the next chapter, however, we are following the detective who is pursuing the boys.

The characters and setting at this level start becoming more symbolic of bigger themes. It pays off for readers to pause and to think whether the setting could be a symbol for a theme or an issue in the lives of the characters and to think about changes in the setting (especially times when the setting becomes oppressive), such as perhaps foreshadowing developments that are not exclusive to the setting alone. For example, when readers find in *Walk Two Moons* that Sal says, "The hot air pressed against my face and the air was like a hot heavy blanket draped on my neck and back," the heat has become a metaphor for the weight of Sal's journey and also a warning signal that previews the snakebite in that chapter.

Characters

Not surprisingly, the characters continue to become more complex and nuanced, but something else begins to happen at this level. Increasingly, the characters are teenagers.

If the reader herself is not yet a teenager, she can sometimes have a hard time empathizing with the characters. When the main character in *Things Not Seen* by Andrew Clements wakes up one morning and finds that he has turned invisible, that invisibility becomes a metaphor for the feeling teenagers often have in adolescence that their parents don't see them for who they truly are. Readers who see this as simply a story about a boy who wakes up invisible miss a huge part of the story.

Also, at these levels, the point of view starts to become even more multidimensional. It starts to be not just interesting but necessary to consider the perspectives of characters other than the protagonist. This is where the unreliable narrator can come into play as well. It is not so much that the narrator can't be trusted, but that the narrator's point of view is incomplete. He or she is often figuring out the past and the present of the story as it unfolds, along with the reader, and there are apt to be many times when a reader feels as if he or she sees more of the big picture than the character whose point of view is presented. Often books at this level require readers to hold on to large casts of characters. Some of the characters who turn out to be hugely important might be adults, so the reader must bring more of an understanding of the complexities of the adult world.

Increasingly, the story is a story and also a statement about the world and life. Very often, the story makes a statement about major social issues such as oppression, injustice, and social norms.

What Kind of Work Is Called for in the Band of X/Y/Z (from *Homecoming to *Monster)?

Books in this band of text difficulty are notably more complex. First, many of them employ a postmodern structure in which multiple genres are included, multiple voices heard. Perspectives overlap but also conflict. Whole chapters, not just short passages, jump back in time. The texts take risks with form and genre, usually using this complex structure to convey ideas, often including the idea that our lives and the world defy any attempt to be pinned down or pigeonholed and the idea that it is not easy to really communicate, to really understand one another. For example, in these texts the narrator is often unreliable. That is, he or she will proclaim things that the reader is expected to realize are not as the person has stated. The unreliability of the narrator mirrors the theme that it is impossible for anyone to be all-knowing, even when talking about oneself. Readers who are working with texts at this band, then, need to be willing to engage in figuring-things-out work while reading.

The expectations on readers go way beyond that. For example, readers of texts at this level are expected to have and to draw upon a lot of knowledge about the world and other books. In this band of text difficulty, many references are left unexplained. In fantasy books at this level, the reader needs to bring a whole wealth of knowledge, often carried over from reading mythology, fables, and other fantasy texts to understand the author's references. It is as if there is an assumption that readers who are working with texts at this band of difficulty are reading other texts related to this one and aware of other sources of information. While reading one book, readers are invited into the canon of literature. These literary references are not essential to understanding the characters and the themes but greatly enhance that reading experience if they are recognized and understood. For example, the epigraph to *Criss Cross, by Lynne Rae Perkins, is a quote from Shakespeare's *A Midsummer Night's Dream, and there are references to that play throughout. A reader not familiar with the play can still read Criss Cross thoughtfully, but one who knows A Midsummer Night's Dream will benefit from that play's treatment of the difficulties and transience of love when considering the characters in Criss Cross and their struggles with identity and relationships. Also in Criss Cross, there are references to Einstein's theory of relativity. One of the characters is struggling to make sense of it. If the reader has no specific knowledge of this complex theory, this is not going to interrupt the story. However, if there is no understanding of the basic concept of atomic science—that the universe is constructed of microscopic atoms—the reader will not be able to appreciate one of the more significant threads in the book.

Readers at this level are assumed to be the kinds of readers who like challenging books and don't want things spelled out for them so simply. In fact, it seems like many books at this level are set up in such a way that they are like puzzles. Even dialogue, which was the aspect of narratives in the lower bands that readers found easiest to follow, can become tricky as characters begin to speak in the vernacular and to use vocabulary from another time and place.

Once you have taken a bird's-eye view of both your children's text level and the challenges present in those levels, you'll have done the analysis of your assessment that can inform your teaching throughout this unit and the year.